The Texture
of Leadership
for Tomorrow's
Church

morph!

Flagship church resources
from Group Publishing

Innovations From Leading Churches

Flagship Church Resources are your shortcut to innovative and effective leadership ideas. You'll find ideas for every area of church leadership, including pastoral ministry, adult ministry, youth ministry, and children's ministry.

Flagship Church Resources are created by the leaders of thriving, dynamic, and trend-setting churches around the country. These nationally recognized teaching churches host regional leadership conferences and are respected by other pastors and church leaders because their approaches to ministry are so effective. These flagship church resources reveal the proven ideas, programs, and principles that these churches have put into practice.

Flagship Church Resources currently available:

- *60 Simple Secrets Every Pastor Should Know*
- *The Perfectly Imperfect Church:* Redefining the "Ideal Church"
- *The Winning Spirit:* Empowering Teenagers Through God's Grace
- *Ultimate Skits:* 20 Parables for Driving Home Your Point
- *Doing Life With God:* Real Stories Written by Students
- *Doing Life With God 2:* Real Stories Written by Students
- *The Visual Edge:* Compelling Video Connectors for Your Worship Experience
- *Mission-Driven Worship:* Helping Your Changing Church Celebrate God
- *An Unstoppable Force:* Daring to Become the Church God Had in Mind
- *A Follower's Life:* 12 Group Studies On What It Means to Walk With Jesus

- *Leadership Essentials for Children's Ministry*
- *Keeping Your Head Above Water:* Refreshing Insights for Church Leadership
- *Seeing Beyond Church Walls:* Action Plans for Touching Your Community
- *unLearning Church:* Just When You Thought You Had Leadership all Figured Out!
- *Morph!:* The Texture of Leadership for Tomorrow's Church
- *The Quest for Christ:* Discipling Today's Young Adults
- *LeadingIdeas:* To-the-Point Training for Christian Leaders
- *Igniting Passion in Your Church:* Becoming Intimate with Christ
- *No More Lone Rangers:* How to Build a Team-Centered Youth Ministry

With more to follow!

The Texture
of Leadership
for Tomorrow's
Church

ethos

Jesus

morph!

Flagship church resources
from Group Publishing

ron martoia

Morph!
The Texture of Leadership for Tomorrow's Church
Copyright © 2003 Ron Martoia

Visit our Web site: **www.grouppublishing.com**

Credits
Creative Development Editor: Paul Woods
Chief Creative Officer: Joani Schultz
Copy Editor: Lyndsay E. Gerwing
Art Director: Randy Kady
Interior Designer: Helen Harrison
Cover Art Director/Designer: Jeff A. Storm
Illustrator: Randy Kady
Production Manager: Peggy Naylor

Library of Congress Cataloging-in-Publication Data
Martoia, Ron, 1962-
Morph! : the texture of leadership for tomorrow's church / by Ron Martoia.
p. cm.
Includes bibliographical references.
ISBN 0-7644-2450-5 (alk. paper)
1. Christian leadership. I. Title.
BV652.1.M366 2002
253--dc21   2002014314
10 9 8 7 6 5 4 3 2   12 11 10 09 08 07 06 05 04 03

Printed in the United States of America.

Dedication

To Valerie...the one who delights my heart, brings joy to the challenge of ministry, and keeps me levelheaded with the hard questions. God designed you just right...handmade for a perfect fit.

Acknowledgments

When I went to my placement director, Dr. Hanson, and told him of the invitation to plant a church, I fully expected a prayer time, some counsel, and a look at the pros and cons. But not Dr. Hanson. He had pioneered seminaries, churches, and missions in Japan. What was I thinking? Anything with the words "plant," "pioneer," or "founder," and he was game. I will never forget his words, "If God hasn't clearly said no, he is saying yes." I was incredulous. Where were the prayer, evaluation, pros and cons? Thanks, Dr. Hanson, for all the wisdom.

This book wouldn't even be possible without the proving grounds of the church I was asked to plant fifteen years ago. I have been the recipient of one of God's gracious churches in Westwinds. To those five founding families fifteen years ago—I thank you for taking the risk! To my parents who were willing to midwife the early years' messes and continue to be hospitable lovers of people and incredible servants to others...I thank you and love you so much. To those early years' people, thanks for your amazing forbearance. For those of you who weathered the transition in the early '90s, thanks for the vision to see what could happen if we finally uncovered and walked in the missional destiny God had for us. To the rest of the now quickly growing Westwinds family—let's buckle in and get ready for the next run God has in store.

I have been endowed with extraordinary servants on my staff; they run with stallion energy, teachable hearts, passionate vision, and experimental openness. Without the current crew of staff and Frontline leaders, many of the ideas in this book would never have been fleshed out.

I have a vast cheering section, led by my dear friends Andy and Trish, who have lifted my arms, encouraged my writing, and, in general, prayed,

coaxed, and prodded me through this adventure. Without their immense expenditures into my life, it would have been an uphill climb. You know who you are...thanks. To my board who has been more encouraging and supportive than is imaginable, I also say thanks.

I want to thank the "Pauls" at Group Publishing. Paul Allen, the editor of Rev. magazine, deserves mention for the original impetus to write articles that were the seminal launching pad for further writing. Paul Woods deserves thanks for his excitement over a book project. Our initial meeting in Phoenix at my graciously provided desert retreat (thanks Rach and Steve) will always be memorable.

For almost fourteen years I have had an executive assistant who is the envy of many of my colleagues. She is the one who makes most of what I do look good. Norma gets credit for making my muddled thoughts comprehensible long before Paul Woods had to deal with them.

Lastly, thanks to my family. It is no secret that without my wife, Valerie, I probably would have thrown in the towel long ago. I love you, honey. To RJ, Skyler, and Ari—this book is a product of your patience with Dad. There were many days you would ask "Workin' on the book again, Dad?" or "Leaving to go to Phoenix again, Dad?" and I would have to cringe and nod my head. I love you three so much. It's now time to make up for lost time, to resume longer wrestling matches, golf outings, chess games, and all the other things you have in mind. Let's go!

Ron Martoia
Cook Bed and Breakfast
Awatukee, AZ

morph

CONTENTS

Morphic Leadership

I first noticed the difference when I was in fifth grade. By then I had several years of elementary school under my belt, and the diversity of teachers had become quite marked. My fifth grade and first grade teachers had a different air about them, and that air created a certain kind of classroom feel. Maybe the similarities were due to the fact that neither of them really had to work but taught because they just loved kids. One was the wife of a bank president; the other was the wife of a prominent doctor.

Maybe the similarities were that they both took individual interest in each child and even took each one out in groups of two and three for dinner and movies throughout the school year. Probably other similarities could be listed, but the real issue, upon mature reflection, is that both Mrs. Abbott and Mrs. Pearse created a certain kind of environment in their classrooms that simply flowed from who they were. The relaxed yet exciting learning environment, the warm and relational interaction, and the affirming yet clear boundaries of their classroom settings inspired a desire to learn and profound respect. Those were my first lessons in how ethos is created. These two teachers' lives and love for teaching and kids created a certain kind of ambience that made the desire to learn inescapable.

I've had the opportunity to see this over and over again in my life. Certain coaches had the same ability to create team ethos; others were miserable to play for. My father was an immensely successful automotive executive, and I grew up around the movers and shakers of that industry. The ability to create a compelling ethos and environment from the flow of an interior life was instantly evident in those few who had it and glaringly absent in those who didn't.

What I didn't know then, I have come to know, own, and trumpet now. The interior life of a leader is *the* formative factor in shaping the flavor and feel of an environment. If the church really is the conduit through which Jesus has chosen to act, then there are few places this issue of ethos and ambience could possibly be more important. *Morph!* is about the inner-life things that need to go on in a leader and leadership team to create the compelling ethos of life change those searching for God so desperately seek. My hope is that you will capture the connection and morph like crazy.

Leadership is changing—the task and the skills, the culture and the

The computer world has borrowed a biblical concept, and we ought to at least use it when appropriate without thinking we are just co-opting a technology term.

people leading. This book is about the interplay of all those changes. The hard part is that someone has to see clearly through all the fog and frenzy. Someone has to see the future, chart the course, lay the plans, architect the team, spawn creativity, and then with perseverance intersect the culture into which we are called to live and speak. In God's plan, that is the role of leadership. Leaders are willing to run the ragged edge of risk taking and do what is necessary to see the church become the full-blown life-development center that God intends it to be.

This is not easy, however. We were not trained to minister in this emerging world in which we live. The views of truth, God, Scripture, and the church are entirely different today than even a decade or two ago. We are living in a morphing matrix. For the church to have a voice in this morphing matrix, she too must change.

The term "morphing" may raise some eyebrows. Lest you think we have detoured into some sort of weird New Age mumbo jumbo, let's define this term as it is very important for the terrain we will traverse ahead. Those of us familiar with the concept of morphing are probably thinking of its usage in computer technology. Even if you are unfamiliar with the technical complexities of how it works, we have all seen examples of it. Morphing is where one image on a TV or computer screen—let's say a truck—changes before your eyes with liquid smoothness into something else—let's say a car. The liquid smoothness is the key. You are actually watching the transformation before your very eyes.

An explanation of the computer technology that makes morphing possible is not necessary. But what is important to know is that morphing happens because the little dots of color that make up the picture of the truck are one by one moved into the configuration of dots that make up the car. When all these little dots are moved into new locations and we view the movements quickly on a TV screen, the changes look liquid.

So what is the big deal? Two things are a big deal. First, the computer world has borrowed a biblical concept, and we ought to at least use it when appropriate without thinking we are just co-opting a technology term. In the New Testament, Paul uses this word and a very familiar compound version of it for the kind of change Christ-followers are to experience in their lives. In Galatians 4:19 Paul says, "My dear children, for whom I am again in the pains of childbirth until Christ is formed in you." The word *formed* in the New International Version is the Greek word *morphe*—where we get our word *morph*.

Not only has the computer world snared a biblical word for her technology, but so has biology. Remember the caterpillar-to-butterfly observation in grade school? The caterpillar underwent a process of transformation called metamorphosis—once more a biblical term in the employ of the sciences. In an often-quoted passage on spiritual growth, Paul says in Romans 12:2a, "Do not conform any longer to the pattern of this world, but be transformed by the renewing of your mind." The word *transformed* is *metamorphe*. This is a relatively rare term in the New Testament. Paul only uses it one other time, in 2 Corinthians 3:18. There are only two additional usages in the entire New Testament. They are in the Gospels where the transfiguration of Jesus is called a metamorphosis.

Here is the second big deal. Morphing isn't only a good image of how spiritual formation needs to occur; leaders need to morph too. In fact, leaders must morph if the church teams they lead and the churches they serve are ever going to morph and move toward greater health and ultimately grow into being a fully leveraged redemption and maturity center for God. Jesus left very clear instructions for the eleven guys left on his team: "Go make disciples and teach them to obey everything I have commanded you" (Matthew 28:19-20).

The whole issue of obedience is wrapped up in the painful but necessary issue of change. When Jesus said, "Teach them to obey," he was essentially saying there are some very crucial areas that require ongoing change and growth. After all, that is obedience, and it isn't just individuals that need to change; so do churches.

What change looks and feels like will come a little later, but we do need to be clear on one thing: Leaders are the ones responsible for the flavor, feel, and direction of the local church. If the leaders aren't healthy, learning, dreaming, praying, and creative individuals, then how are we to expect the church to be any of those things?

Most leadership books tell us that everything rises and falls on leadership. If that is even partially correct, the morphing going on inside the leader is critical to the morphing that could go on in the organism of the church. A changing, healthy, growing leader cannot help but have a team and church that slowly, over time, takes on that kind of ethos. The connection between self-leadership, the leadership team culture, and the feel and dynamic of the church are tightly woven but often overlooked.

After a quick glance at the sea change going on around us, we will turn to the first section and address inner life issues: the inside issues of self-leadership that every leader needs to be attuned to for effective ministry in

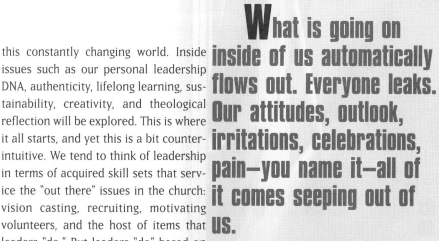

What is going on inside of us automatically flows out. Everyone leaks. Our attitudes, outlook, irritations, celebrations, pain—you name it—all of it comes seeping out of us.

this constantly changing world. Inside issues such as our personal leadership DNA, authenticity, lifelong learning, sustainability, creativity, and theological reflection will be explored. This is where it all starts, and yet this is a bit counterintuitive. We tend to think of leadership in terms of acquired skill sets that service the "out there" issues in the church: vision casting, recruiting, motivating volunteers, and the host of items that leaders "do." But leaders "do" based on who they are. Doing flows from being. This makes the inside leadership issues the key point of departure for our outside activities.

Out of the interior life of the leader flows a certain kind of aura, ethos, and culture. I call this the leadership "leak." The concept may sound mystical and ethereal, but it is the leak from the leader and leadership team that creates what we call ethos or organizational culture. What is going on inside of us automatically flows out. Everyone leaks. Our attitudes, outlook, irritations, celebrations, pain—you name it—all of it comes seeping out of us. We have all experienced it. There are certain people who always seem to have a toxic leak. You know who they are, and truth be known, you avoid them like the plague! The opposite is true as well. Some people always seem to bring encouragement, high expectation, and health to the table. They ooze and leak that disposition.

Leaders are no different. Who they are—for better or worse—directly impacts the flavor, feel, and health of a local church. This leak creates a certain feel and is decisive in who ends up attracted to or distanced from your team. The feel is then passed on and developed in the team, and that in turn determines the feel and flavor of the church at large. Is this intangible? No, the "feel" is very tangible but invisible, that's the nature of all organizational culture. This critical link between the interior life of the leader and the church ethos is what morphic leadership is all about.

Since we as leaders and our leadership teams significantly shape the culture of the church, we will be looking at things such as an expectant environment, the theology and practice of creativity and innovation, worship experience design, how change happens, team resource brokering, and a host of other things that give texture to church culture. Morphic leadership is a double-entendre about two morphing movements: the interior morph of the leader who has the goal and outcome of being a catalyst for the morphing of those people, teams, and the church culture around them.

Morphy

Our Morphing Context

As a grade school boy in the 1970s, I saw a brief film called *Future Shock*. The film was about how our society would have to deal with the massive technological changes just around the corner. These changes were to have significant impact on the social and relational fabric of our lives. I went home that night thinking, "Wow, if even a few of those things happen, the world will be a totally different place to live in." Little did I know on that grade school day that I had just been exposed to Alvin Toffler, one of the brilliant futurists of our generation.

Consider these kinds of shifts all happening within a space of a few years. Think about the early '70s—no VCRs, pocket calculators, LCD watches, or personal computers. It's hard to imagine life without those things, and yet those were just the beginning of the gadgets that have transformed our lives to ever-increasing levels of electronic techno-mania. I get my e-mail on my cell phone. With my iPAQ Pocket PC, I beam via infrared our agenda or a book review to other staffers in the room. I read the latest e-book, watch my handwriting transform into a Word document, or surf the net in the airport while I wait for a flight. I composed this entire book on my 3.75-pound notebook computer that has hundreds of times the speed and storage of that first IBM desktop PC-XT introduced back in 1983 when both my wife and I were employees for IBM.

The changes we've seen are mind-boggling, and the projections of what's ahead are equally incredible. Imagine a paper-thin sheet of plastic with a phone line coming out that, when plugged into a phone jack, downloads one of thousands of hourly updated newspapers. The ability to tap your favorite local rag will be

The changes we've seen are mind-boggling, and the projections of what's ahead are equally incredible. only moments and pennies away. Imagine grade school students receiving e-book readers at the beginning of every school year with all their textbooks preloaded, along with several hundred reference books for research and reading.

Move into the church arena. Picture credit/debit card scanners passed down the aisles of our churches for the offering, right along with the old basket. Consider individual, thin-panel computer screens at each church seat that allow the attendees to choose which customizations they prefer to view, in addition to the live worship experience in front of them. They may choose a looping animation of spectacular colors, a linear outline of the message as it's delivered, scrolling pieces of art supporting each worship segment, or the logged-in prayer requests of fellow worshippers seen in real time as they're entered into terminals throughout the worship space.

Changes in the New World

Just around the corner for millions of people is the next best thing to being in the actual worship location. Satellite technology enables whole services to be piped to remote locations. How long before that will be displaced by life-size holographic projections, making you feel as if you're actually present?

The potential changes are limitless for both society and the church. Most of these possibilities don't need any new technology; simply the will, the funding, and the desire to make them happen if they seem missional for the church. If this is what is available now, what will the possibilities look like with new emerging technologies? A recent sketch for a series we did called *Intersecting Our Native World* had somebody join in our church service live through contact lens implants that picked up our satellite link. Sketch today—reality tomorrow?

These kinds of changes are just the tip of the iceberg. How commerce, information, knowledge, education, and even just basic living conditions are impacted by much of this technology is quite easy to see. However, less visible changes are going on within our society—the softer issues like our views of truth, community, personhood, and God, for example.

What's the role of the church? How will the mapping of the human genome make the abortion debate look like ethical kindergarten? How does rampant consumerism impact the way people perceive church? What about the increase of brokenness within relationships and how it should affect the basic program offerings within our ministries? How do our views of personhood and individualism relate to our gospel proclamation and church service design? Electronic technology is a very visible and interesting change going on around us, but other cultural, attitudinal, and spiritual shifts are no less real and just as critical.

Still to receive honorable mention is the pace of change around us. Hardly an area of life is left untouched by radical change. But the pace doesn't seem to ever slow down. We've moved from a bygone era of continuous change to discontinuous transition.

Electronic technology is a very visible and interesting change going on around us, but other cultural, attitudinal, and spiritual shifts are no less real and just as critical.

A scrambled egg in the frying pan is experiencing continuous change as it's heated over low heat. The slow rise in temperature is at any time reversible. Simply removing the egg from the heat will stop the continuous heat-up. But there comes a time when the process reaches irreversibility, and the egg experiences the transition from a liquid state to the scrambled state. Removing it from heat, even putting it in the freezer, can't reverse the transition through which the egg passed.

The fried egg demonstrates why the kind of change we're experiencing is often so radical and disorienting. We're experiencing lots of scrambled egg transitions.

The Dow Jones sees the changes. In October 1999 the Dow dropped some of the old standbys that were quickly moving to the margins: Sears, Union Carbide, Chevron, and Goodyear. What went in the places of the department store and the petrochemical companies? Microsoft, Intel, Hewlett-Packard, and The Home Depot. We're living in a morphing matrix.

Absorbing the Changes

How will these changes impact the church? This isn't an issue of "if they will"; they profoundly do so already. The more important question is how *should* they impact the church, and how do church leaders understand these monumental shifts in our culture? What do they mean for ministry in the emerging future? This era into which we've been invited by God to make his Son, Jesus, known could hardly be more complex or exhilarating.

The current cultural shifts mean our ministry context is changing. The days are long past when arising on Sunday morning to dress in Sunday best and arrive at church prim and proper was the standard and assumed experience of the average American. For the vast majority of baby boomers, church attendance was rather typical. An unannounced inversion seems to have taken place, however. In talking with twenty-somethings, a very small percentage of them have grown up with a church experience. Many of them have absolutely no religious moorings of any sort. There seems to have been a shift somewhere in the transition from boomer (those between 39-55) to buster (those between 24-39).

While we need to be very careful of the sweeping generalizations often used in typical demographic labeling, the fact that major change is afoot is hard to ignore. Though pervasive, this shift was unannounced, undetectable, and remains rather nondescript. Noting this shift with very descriptive images, Leonard Sweet says, "If you were born before 1962, you are an immigrant. If you were born after 1962, you are a native."[1] I'm not sure what you are if you were born in 1962. I guess you're stuck at the border crossing.

Reading the Changes

A major responsibility of the leader is to know and read the cultural currents and then figure out, innovate, and create a way for the church to stay at a position of intersection with culture. The Old and New Testaments each have often-quoted texts that encourage this kind of cultural savvy and interface. First Chronicles 12:32 says, "Men of Issachar, who understood the times and knew what Israel should do." Here was a group who were sign-readers and cultural observers. They went the next step, however; they knew what they were to do, given the context they observed. This is 21C leadership.

> **A** major responsibility of the leader is to know and read the cultural currents and then figure out, innovate, and create a way for the church to stay at a position of intersection with culture.

Paul presents ministry with the same kind of pragmatic outlook. To think of ministry in practical terms, in categories that get us to a bottom line, seems almost sacrilegious in some circles. But Paul was crystal clear in 1 Corinthians 9:20-22: "To the Jews I became like a Jew, to win the Jews. To those under the law I became like one under the law (though I myself am not under the law), so as to win those under the law. To those not having the law I became like one not having the law (though I am not free from God's law but am under Christ's law), so as to win those not having the law. To the weak I became weak, to win the weak. I have become all things to all men so that by all possible means I might save some."

Paul changed methodologies whenever necessary to make sure the idiom, the language, and the metaphors were all comprehensible and connecting with his audience. He had a clearly defined goal to win some. He had no delusions of grandeur that he would win everyone. His goal wasn't "keep everyone happy" or "make sure everyone agrees with my approach." This makes total sense when we think about ministry from an effectiveness perspective, but when seen through the territoriality of traditions, liturgies, and sacred cows, the common sense of it all is no longer so common.[2]

I was working out early one morning before attending a recent theological scholarship conference when I met a professor from a very conservative Bible school. Over the loud volume of the morning CNN broadcast, we exchanged the typical "what do you do" information. He confided his previous misgivings about all this "contemporary ministry stuff" and then **Biblical interpretation is helpful only when coupled with cultural interpretation.** quickly added, "But I think I'm seeing things differently these days." Amidst the rhythmic squeak of our treadmills and dripping beads of sweat, he began to recount the requirements of the students at his school: church every Sunday morning, every Sunday evening, and every Wednesday night, plus attendance at four required chapel services weekly. He then made two profound observations. "I think our students are getting way too much religion; they seem to be more committed to serving a system and rules than being in relationship with Jesus." He had concluded that his school was preparing students for protecting a carefully scripted tradition but not for learning how to read the times and translate the gospel into a comprehensible message.

Biblical interpretation is helpful only when coupled with cultural interpretation. First-century Galilee spoke Aramaic and Greek. If Jesus had come speaking French, his message would have been squandered and lost. Is the church speaking a foreign language or the language of the times?

Leading at the Intersection

Cultural interpretation and intersection are leadership responsibilities. A leader unwilling or unable to do good cultural reflection will put the church on a trajectory toward obsolescence. Many of us shy away from this task and for good reason. A formidable host of factors have to be considered as each local church looks at its cultural point of entry. Every local church has unique gifts, a unique leadership style, a unique contribution to its local community, a mission that's hopefully rooted in the Great Commission, and a vision for how to accomplish it that's as unique as a set of fingerprints.

Every community has a unique culture, demography, interests, and lifestyle. This puts the leader in a very important role as a master of intersection. It requires as much facility in biblical exegesis as cultural exegesis, as much attention to careful biblical reading as to carefully reading the cultural context.

The quintessential example of genius intersection is, of course, the incarnation: God's presence, voice, and message piercing and penetrating 1C culture. As we simply observe the potency of the incarnation, several things come to mind. God sent Jesus as a person. God could have sent the message packaged any number of ways. He didn't choose a CD player to herald the good news, a Web page that automatically pops up every time someone logs on, or an MP3 download into our ear canal.

The fact that he sent a person bespeaks God's desire to be relevant, understandable, approachable, and relational. Jesus came dressing in the garb of the day, speaking the language of the time, eating, sleeping, sweating, and having body odor. He was someone everyone could approach. The message he embodied was eminently understandable but radically controversial for the religious leaders of the day. They didn't like the package God chose. They preferred the packaging of a political king and were initially irked and then outright outraged that Jesus would suggest anything else. Jesus said the current religious system was bankrupt and the leaders of the day were more interested in status quo protectionism than with missional destiny (Mark 7).

The church has to take its cue from God's Word. The job of cultural intersection will call forth the very best leadership the church has to offer. It will call forth the very best leadership you have to offer. The task is certainly daunting but the potential kingdom advance incalculable.

The church today has the potential to be engaged in an adventure of apostolic importance and prophetic potency. But it will require leaders and leadership teams who are unwilling to let their liturgies calcify and their structures smother the Spirit. The church can't hope to protect itself from the onslaught of "the world" by the futile attempt to create a haven of consistency amidst a culture of turbulent and virulent inconsistency. Such tactics will only produce an illusion of comfort that is increasingly out of date and hastens the entrance of hospice into our terminal condition.

Such tactics will only produce an illusion of comfort that is increasingly out of date and hastens the entrance of hospice into our terminal condition.

I'm currently working to help another church that is just coming to grips with this issue, and whether or not she turns the corner is still a matter of speculation. Will she be shackled to the past or poised for opportunities appearing tomorrow?

Tim called me one day for lunch. After attending our leadership conference a couple months earlier, he had decided to follow up with a meeting at a local grill. He and I had interacted before but on a very limited basis. He had only been in his current context a year and a half, and he was still looking for more connection. Tim was in a traditional mainline church. Not much had changed in the last thirty years except attendance. They had gone from nearly a thousand in attendance in the 1970s to about 280. Other than that, everything was pretty stable, solid, and nearly fossilized.

As our waitress grated fresh Parmesan over our bowls of pasta, I asked Tim what was cooking in his neck of the woods. He said, "Ron, I know you're going to find this petty and even a bit humorous, but when I decided to go without my robe (typical Sunday attire in his tradition), you would have thought I'd asked people to sacrifice their firstborn." We both chuckled but knew the stakes were high. If changing something this small in the interests of being more approachable to new unchurched people caused this much stir, how were the really important changes going to be received?

morph

Some of the people in the congregation were incensed; the staff was inundated with complaints and dumbfounded on how to handle it. They found themselves at an interesting and challenging place. Would they alienate the complainers or pacify them? Would they help explain the rationale for the change or buckle under people-pleasing pressure? As you can imagine, this is just the beginning of the kinds of changes on the horizon that this team would like to implement. It illustrates the kind of obstacles facing leaders today.

This isn't a book on how to connect the church with culture. Several good volumes have explored postmodernity and even how the church sits within it.[3] This volume explores the leadership issues arising in this new world—the significant personal, internal issues and how attention to self-leadership creates a certain type of feel, expectancy, and outlook in a congregation. We'll also examine how to make people resilient and adept at exploiting these changes for more effective and dynamic ministry.

Several things are noteworthy as we look at the cultural landscape in which the church voices its message and lives its life. This will serve as a quick sketch, providing backdrop for self-leadership issues and how these impact church ethos. While many could be listed, these four are central to the unfolding of the following chapters.

Truth in Question

Near the top of the list is truth; for many, it's no longer absolute. Truth is often defined in personal and private ways. If it works for me, then that's good enough for me. The idea of an overarching framework, out of which truth claims should be checked and evaluated, no longer dominates. What does this mean for the church?

The idea of an overarching framework, out of which truth claims should be checked and evaluated, no longer dominates.

The implications are broad and unavoidable. Apologetics have to be rethought and augmented. The days of a strictly evidentialist approach are probably long gone. An evidentialist approach will have to be wedded to a relational one that allows the questioner to see a different kind of life—a life he or she may long for but be uncertain how to experience.

This has clear implications for those weekend talks we give called the sermon. People are looking more for a path than pontification. They long for a path pointing them toward spiritual discovery—discovery those of us in the church are still experiencing with humility. Pontification that has the smell of doctrinaire arrogance is simply the phony turn off many outside the church have come to expect from those of us inside the church.

Chad and Christina are a good example. Chad and I had numerous golfing encounters before our first spiritual lunch engagement. As we walked green, lush fairways, we had covered all the basic things you can talk about: what he and I did for a living, family matters, and given my vocation, spiritual things as well. Chad and Christina had come to a Christmas Eve service, but that appeared to be as close as they wanted to get to church. Our first lunch was his opportunity to unburden his mind and heart. He just couldn't buy the "pat answers," he said. "I want to explore all this carefully, and my concern is that there simply isn't a place that will allow me to work through the process, ask my questions, and discover the answers."

Chad isn't alone. Though an intellectual, his questions weren't primarily of that nature. He wanted someone to point him down the right path and let him wrestle the issues to the ground. Christina was a little different case. She was convinced they would try church if "my kids don't get brainwashed into believing this 'Jesus is the only way to heaven' stuff."

A year and a half later, they're relatively consistent attendees at Westwinds and are slowly getting involved, cautiously exploring, and becoming noticeably intrigued by those around them. Can I say where they are in the process? That's a question I used to ask. I am now convinced it's wrongheaded and unanswerable. I've decided that the point is they are still in the process.

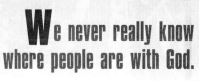

We never really know where people are with God.

We never really know where people are with God. In fact, a good deal of the time, we aren't even sure where we are in the process. They were simply looking for someone, some church to show them the path. They were looking for a group of people living intriguing lives that they could observe, question, and then "do life with." Slowly their lives are morphing.

Experience Cravings

The issue of experience is a second major cultural player that's affecting church ministry in this new millennium. Experience is a premium commodity. Whether it's going to the Rainforest Café for a meal or shopping at an REI Outfitter complete with mountain-biking track, seven-story mountain climbing wall, and mechanical ski slope, we're a culture that's craving experience. From Chuck E. Cheese to adventure travel, there's something for all ages and all price ranges in the new experience economy.

Our TV viewing also screams experience. The dominant afternoon programming of the '80s was the soap opera. In the '90s it was the talk show. With the shift from vicarious living through the fabricated soap characters to the real-life storytelling of the talk show, we've moved from representation to participation. The wild success of *Survivor*, *Fear Factor*, and other reality TV shows demonstrates our desire for the real and our craving for experience. Who could have guessed that more people would watch the season finale of *Survivor* than voted in the Bush/Gore presidential election?[4]

Enter the church. For most people, there is a major disconnection between their day-to-day lives and the fifty-year time warp they enter when they walk through the front doors of the church. Does this mean we should simply entertain? acquiesce to the culture? let the "market" determine what we say and do? These are critical questions to explore later. But the fact that it is an issue means it must be investigated. And the fact that it's on the terrain of our culture means it is an issue that leaders must wrestle with and take into consideration as we chart the path into the future.

Everything Has Gone Hyper

Hyper-choice is a third hot issue. Do an informal survey of the mundane. At my local mega-supermarket, I find over sixty different potato chip possibilities. That isn't snack options—pretzels, popcorn, and cheese curls—it is strictly potato chips. And toothpaste? There are forty-six options.

So what, you say? This kind of choice in almost every department of life leads to a "demand for choice" mind-set.[5] What you don't have or know about, you don't miss. If the only chips in existence were standard potato chips, no one would complain if there weren't kettle chips, ridged chips, low-fat chips, or natural chips. But if you walked into a store today and

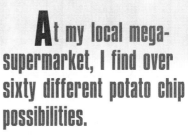

At my local mega-supermarket, I find over sixty different potato chip possibilities.

all they offered was one choice, you would feel cheated as a consumer. What does this hyper-choice mean for our churches?

The increase of options has a closely associated phenomenon leaders will have to tangle with in the future—megastore swallow-up. Lowe's and The Home Depot have swallowed up a good deal of the mom and pop hardware stores. And of course that's only the beginning. Wal-Mart has done the same thing.

Maybe the implications aren't instantly transparent. But their impact is being felt. Even the average person in small town USA is getting increasingly accustomed to one-stop shopping where convenience and options are at their fingertips. Like it or not, this outlook has migrated into the church arena.

Interestingly, these large megastores recognize that their mammoth size cannot create an impersonal feel. If you go to a Sam's or Lowe's, you'll be warmly greeted by someone at the front door. Customer service in these places is a top priority.

How does the church measure up? The issue of feel, and the warmth or lack of it, are constantly voiced by visitors. This has always been an issue for the new person trying to "break into" the church. The common critique of churches being cliquish, cool, and tough to connect with is most likely ancient. But our "customer is right" culture heightens this struggle to new levels.

Does the church offer just one service time? What about different-flavored services? Is the church a one stop shopping megastore, or is it a small mom and pop operation? Are there great kids' ministry options, junior high programs, a cool high school ministry? What about single parents' support? The list goes on and on.

Some people may prefer the intimacy and feel of a small church with seventy-five people. But that size church can't provide the one-stop shopping the statistics seem to say the churched and unchurched public craves. This isn't an apologetic for "large church is better church." It's merely an inescapable observation and a huge leadership issue. How is a leader to remain missionally faithful but intersect a changing culture in a way that invites investigation and engagement?

Spiritual Interest: Friend or Foe?

The fourth major cultural tide leaders must surf is the increased interest in spiritual things, but not necessarily Christian things. This seascape is fraught with all sorts of powerful waves that all have capsize potential. Think about the increase of interest in psychics. Who would have thought even five years ago that you would be able to dial a 900 number and receive an "individualized" tarot card reading? Who would have guessed the Harry Potter series would be equally read by kids and adults and set all-time records at the box office? On any given day you can tune into Oprah and catch any number of guests peddling the latest Zen, New Age, or pure self-help material. Interestingly, today's Oprah guest may set forth glaring contradictions with the previous day's guest, but in an age of redefined truth, we are encouraged to embrace it all. It doesn't seem to be a problem for most. What are we as leaders in this culture called to do in this melting amalgam of spirituality?

The distinction between religion and spirituality is commonplace. Robert Wuthnow chronicles this phenomenon in his recent volume *After Heaven: Spirituality in America Since the 1950s.*

If spiritual interest is on the rise and yet the church isn't the dominant location for exploring this interest, then doesn't this tell us something as leaders?

It seems relatively clear that this distinction shows a disdain for "organized religion," even though the flip side isn't disorganized religion. The alternative seems to be something more personalized, spiritual, practical but mystical, a genuine experience with something transcendent. Again the implications here are hard to escape.

If spiritual interest is on the rise and yet the church isn't the dominant location for exploring this interest, then doesn't this tell us something as leaders? Leonard Sweet says this is the fourth spiritual Great Awakening in American history, but it's the first led outside the church.

22

For the church to get and stay on track, it will take leaders—morphic leaders who intimately feed the feel and flavor of their churches—willing to undergo the radical changes at the personal level. The day the church is taught by gifted teachers, led by gifted leaders, served by gifted servants, administrated by gifted administrators (you get the point), will be a day the church begins to fire on all eight cylinders and becomes the salt and light God designed her to be. Nothing short of this kind of vigilance will solve the problem of those outside the church looking to other sources for spiritual guidance.

We in the church have often lived uninteresting, unintriguing, and inauthentic lives. It's no wonder people outside the church have no reason to check it out as a source of potential spiritual experience and answers. Our churches need to morph to meet a morphing culture.

The Power of a Well-Placed Question

Solomon says in Proverbs 20:5, "The purposes of a man's heart are deep waters, but a man of understanding draws them out."

We would do well to consider the intent of this little passage. Early in my doctoral program I was exposed to Bobb Beihl. As a consultant focused in the area of master planning, Bobb was constantly asking well-placed questions. He never seemed to just ask a few average questions; he asked lots and lots of insightful ones. I thank God for Bobb. I've been saved from numerous headaches and potential miscues by using his battery of questions.[6]

In good Bobb Beihl form, I'd like to encourage you to do the work of reflection and journaling as you head through this material. You'll discover and uncover so much more about yourself, your values, and what makes you tick. The sections called InnerAction at the end of each chapter will help you uncover areas needing more work, plus areas you can celebrate and build upon. Hopefully the questions will catalyze inner reflection and lead to action.

Leaders, prepare for the journey. May inner-action begin the morphing.

InnerAction

1. In your ministry context, what elements of these cultural shifts do you see? How are these shifts positively or negatively impacting your ministry effectiveness?

2. Are there other cultural currents not discussed here that are impacting your ministry arena? (See the observations of someone like Gerard Kelly in *Retrofuture*.) What will these changes do to your future planning?

3. Where are you on the cultural interpretation front? Are you tuned in? What are the last five cultural pieces you've read, and what actually changed in your ministry as a result of those insights? What cultural pieces have you discussed as a staff, and what brainstorming emerged?

Endnotes

1. Leonard Sweet, *Carpe Mañana* (Grand Rapids, MI: Zondervan, 2001), 14.

2. I have to credit my dad here, Ronald J. Martoia. As a corporate and executive consultant, he has said for years that common sense is really not all that common. If it was, we wouldn't have so much nonsense. I had the privilege of growing up in a context in which simply by osmosis I should have become a leader. I thank my parents for the greenhouse context.

3. Chuck Smith, Jr., *The End of the World...As We Know It* (Colorado Springs, CO: WaterBrook Press, 2001). Brian D. McLaren, *The Church on the Other Side: Doing Ministry in the Postmodern Matrix* (Grand Rapids, MI: Zondervan Publishing House, 1998, 2000). Leonard Sweet, *SoulTsunami: Sink or Swim in New Millennium Culture* (Grand Rapids, MI: Zondervan Publishing House, 1999). Leonard Sweet, *Post-Modern Pilgrims: First Century Passion for the 21st Century World* (Nashville, TN: Broadman & Holman Publishers, 2000).

4. Taped session of Leonard Sweet at SimpleComplexities Conference, October 2001.

5. Gerald Kelly, *Retrofuture: Rediscovering Our Roots, Recharting Our Routes* (Downers Grove, IL: InterVarsity Press, 1999), 68.

6. Bobb Beihl has a couple of great examples of his question-asking prowess. Bobb Beihl, *Increasing Your Leadership Confidence* (Sisters, OR: Questar Publishers, Inc., 1989). Bobb Beihl and Ted W. Engstrom, *Increasing Your Boardroom Confidence* (Phoenix, AZ: Questar Publishers, Inc., 1988). These are simply must-reads to better learn the art of question asking.

morphi

INNERMORPH

Gary, a pastor friend, called me on his cell phone on the way back from a personal retreat. He was flying high and wanted me to share his excitement. Gary's church leadership team, along with several other churches in the area, had attended our monthly leadership training event a month earlier. Out of that experience, he had pursued a recommended resource, taken a personal retreat, and was calling on his return trip home to fill me in. "This has changed my life and ministry for good. There are going to be some changes. There just have to be if I'm going to stay and serve this church. But, Ron, a lot of the changes are really changes in me. They can't change and grow until I change and grow."

We only talked for a few minutes that day but had a real down and dirty discussion the following week. What Gary was wrestling through was the same thing I'd wrestled through a few years earlier. Changing a church isn't really about changing a church; it's about growing the leader(ship) of the church. It's about morphing.

Technology and Biology Go Biblical

When the technology of morphing was introduced in music videos in the early '80s, we were all fascinated. A computerized image, through liquid smooth changes, is "morphed" into another entirely different image. Then in the '90s Dodge and Gillette commercials morphed everything from brilliant red sports cars and trucks to faces of various ethnicities getting ready to shave. It was simply fascinating.

We've already made mention of how biology and technology have employed biblical terminology. Whether we're speaking of the caterpillar-to-butterfly metamorphosis or the dot-by-dot, pixel-by-pixel change when a computer image morphs, incremental transformation is the focus.

This is Paul's basic image. As we grow and experience transformation, the New Testament says we are morphing. Paul said it was his desire to see Christ formed (morphe) in the Galatian Christ-followers (Galatians 4:19). He longed for a point-by-point, pixel-by-pixel, cell-by-cell change. Morphic leadership is about changing (transforming) the leader so the organism of the church can morph as well.

When we think of growing our leadership, we usually think in terms of becoming a better time manager, motivator, speaker, or strategic planner. Rarely do we assume leadership growth as fundamentally deep change in the inner life of the leader. Leadership is about connecting with our God-designed essence, our core inner shape, and then leading from that center. Leadership is first an inside job.

Morph of the Leader—Morph of the Team

For a long time, we've heard "Speed of the leader, speed of the team." I believe it, I try to teach it, and hope I model it. But the stakes are higher. Speed is just as essential as it has always been, but the need to work smarter, not harder, ranks right up there too. But more than that has to happen for the church to catch the full gale the Holy Spirit wants to blow through it and into the world. So I update the old adage: Morph of the leader, morph of the team.

The emerging church needs morphic leaders who are determined to experience radical transformation. When that transformation happens, it flows into the teams they lead and the churches they serve. This is where the hard work of leadership must start if we're going to lead with all diligence, earnestness, effort, and zeal as Paul challenges us in Romans 12:8.[1] Changing the church and other people is impossible; that's God's business and quite out of our control. What *is* within the domain of our responsibility is our own health, growth, and morphic dynamic. God is going to build his church by changing me.

The New Testament paints the radically transformed life as the goal of all Christ-followers. The necessity of morphic change in the life of the leader should be seen as even more critical. I may have a slightly slower download time than some, but making this connection was really profound for me. I saw leadership as something "in addition to" my relationship with Christ. In reality, it was part of the morphing image. Leadership was flowing and morphing out of my interior deep change.

Chips and Salsa Therapy

This realization was hard and painful for me. While at a conference, it took a dear friend, two long evenings of Mexican food, and hours of discussion for me to come to grips with some of my own personal immaturities. I'm not against offices and clinical settings, but who can beat Mexican food and chips and salsa for a therapy session?

I met Mac, an Episcopal rector, in my doctoral program, and the role he would play in catalyzing growth and health would prove to be a turning point in my life. He was the catalyst for my first deep aha. I've built upon it numerous times since. Some of the toughest leadership calls I've had to make were related to unpopular decisions I knew would go against the wishes of certain people in the congregation. Every leader comes to some point in his or her personal development where he or she will be challenged to do what is best for the whole, even when it's unpopular with a small group or individual.

Mac had quickly identified a deep people-pleasing idol in my life. I was essentially paralyzed in making a decision because one woman had issued me an ultimatum: She would leave if I didn't do things her way. What was churning at subterranean levels in me was much deeper, though. It was essentially about pride. My thoughts worked something like this: "If this lady gets ticked at me, the chances are she'll tell some other people. As soon as she does, what will other people think, and how will I know what she said? I'll then look bad in front of how many people?" Those are the beginning ruminations that escalated from there and took on a life of their own. "Now there will be a group of people who don't like the call I made and also don't like the way I've treated their friend [the ultimatum giver]. I'll lose credibility, and worse than that, I'll be unable to defend myself." Have you ever had these demons lurking in your head? This is people-pleasing, and I had a good case of it.

Every leader comes to some point in his or her personal development where he or she will be challenged to do what is best for the whole, even when it's unpopular with a small group or individual.

Looking back, it seems absolutely foolish and embarrassing that I would even consider allowing one person or group of people the power to hold the entire church hostage. But in those early days, this was the kind of thing out of which sleepless nights were made. With wise counsel I came to conclude that this tough decision was tough only because I was concerned about her perception of me and the potential ripple effect it might have on others. On every other count it was a wise, missional, "best for the church" decision. Mac told me something that would forever change my leadership life. He said, "Ron, if this is a hard decision to make now [we were a church of about 200], think how frequently you'll have to make this decision when you're 700 [which was the size of his congregation at the time]. You need to determine if you have the stomach for leadership. You can choose ulcers or trust in God's choice of you as a leader." How right he was. Those two dinner therapy sessions proved life-changing.

I had to settle in my mind whether emotions would dictate my decision making, a few vocal detractors would run the church, or I would really lead. This was a critical turning point for me and has impacted my leadership on nearly a weekly basis. What would have been ulcer-producing situations back then happen very frequently now. The tickle in my stomach is still there, emotions are still felt, but they don't provide the North Star for the issues I have to navigate. Callous insensitivity may be a possible flip side to this coin, but it isn't a viable ministry solution. It won't contribute to maturity.

Real leading requires sorting through input, evaluating sources, seeking God's best in his Word and his internal promptings, and, if in doubt, checking the decision against others with wisdom and years. My discussions with Mac prompted a morphing moment when interior leadership immaturity had to be identified and dealt with in me if I was to progress into the leader God wanted me to be. I returned from that conference and took what proved to be the first hard steps of emotional maturity that essentially translated into leadership lessons. God was shaping me; I was becoming a morphic leader.

From Pepto Bismol Churning to Inner Learning

With courage buoyed and phone support from Mac for the next several weeks, I can honestly say this is when my real leadership growth and emotional maturity began to track. This was the first time I had pictured myself as a leader...a spiritually gifted leader. To see myself as a pastor? No problem. A teacher? Most certainly. But a leader? It wasn't my self-understanding. I went through plenty of Pepto Bismol and Tums in those early days. I'm ashamed to say many sleepless nights were the result of my inability to simply grow up and make hard decisions. Inner life growth is the core of leadership development.

This leads to one of the key reasons that leaders have to grow up on the inside and experience deep change. When Westwinds went through a challenging time, often it could be traced to me going through a challenging time. Our low spots as a church were often a reflection of low spots in my maturity curve. This is not meant as a guilt-inducer for those in tough leadership times. Leadership is a complex art form, and one new skill can't fix all the complexities that arise. But it's safe to say when we are heading through bumpy waters as a church, we need to be a bit more introspective in asking "What is it in my leadership or leadership team that may be promoting this difficulty?"

When Westwinds went through a challenging time, often it could be traced to me going through a challenging time.

I have learned that I'm not alone. A large number of people go into pastoral ministry because they really want to help people. That's precisely the two-edged sword that causes so much trouble. On one hand, you want to please people, serve them, and keep them happy. On the other hand, that becomes pathological if we aren't careful. Ulcers and sleepless nights later, we realize the applause meter of our church attendees guides our whole outlook in life and has a fairly powerful stranglehold on our decision-making apparatus.

We've grown over fivefold since those Mexican restaurant therapy sessions, and I've had to learn to make unpopular calls on a much more frequent basis. Mac was as prophetic as he was insightful. God is interested in morphing his leaders because the overflow of that change will "leak" into the ethos of the church. The emotional growing up I've done since then continues and is far from over, but ulcers are a thing of the past.

Once I realized that change in the church organism is an outflow of personal transformation, the task of leadership took on a different coloration. This was exactly the same dawning Gary was beginning to share when we talked that sunny afternoon on his cell phone. The biggest changes in the church needed to take place in him. Once that was underway, the leak of new vision and values and the crafting of a new church ethos were simply inevitable.

Walking through this maturity experience illustrated for me why I needed to have a small group of guys in vocational ministry who were developmentally far ahead of me. These are guys who over the years have been encouragers and have provided compasslike direction when I was confused or unclear. Sometimes these have been simple "you need to grow up" sessions. Other times these were "thinking it through out loud" sessions. But whatever the need, they have been critical in helping me through difficult times and keeping me healthy. Plenty of times I have called to say, "I'm not thinking in a healthy way; help me sort this out." Everybody needs a small group of guys or gals like this to keep the heart and head clear.

Informational Versus Transformational

The world in which we live places a high value on information—amassing it, managing it, and being aware of it. We pick up a subtle message very early in our schooling: Information acquired is what wins the day. Take my school experience, typical probably of most of ours. How long did it take me to figure out that school tests were essentially about short-term memory skills? By third grade I'd pretty much beat the system. Hone your ability to store information the teacher said you would need to spit out on paper, take a test, score a good grade, and start storing the next round of data.

We all came to realize that the better our short-term memory, the higher our grade. What was actually learned and integrated into life was a rather secondary issue, if it was an issue at all. High school and college are simply the same basic scenario with the stakes a bit higher and the cost of being in the classes higher too. What is the summary taken away from all this? We come to equate the intake of information with transformation.

What happens when this migrates church-side? We have information/transformation confusion. In the Sunday school classroom, we teach and assume that memorized Scripture, daily devotions, and a regimen of prayer bring life change. And while this is possible, it may also do nothing but lead to a calcified, legalistic pattern.

Move down the hall to the office of the pastoral staff. They often share the same subtle confusion. I am hardly finger-pointing. It's a picture of my life not long ago. This is exactly why we need a less program-driven and technique-fix model of leadership development. Instead we need an interior development program that helps leaders uncover their deepest core design and then tools them to build on it. Vibrant leaders can't create environments that are anything but vibrant.

This glance into the inner working of leadership is counterintuitive in our seminar-driven, principle-extracting, "higher education" model of learning. I confess that I had the '90s seminar-junkie mentality. Attend a conference, grab some resources, go back and blow away your elders with all your new ideas, experience frustration because no one else could quite "get it," and then trot off to another conference to find something that might fit better and meet with less resistance. I have to admit that I've done it more than once.

I think seminars are invaluable, programs essential, and resources the lifeblood of any ministry team worth its salt. However, all those things could be well in place and a church still miss the health and growth mark. The obvious disconnection happening in my head in those early years of ministry was that techniques and skills don't change my life or the life of anyone else. They are simply vehicular transportation. Life, health, and growth are about interior issues, the inner ordering of the leader's life. How could the life, health, and growth of the church organism be anything different?

Space-Feel Architecture

I've become increasingly convinced over the last decade that the most profound change a church will ever see is spawned by the deepening maturity, emotional growing up, and the quest for lifelong learning of the point leader and leadership team of a church. Why? The "space-feel" of a church may be the most undiscussed, critical indicator of a church's health. The space-feel in a church—that intangible, tough to put your finger on ambience—is the dominant attraction or repellent of people walking into your church for the first time.

Who and what defines that space-feel? The leadership core of a church— the point

30

leader, the staff, the unpaid core of servants in small group leadership and ministry team directorships—define, refine, and remake the "feel" of the church.

Essentially, leaders are architects. We don't build buildings, but we do design space. The space is invisible, but it is very, very tangible, and it is felt. We need to conceive part of our leadership responsibility as being space-feel architects.

This ethos or feel is what management literature calls organizational culture: those unspoken rules of how things work, what values we hold, how we treat each other, and how conflict is handled. We've paid far too little attention to it in the church. First, because it is invisible and largely composed of tacit rules and assumptions, organizational culture is tough to define. Because it's tough to define, training people and orchestrating change in culture is difficult work. Second, the work of self-leadership is very hard, painful, and slow-going. Those two things have contributed to a significant amount of ignorance on this issue within our churches.

If people entering our churches can instantly "feel" the flavor, temperature, and tenor of the culture, then how do we attempt to shape and sculpt that feel into something that is inviting, expectant, and thick with the compelling presence of God? The feel of our churches has always been critical, but our current postmodern location makes it even more so. In the past, the church may have been evaluated on the basis of the organ and organist, the preacher's ability to deliver the goods, or how good the children's sermon connected with the kids. If these things were up to snuff, then "joining" was the thing to do. Those days are largely over.

I was recently at a conference in downtown Atlanta. While walking through a food court in a high-rise mall complex, I was struck by how many of the food businesses were out in front handing out samples of their lunch fare—Chinese samples, cheese steak hoagie samples, California wrap samples. There's nothing unusual about samples, but I'd never found this in a mall food court with fast-food chains. I asked one of the vendors the rationale. His words? "People want to sample before they are sold." Lesson learned. Church visitors are exactly the same.

We now find people who are far more deliberate and discriminating in their church selection process. This is especially true of those who have never been in a church or are reconnecting after a decade-long hiatus.

> **"People want to sample before they are sold."**

Visitors aren't attending the churches they grew up in as kids or the denominational choices of their parents. People investigating church are looking to connect with others, and some are looking for the transcendent, and usually in that order. They are far more apt to want to "belong" before they experiment with "believing." They want to sample before they are sold. This makes the issue of church ethos exceedingly critical. If they are simply sampling to see if they want to "buy in," then the feel they experience every week is crucial.

Some church consultants say people decide within the first two to five minutes whether or not to attend a church again. The point? It isn't message, music, or media. It is ethos...pure and simple. When we have done informal surveys of visitors who have been around a few weeks and say, "Tell us about your Westwinds experience," or "Tell us what you think about Westwinds," either inquiry seems to get the same basic response. People describe what they are feeling from others in the lobby and what they feel like when they leave a worship experience. In short, they almost always comment on the tangible, though invisible, feel of ethos.

The inner morphing of the leader is so critical because what is going on inside us automatically overflows into the space around us. What leaks from the leader and leadership team of the church does more to sculpt ethos than any other factor, including preaching, music, and the rest of the arts.

What do we know about the leak? Over the last several years, I've made several observations.

Leak Laws Observed

All of us leak; this is the first leak law. While this may be stating the obvious, the implications are not so obvious. In a typical view of leadership, we model, we cast vision, we get people on board, and if we do it all correctly, the soldiers charge the hill and we accomplish the mission.

All of us leak; this is the first leak law. While there is some truth to this, it places too much emphasis on the leader. All people leak, which shows why the leak of the leadership core team to the rest of the group is so important. In other words, the leak of one is not what creates the feel in a church. It is the leak of a critical mass of people. The leak of the leadership core is important precisely because over time this will be the leak of the larger group.

Second, leaking has pervasive effects. When enough food coloring is put into the white powdered sugar frosting my kids and I put on graham crackers, the food coloring permeates all the frosting, not just a little corner of the frosting bowl. This principle has obvious implications for everything from creating an expectant environment for God to combating the gossip goblin.

A corollary to this second leak law is that negative leaks seem to permeate quicker. Most of us in ministry will readily acknowledge this one. Negative gossip spreads like fire. Cantankerous comments grow like cancer and seem to unearth every disgruntled person within a three-mile radius.

Third, leaking is usually unconscious and unintentional. Here is an important point. Most people do not set out to infect or endear someone with their attitude, demeanor, or story. But it happens anyway. This may be one of the more difficult yet powerful things for us to learn about the leak. The effects of leaking are as insidious as they are subversive. Here is a point worthy of training—leak awareness. What are you leaking? And even more important, how are you leaking?

Fourth, leaking can't be faked or fabricated long term. Our church culture is something we've woven like fabric—thread-by-thread, action-by-action, attitude-by-attitude, and story-by-story. Church culture is church specific and, therefore, unique; no two are alike. We can put some window dressing on changing our culture by trying a fix-of-the-month or program-of-the-week. The reality is that leaking starts on the inside and flows out, not the other way around.

Morphic leadership means profound interior transformation, and it forms the basis for seeing culture change with lasting results. Programmatic fixes, new skills acquired, or better visions cast are all well and good, but they can't change the feel of the church culture in any lasting way. We've had to learn this many times and in many ways. Part of the job of the morphic leader is to tune in to the cultural frequency of the church and see if it's where it should be. We had to inject some life when we realized our church "feel" was that of busyness.

The Case of Mistaken Core Values

After some informal surveying, staff discussions on a retreat day, and board input, we came to conclude that our "feel" as a church was simply busy. We were ten years old and had been meeting in schools the whole time. We had to do everything in "portable mode," and we developed a very efficient way of getting all of our gear set up and torn down for our church services. The result? We were experiencing major collision between our church ethos and our stated values. Our first stated core value is "All people matter to God."

All organizations (churches included) have stated values and values in practice. When the values in practice aren't aligned with stated values, we'll have a credibility gap. We'll create a culture that says one thing but models something else. That was exactly our problem. We had a stated value, but in practice our value was that setting up and tearing down is more important than creating community with new people.

Our intention had never been to marginalize visitors. But picture our leak laws at work. We were unconsciously portraying in our attitudes and actions a scurrying around, a busying of ourselves with physical property considerations. The more people we enlisted to help in the tear-down process, the more people we removed from the "mingling with visitors" system. We were sending the wrong message. Our "busyness" was read as "unfriendliness." Even more important, we actually were told that some people thought acceptance meant serving like crazy.

Leak Awareness

We've mentioned in passing the two primary ways our interior lives leak—our disposition and our story. Our attitude, countenance, and approach toward people have direct bearing on how others see us. This is usually confirmed by the story we tell. Story or narrative, as used here, is a broad category capturing the essence of what we are sharing at any given time.

All of us have bad days from time to time. No one expects us to be perfect or have plastic grins pasted over our mouths 24/7. Leaking can't be faked long term anyway. Over time, however, our basic demeanor and story show others who we are, what we most deeply believe about God and others, and whether we see the world through a glass half empty or half full.

The "over time" component is the important part of the equation here. The collective "over time" demeanor and story of our church attendees is what creates the overall feel in our church. Our leak laws come to mind again. All of us leak. Leak is unintentional, leak is pervasive, and you can't fake it.

Almost everything written these days mentions the role of story in the post-modern world. One thing needs to be said concerning my usage of it here. Far from being merely a pop fad, Jesus used story all the time. In fact, Matthew 13:34 records that Jesus did not say anything to the crowds without using a parable. Jesus knew the power of story. We often think story is for the uneducated and more childlike in our midst and propositions are for the more intellectual. Apparently, that's not true.

Leak is unintentional, leak is pervasive, and you can't fake it.

All of us are experts on at least one thing: our story. We know better than anyone else what has happened in our lives and how the main character in the story feels and thinks. Our story is the most compelling and persuasive thing we can give people about God's activity in the world. God's invitation, our response, and God's profound changing of us are all-powerful and compelling.

Furthermore, have you ever met anyone who didn't want to tell his or her story—that person's woes, pains, and one-upmanship experiences? Go to a nursing home or a retirement center. You'll get the picture. Here's where we have a swinging door as Christ-followers. The ability to listen and share stories is the way people come to follow Jesus.

Maybe now the connection between interior morphing and the culture of our churches is becoming clearer. How can someone who is growing with God, experiencing answers to prayer, seeing spiritual conversations started with new questioners, and feeling a deepening sense of community in his or her relationships not leak healthy stuff?

Obviously, growth at this level means dealing with our dark issues of pain and brokenness and addressing our fractures and wounds. But the person in the process of moving with God toward health has a compelling authenticity that is impossible to hide. Certainly rough waters have to be sailed at times. Tough days do hit. But the steady ride and slow burn of dynamic morphing can't be hidden.

Unfortunately, the opposite example is readily available to most of us. We all know people who leak toxic ooze no matter what the day or season of year. They have a story all right, but it is more like a virus you want to avoid. They just don't seem to shake it. These are the chronic VDPs, as Gordon McDonald calls them,[2]—the Very Draining People who do nothing to contribute but do all they can to drain as much from everyone else as possible. The spread of those toxins can be contagious if not caught early and can infect an entire church ethos, especially in smaller congregations.

The person in the process of moving with God toward health has a compelling authenticity that is impossible to hide.

In the next few chapters, we'll explore the inner life issues we need to be aware of as leaders. In the later chapters, we'll look at components we need floating around in our church culture if we are going to see spiritual formation and a church ethos that is compelling and engaging. Those willing to experience the challenge of personal morphing will see their leadership rise to an entirely new level. As we morph so shall we leak. Morph on!

InnerAction

1. In what areas are you morphing right now? How has it gone? What does this tell you about how to help other leaders on your team who you may need to coach through similar situations?

2. Do you have any "Mexican restaurant therapy sessions" you can point to, any mentors who have helped you sled through difficult waters? If not, why not, and how can it be remedied? If so, what is next on the docket?

3. Where can you see connections between your personal growth and the ministry context you serve? How can you position yourself before God to increase the incidence of this happening? How can you help your team experience the same thing?

4. What leak laws hit you the hardest? What does your leadership team think are the most important insights for them? What can you concretely do to heighten the leak awareness in yourself and your team?

5. What in your church culture is less than optimal for the first-time visitor in your church? What does your team say about the overall feel of your church? What would first-time visitors say if you had the courage to survey them and they had the courage to be honest?

Endnotes

1. "If it is encouraging, let him encourage; if it is contributing to the needs of others, let him give generously; if it is leadership, let him govern diligently; if it is showing mercy, let him do it cheerfully" (Romans 12:8).

2. Gordon MacDonald, *Restoring Your Spiritual Passion* (Nashville, TN: Oliver-Nelson Books, a division of Thomas Nelson, Inc., Publishers, 1986), 84.

CELLULAR LEADERSHIP: THE COUNTER- INTUITIVE MOVE INWARD

The current weekend set of talks I am giving is on the topic of replication. This weekend my talk was built around 2 Peter 1:3-9. All preaching brings us face to face with the text and how it is actually being lived out in our lives. But I was reminded in a rather serendipitous way that this text holds a bit more octane than most for me.

As I was digging around in an old box, I discovered a copy of a Bible study I had prepared when I was fifteen years old (not that long ago, I might add) for the Bible study group I led of a bunch of other thirteen- to fifteen-year-olds. This was one of those first indelible passages I had learned as a young believer. In that study I wrote, "If there is nothing else we do with this passage, we must at least become promise fanatics. God's promises are the way he gets us to experience more of him and less of the world, and that is something we will need to do forever." That comment from twenty-five years ago was riveting. I had to ask myself—in the midst of all the strategic planning, staffing complexities, troubleshooting, new ministry initiatives, and so on—am I a promise fanatic? Am I trying to experience more of him and less of the world? Over an old box of Bible studies, I perchance (or was it perchance?) uncovered God, and I had one of those "Is the main thing the main thing, Ron?" experiences.

Leadership is certainly about leading something, somewhere, somehow. But is it possible that our leadership focus on external activities makes us lose sight of the deeper, more fundamental issues? At the most basic cellular level, leadership isn't first about the complex organism of the church; it's about the complex world of basic building blocks in a leader's life. How leaders model health, wholeness, and alignment is where the leadership challenge begins. As a chef, I know the value of herbs permeating a dish, of marinades spreading throughout meat. Being a promise fanatic and experiencing more of God and less of the world is a marinade I can never afford to be without.

What is it about leadership that you believe at the most fundamental cellular level? To help you think through what leadership is, see the appendix at the back of this book, "The First Strand of Leadership DNA." Most of us have never been challenged to begin thinking about those deep beliefs. Once we have a working definition of leadership, then we need to think about those deep beliefs that shape almost every move we make.

A couple of years ago Dee Hock, founder of Visa International, wrote a book called *Birth of a Chaordic Age*.[1] In it he details a surprising redistribution of leadership focus. This insight proved to be so keen that Leader to Leader, the Drucker Foundation leadership magazine, excerpted this core idea for a feature article.[2] He relates asking scores of people where their leadership energy is to be spent. Almost universally, he got a response that leadership is about leading and managing subordinates. Their self-conceived understanding of leadership was to get others in line, help them catch the vision, charge the hill, and accomplish the goals.

Hock says this is all wrong. If leadership focus isn't primarily a glance downward toward subordinates, then what are the other possibilities?[3] After going through the possible candidates for our leadership attention—peers, superiors, and subordinates—he states all of those as only secondary in importance.

Moving In

He makes the audacious claim that as much as 50 percent of a leader's energy should be spent on what he calls self-leadership issues. Only after managing and leading self can we hope to lead laterally, lead up, and then, and only then, lead our subordinates. And that is Hock's pecking order. The leading of subordinates should only get about one fifth of our time if we're leading appropriately in the other spheres, says Hock.[4]

Whether the 50 percent number is a good estimate or even measurable is certainly debatable. What should be clear, though, is that inner leadership must be much more front and center in our leadeship

> **Only after managing and leading self can we hope to lead laterally, lead up, and then, and only then, lead our subordinates.**

development plans. Leadership is more about self-leadership than leading followers. Leadership is more about interior morphing than outer management. Leadership is more about a profound sense of growth in myself than getting others to do what I want them to do.

Solomon, in Proverbs 4:23, makes a comment rarely applied to leadership: "Above all else, guard your heart, for it is the wellspring of life." We don't tend to think of leadership as a heart issue. For most, leadership seems more head, more analysis, more systems thinking, more programmatic solution-finding. Leadership is certainly all of that and more. But that isn't where deep leadership issues start. They start inside us at subterranean levels and slowly surface.

The heart is where the core of who we are is discovered. Of course, we don't really think our identities as people are somehow mystically located in those fist-sized muscles that are responsible for the pumping of oxygenated blood throughout our bodies. Solomon is saying our deepest longings, aspirations, wiring, and visions are not just deep down inside us, but they are a spring automatically bubbling out of us.

Essentially, this is also the connection Jesus makes. Matthew 12:34b-35: "For out of the overflow of the heart the mouth speaks. The good man brings good things out of the good stored up in him, and the evil man brings evil things out of the evil stored up in him." What we hold to at the deepest levels will fundamentally shape our leadership lives.

Right Person, Right Place, Right Time

Leadership is the catalyst for releasing God's "what ifs" in others. Apparently, God is totally fine with leadership coming in all shapes and sizes. The uniqueness we bring to the leadership task is what God uses to his advantage by placing us into snug-fit contexts. So we must make no mistake about it. Leadership is about God releasing his outlandish hopes and dreams through a certain personality, in a certain context, for a certain time, with a certain people. That last phrase is very important, for ultimately leadership is relational.

> **Leadership is about God releasing his outlandish hopes and dreams through a certain personality, in a certain context, for a certain time, with a certain people.**

This releasing of God's "what ifs" requires a profound personal belief in people. I confess that it isn't a belief that comes naturally either. The dark tendency most of us have as fallen creatures is to instantly and continually do comparisons with others. Right away we enter into an internal dialogue about what we think of the way they're dressed, how they look, and what attitudes they are displaying.

That dark tendency stands in direct competition with the accurate belief that

God would like to do something outlandish through them. God would like to even exceed *their* wildest imagination. God has a sense of humor. Notice he didn't say, "*Your* wildest imagination for them." God knows there's a tendency to hope for someone else's best as long as it's just a bit less than our best. Paul had to admonish the Corinthians to rejoice when one rejoices and to mourn when one mourns. Apparently, Paul knew that the human tendency was to invert those two responses.

A deep belief in people and God's best for them, in his purpose for them, and in his incredible plan for them births endless wonderment in a leader. A morphic leader wants to continually hold up God's wonderings in front of each person and, in so doing, show them what God thinks could be. This takes a noncompetitive, deep sense of God's best for everyone.

I have countless notes in my files of people who I've been around for a lot of years now. They have only recently come to see that the slow drip of encouragement in their lives is actually shaping whole new lives for them. Endless wonderment of what God could do if a person got aligned with God and his purposes is a bedrock value we must have and own.

Our tendency is to look for people to develop as leaders. And some people are specifically gifted in leadership. Senior leaders must first be concerned to identify who those are and spend the bulk of their time developing and investing in them. But because of what I've seen in the power of *paraklesis*, coming alongside to encourage others, I'm convinced that everyone has the ability to engage in paraklesis themselves and become profound encouragers who leave indelible marks on all sorts of lives. For more on paraklesis, see the appendix, "The First Strand of Leadership DNA."

Maybe we spend too much time looking for the leader "in the rough" instead of roughly shaping a leader and, in the process, discovering she is one. I stand persuaded that even those without the spiritual gift of leadership can still exert tremendous leadership through *paraklesis*, just as the average Christ-follower can see people come to Christ, even if his or her effectiveness isn't the same as the one with the spiritual gift of evangelism.

Here is one of those bedrock beliefs. Everyone has encouragement ability. It can be learned, cultivated, and operated at every level and department of life. I already said that doesn't mean everyone has the spiritual gift of leadership, but everyone has the ability to encourage others in their God-designed destiny. A belief like this impacts my speaking, leadership exchanges, staff development, wandering in the lobby, and interchange with little kids who leave runny nose marks on my pants when they give me a hug. Encouragement or lack of it

> **Maybe we spend too much time looking for the leader "in the rough" instead of roughly shaping a leader and, in the process, discovering she is one.**

leaves indelible markings on the life of every human. Encouragement is one of those catalysts that release God's "what ifs."

Encouragement is morphic. It deeply molds, shapes, and contours what we believe about ourselves, what God thinks of us, and what he wants to accomplish through us. The great leader John Gardner, who has served seven presidents in various capacities, gets at this as well: "If one is leading, teaching, dealing with young people or engaged in any other activity that involves influencing, directing, guiding, helping or nurturing, the whole tone of the relationship is conditioned by one's faith in human possibilities. That is the generative element, the source of the current that gives life to the relationship."[5]

Granted, Gardner's emphasis here is on human possibilities; ours is on God's possibilities. But let's not miss the meat. He says the whole tone of our relationships as a leader is conditioned by this deep belief. He calls it faith in people.

Unraveling Our Own Strands

Several strands of DNA converge to create our leadership uniqueness: leadership definition (discussed in the appendix, "The First Strand of Leadership DNA"), discovery of God-designed destiny, and the deep beliefs we hold about people and the leadership task. Leadership definition has broad impact on who you are and how you lead. Your sense of destiny and the distinct shape of God's gifts in you also imprint uniqueness.

Leadership must start with and be shaped by our hearts. Robert Greenleaf's classic *Servant Leadership* is an effort to make it clear that leadership is more about a state of being than a set of activities.[6] His contribution is a profound bell-ringer for me. He challenges the leader to choose to serve. Without the choice to serve, any leader's capacity is profoundly limited. This is rooted in Jesus' "the greatest of all is the servant of all."

Is one of our deep-seated beliefs a call to serve or to have fun building an enterprise? This is always a good question to check in on periodically. I confess that when I get frustrated with a young staff and they start to seem high maintenance to me, God invites me off my high horse to reflect on my heart posture and reason for doing what I do. If we believe encouragement is the mode for releasing God's "what ifs," then my impatience is a lapse in keeping the main thing the main thing.

What about defining our "what ifs"? What is our deepest God-designed destiny? Self-leadership is at least being aware of what we sense we're called to become and accomplish, given who God has made us and where he has placed us at the moment. Learning to align with our deepest God-designed wellspring sets us up for a life of deep satisfaction and the advancement of God's purposes in the earth. Satisfaction is forthcoming because we're doing and becoming what God intended from the very beginning. We advance the purposes of God because we're doing what he has designed us to do. As a result, we receive God's breath and blessing on our work. This is nothing short of discovering our purpose for being.

We advance the purposes of God because we're doing what he has designed us to do.

This isn't an easy journey. Getting in touch with our unique gifting is sometimes harder than we might imagine. We're so ill-equipped to look inside. Almost everything in life has taught us to look at externals. None of these, however, can align us with the inner crafting of our heavenly Father.

Building on Islands, Not Valleys

This is also important for how we see ourselves and how we invest our time in personal development. Peter Drucker, the founder of modern management and Christian business statesman, has made it an almost commonplace saying that we should build on islands of health and strength. This, too, is a counterintuitive move. The natural tendency is to seek ways to strengthen our weaknesses so we can be well rounded. We hear parents, teachers, and coaches talk about the need to be well rounded. But it's probably not God's ideal. It appears that Drucker has simply popularized—and even made famous—a biblical principle.

To invest our time, money, resources, and energy to get all our weak areas up to a baseline minimum leaves us no room, time, money, or energy to source and develop our strength. The result is quite obvious. Strengthen weaknesses, and you'll be an average generalist. Spend time developing the treasure God has invested in you, and you soar as a crucial and high-impact player in God's economy.

We need to be reminded that God didn't give everyone a modicum of every spiritual gift so we all could do a little of everything pretty well. He gifted us with very specific gifts and purposes. It's up to us to discover them and fully use them for kingdom value. This isn't permission to simply write off ever engaging in those things that all Christ-followers are responsible to do. It's a challenge, however, to see alignment with our divine design as a major priority in effectively carrying out our leadership imperatives.

All of us are mandated to share our faith with those far from God. Just because we don't have the spiritual gift of evangelism doesn't mean we can simply state that it isn't a strength and, therefore, spend no time being trained to better share our story and God's. If we really don't have a knack for teaching and facilitating small group discussions and really do have an obvious ability using computer technology to develop digital art, then we ought to take classes, get mentored, and explore the best way to use this gift in the employ of God's kingdom. Our visual age may very well see the digital artist be at least as important as the biblical teacher.[7]

There's no Christian responsibility that says all Christians must facilitate a small group or teach a Bible study. Unless we come to grips with how God has made us, gifted us, and designed us, we'll never see ourselves the way God sees us and never ask how to best employ what he has given us.

Viral "Excusiosis"

Jeremiah's life is one of many examples that could be cited. Jeremiah 1:5-10: "Before I formed you in the womb I knew you, before you were born I set you apart; I appointed you as a prophet to the nations.

" 'Ah, Sovereign Lord,' I said, 'I do not know how to speak; I am only a child.'

"But the Lord said to me, 'Do not say, "I am only a child." You must go to everyone I send you to and say whatever I command you. Do not be afraid of them, for I am with you and will rescue you,' declares the Lord.

"Then the Lord reached out his hand and touched my mouth and said to me, 'Now, I have put my words in your mouth. See, today I appoint you over nations and kingdoms to uproot and tear down, to destroy and overthrow, to build and to plant.' "

> **"Excusiosis" is the disease of second-guessing God by offering excuses as to why his plan must be mistaken, misplaced, or ill-timed.**

Jeremiah had a very specific DNA. God had a clear plan for Jeremiah and had gifted him for the particular mission. Furthermore, Jeremiah had to come to grips with the magnitude of what God was asking him to do. Jeremiah had a profound case of "excusiosis." "Excusiosis" is the disease of second-guessing God by offering excuses as to why his plan must be mistaken, misplaced, or ill-timed. Jeremiah thought he was too young, an inept speaker, and generally scared silly about the scope of what God had in mind.

Jeremiah isn't the only character who felt this way. Noah, Jonah, Moses, David, and Paul could also be examined. Time after time what emerges is that our calling is often intimidating in magnitude, demanding skill sets we don't think we have, and at times in our life we feel are inopportune. This is nothing short of mastering our purpose for being—the reason God set us on the planet.

Our deepest beliefs about life, people, change, spiritual formation, and the role of prayer all reside deep down inside. Solomon's admonition is to pay careful attention to this because, like a wellspring, it will automatically bubble to the surface.

The number of times I've seen leaders mismatched with their ministry post is heartbreaking. Actually, it's not just ministry posts having this problem; you can find it in the marketplace as well. Imagine getting up to face the day, and the dominant feeling is "I'm not well placed in this job. I don't like what I do day to day. Will I waste my whole life doing this?" Misplacement of this magnitude is even more tragic in ministry.

Leaders who feel displaced, and yet attempt to lead others in the discovery of their divine design, put the church in a very precarious position. I know plenty of guys in lead ministry posts who feel that their fit with that particular church tradition, local setting, or simply that local congregation is far less than ideal. Don't construe that "less than ideal" means they're engaged in a difficult ministry. Everyone has difficulties in ministry. I'm referring to the genuine mismatch of the mission, vision, and values of a point leader with the mission, vision, and values of the congregation.

Unfortunately, due to faulty understandings of "call" and servanthood, many church staff persist in misplaced positions. The harm to them, their congregations, and the advancement of the kingdom is incalculable. There is no doubt that better training on the front end could do a lot to prevent this kind of misplacement and promote better congregation/leader fit.

Every leader has a unique DNA. Leadership DNA determines the kind of ministry giftedness, vision, context fit, philosophy of ministry, personal values, and leadership philosophy and style. When and where are leaders trained to get a handle on these issues? Rarely are they wrestled to the ground prior to taking a first job or ministry position. The tools for sorting the complexities of leader/church fit are few and far between.

Personal Fit

Once you've settled on your leadership definition, the next step is to uncover the unique shape of your divine design. What's the personal mission God has given to the leader? Of course, some of this will be refined and honed only in the context of ministry opportunities. No one would suggest that all this can be figured out in a sterile environment apart from the actual ministry context.

But so much more could be determined prior to the first placement. What is the basic giftedness of the leader? Is the dominant expression shepherding, teaching, or leading? Is this person cut from point-leader cloth or is he or she more like a number-two support player or a good team developer or a creative visionary? What about established church versus entrepreneurial plant? Is a traditional context or a highly creative one better? Is the preference toward being cut loose or highly managed? a team player or better at the solo work? Is the leader wired to be a shepherd or a team architect and developer? Since most of these questions aren't asked on the front end, they have to be asked in the middle of ministry appointments where congregations get to suffer the mud of self-discovery.

All of these questions only begin to get at the options in front of every leader. Yet in the traditional educational pipeline, these aren't the dominant questions being asked. This may explain why there's an increasing emphasis on homegrown leadership. In the homegrown alternative, these issues are identified as a person in the marketplace serves in an unpaid servant capacity. Over time they find such a great ministry/giftedness fit that they decide to make this a lifetime pursuit. Ideally, this should be what the internship accomplishes in the traditional training model.

As a fifteen-year-old coming to Christ, going to a Christian undergraduate experience, and then off to seminary, I was never once put into the place of asking, "What's God's mission for my life? How are my dominant gifts expressed? What kind of context would I best serve, and what kind of church could receive the maximum benefit?"

Failure to ask these questions is hurting the church and the kingdom, too. Self-leadership starts by asking, "What are my dominant gifts? What's my God-designed mission in life? Where will that be most advantageous for God?" I know many will say, "I'm simply called to be a pastor or missionary or teacher." But the nuanced possibilities are where the real fit issues crop up.

Is the Main Thing Clear?

I was on my way to have breakfast with a local pastor who was seriously struggling with his ministry post. Cal had been in this mainline church for four and a half years. Over typical Cracker Barrel fare, we discussed what a missional church looks like. I said to Cal, "During your time here in Jackson, how many people have you seen come to Christ?" He never wavered or even thought about it. He said, "To my knowledge, not one."

Of course, we never have any way of knowing who, how, or when anyone is touched. But if, in the course of that period of time, there was no sense at all that anyone had surrendered their lives to Christ, his visible wince made it clear there was a neglect, misunderstanding, or simple disregard for the Great Commission.

My follow-up question was more congregational in focus. "Would those in your church know, identify, or invite nonchurched people to your services?" His response was equally quick this time. "Ron, I am not sure if they even think about unchurched people." Further probing revealed that Cal had discussed the Great Commission, but the congregation's role in fulfilling it had never been pursued. He knew that he was dissatisfied but couldn't identify why. His dawning was about to arrive. His agitation was largely out of a wheel-spinning, uphill climb that was dissatisfying at its root.

My dawning had come several years earlier. I had never asked the questions "How am I wired? What does how I feel look like? Biblically, how does it look? How does it fit with my temperament and ministry location? What is possible in this context?" Coming to grips with who I was played an important role in discovering how to get Westwinds on track and best use my gifts.

Six years into the church plant, we'd grown from five families to about two hundred people. Sounds good on the surface, but numbers don't tell the whole story. Almost all the people in attendance were already Christians when they came to Westwinds. In the first six years, to our knowledge, only eight people had come to Christ. At that point, I was coming to the same type of dawning Cal was now experiencing.

Quite frankly, we couldn't expect any better results. We had absolutely no focus on being a church moved by God's heart for mission and for people far from God. I had thought that I was going into academics, but God had redirected me in what appeared to be a last-minute course correction. It left me feeling a bit unprepared for my first post.

Those first six years, we did the only thing I knew to do—train and teach the saints with the best Greek-text-based, expositional sermonizing I could muster. Church services had the feel of a seminary class, complete with incomprehensible language and a little music thrown in. We look back and laugh our heads off now. As seminarians we often found class boring as all get out. Why did I think adding a little music would make the average marketplace person or stay-at-home parent like it any better, let alone understand it?

There was little Great Commission fulfillment about what we did in those days. We were training people, but we were not reproducing ourselves in the lives of those who needed Jesus. This realization was the catalyst I needed to really ask the questions "What have I been made to do? What's my reason for being?" This was a portion of my foray into the inner life issues I needed to settle. This was part helping Westwinds align itself with God's Word and part uncovering my creative entrepreneurial gifts and sense of mission.

Context Is Almost Everything

Here's where the profound connection meets between who we are and what we do. Deep effectiveness begins when the gifts of a leader and leadership team find the right home in the ministry context being served. This may not be so intuitive. With reflection, though, it seems clear that we will most naturally lead, experience passion, and sustain motivation when we're deeply aligned with what is most core to our being. This is cellular leadership. This may sound as if the chances of leaders getting aligned in the right context are slimmer than winning the lottery. Not true.

There are obviously two ways of looking at this. The leader or staff may work to find the right fit on the front end with a congregation in which gifts and goals of both are clearly similar. The other alternative is that the leader mediates the mission and vision of the local church through his or her sense of destiny and gifting and, as a result, shifts the trajectory of the congregation.

Mission and vision always carry the fingerprints of someone or something. For some churches, the forefathers are the mediators of the church vision. Protecting

Deep effectiveness begins when the gifts of a leader and leadership team find the right home in the ministry context being served. yesterday is the highest priority. In other situations, it's denominational distinctives that filter how the vision is experienced. In still other church settings, it's a carefully articulated biblical mission and vision statement. This often has the feel and flavor of the point leader and leadership team. When the key leader's DNA doesn't align with mission, vision, and values, the misfit will almost always lead to ineffectiveness and discontent.

Some may say this sounds like if you can't get a church to do what you want, it must be a bad fit. That isn't what I'm saying here. Leadership at the cellular level requires that the leader know who God has made him or her to be. Then the leader does all he or she can to either find a context seeking those kinds of genes or mediate church mission and vision in such a way that the church benefits from the best God has put in that leader.

Moses captured a vision from God, and it took into full account his gifts, temperament, abilities, and weaknesses. Paul's leadership was of an entirely different sort, and his mission and vision in life were very different as well. Each leader's DNA is central to fully leveraging who God has made that leader to be.

Think about the implications this has for what leaders leak to those around them. If leaders are tuned to their unique leadership genes and gifts, it's rather obvious they will, in turn, be hiring and training their teams to do the same. This promotes further leak. Staff leaders encourage others to find their genuine niche. They know how to assist in the process because they've gone through the process themselves. You can't take people where you haven't traveled before. Our sense of purpose in life is just the beginning of assessing our leadership DNA.

Co-Missioning: The Nexus of Leader and Context

How does a sense of personal mission fit with a local church mission and vision? We need to learn the fine art of co-missioning. Several things need comment here.

First, a personal sense of destiny may be very broad or narrow. I think it's safe to say this is as individual and distinct as each person. The analogy to DNA is wholly appropriate. I admit that I was never forced to consider this until I was into my doctoral classes and was asked to write a personal mission statement and philosophy of leadership paper. This exercise was part of the catalyst provoking my discontent with our lack of conversion growth in the early years of Westwinds.

I want to invite you to take the time to consider a solitude retreat for the InnerAction with this chapter. Until this issue is settled about who God has made you to be and what he wants you to accomplish, little else will matter.

I struggled with the change of ministry direction that I experienced in the last months of my seminary experience. My change from academics to pastoral ministry and church planting was unsettling. What about my sense of call? What about "God's hand on my life"? It took me six months in 1991 to land a clear, concise, but deeply rich mission statement.

My personal mission wasn't vested in church ministry; it was rooted in being a transformational architect. I had gifts in designing and building biblical models for life change. The dominant expression of those gifts is in the local church in the form of a fifteen-year-old church plant. My gifts are also well used in the context of church consulting, personal coaching, and hosting leadership and creativity conferences. As a transformational architect, I coach people toward irresistible life change and influential life work. I get jazzed by, lay awake at night over, and spend my best creative brain juice on helping people and churches develop full lives and achieve alignment with their life purpose.

Jesus didn't leave much room for speculation as to the role of the remaining eleven guys.

On the church front, mission isn't so open to exploration. Jesus didn't leave much room for speculation as to the role of the remaining eleven guys. Quite simply, he told them to go out and make disciples, incorporate them into the local church through baptism, and teach them to obey everything Jesus commanded.

The basic two-prong reason for the existence of the church is making new disciples and bringing them to maturity. This is simply a nonnegotiable. Any church that has any other agenda ahead of these two prongs is simply on a tangent to the main mission Jesus left for the church to accomplish.

Getting the Two Straight

The issue of local church vision is a bit different. A simple distinction is that a mission defines *why* we exist and a vision defines *how we will accomplish* the "why we exist." This is where the DNA of a leader and church need to meet.

I have a friend in Kansas who shares the exact same mission as Westwinds. He is motivated and compelled by the Great Commission. But our similarities end there. Our visions of how to accomplish the mission are worlds apart. He's in a high church context that has the vision of using the beauty of traditional liturgy, the fine arts, and things like the *Alpha Course* to reach people outside the church, and he weaves them into the life of his local congregation.

At Westwinds our vision is to use a variety of fresh formats. With a high aesthetic and artistic emphasis, we want to present Christ in caring, creative, and credible ways. The flavor and shape of our worship experience is radically different from his liturgical church setting, even though our missions are the same. I'd be discontent, given my particular creative DNA, in his high church context, and he wouldn't be excited about the use of digital art and alternative worship experiences with scent, layers, scrolling video loops, multiple TV monitors, and ambient music throughout. Cellular leadership means looking down into the most basic building blocks of the leader's cells and asking, "How have I been designed, and what is the best way to see that manifested for God?"

Making It Personal

Uncovering your God-designed purpose is a deeply spiritual experience. We need a proper view of who we are. We tend to view ourselves as humans having a spiritual experience. A biblical worldview says we're embodied spiritual beings having a human experience.

You need to remember why uncovering your sense of missional destiny is so important. We need the breath of God's Spirit on our lives, and we need to align our personal mission with the ministry of our local contexts. Mission-statement writing exercises service your ability to help others through the process. Our unpaid servant leaders, our congregations, and our youth and teens need this coaching. Leaders who get to the cellular level will have the ability to walk others through it. In a world where pastors and missionaries are "called" and every other vocation is supposedly open for the choosing, mission and purpose statement writing are desperately needed.

InnerAction

1. What are the six to ten core items on how you would like to do the journey with those around you? What is your leadership philosophy? What are the ministry nonnegotiables that will draw a line in the sand? What are the things that make you weep, beat the table with your fists, laugh, or experience deep waves of compassion? What excites you most about ministry? If you could write your ministry description, what would it look like? How aligned are you with that sketch? What prevents you from doing exactly what you feel God is calling you to do?

2. If you don't have a clear purpose or mission statement, here's a way to start the wheels turning. Block a four-hour retreat time. This will be the first of several solitude times for reflection. If you don't have a good leather journal, buy one. You need to be free from cell phones, kids, and any other distractions. No Internet. No music.

After some time of prayer and asking for God's guidance, read Jeremiah 1:1-10, and meditate on Ephesians 2:10. Slowly begin answering and jotting thoughts generated from the InnerAction questions. Keep three different areas: One section for your mission statement thoughts, one section for your core values, and one section for your thoughts on what the church would look like if it became all God wanted it to be. Patience for the process is critical to depth. This first four-hour solitude stint will be simply the launching pad.

3. In subsequent weeks of prayer and meditation times, you need to continue jotting thoughts, refining phrases, identifying passages of Scripture that hit you with freight, and deleting phrases and ideas that have been incorporated or refined. As this process happens, pay attention to your emotional state. What phrases, ideas, and thoughts really get you excited? get you dreaming? get you hoping? Over the space of several months and genuine effort, you'll identify who you really are, the purpose for which you've been made.

4. Sometime in the process, you may want to do one or two exercises often used to get us most in touch with our deepest core. The "Eightieth Birthday Party" is a powerful experience. You're invited to an eightieth birthday party with well-known community leaders, dignitaries, news people, national magazine writers, and government officials. At this party you're seated at the head table, and you realize it's your birthday party. In addition to the flowing laughter from those roasting you, for the next several hours, many people from the impressive guest list go one by one to the microphone and begin to tell stories of the great person of character you are and the great accomplishments you are leaving as a legacy.

What would you want those guests to say about the person you have become? What would you like them to say about the accomplishments and legacy you're leaving? What's left is to design a plan to help us move from where we are to the picture of where we'd like to end up.

5. A second exercise accomplishing a similar thing is the "Five Year Exercise." If you knew you would only be on this planet for five more years, what would you change about who you are and what you do? In other words, are you actually doing exactly what you think God wants you to do, or are you hoping someday to magically land in it?

Endnotes

1. Dee Hock, *Birth of the Chaordic Age* (San Francisco, CA: Berrett-Koehler Publishers, Inc., 1999).
2. Hock, "The Art of Chaordic Leadership," Leader to Leader (Number 15, Winter 2000).
3. Hock, "The Art of Chaordic Leadership," Leader to Leader, (Number 15, Winter 2000).
4. Hock, *Birth of the Chaordic Age,* 69.
5. John W. Gardner, *On Leadership* (New York, NY: The Free Press, a division of Macmillan, Inc., 1990), 199.
6. Robert K. Greenleaf, *Servant Leadership* (Mahnah, NJ: Paulist Press, 1983).
7. Which, by the way, is one of the 21C giftings of Bezalel and Ohaliab (Exodus 36:1).

CHAPTER FOUR

SOUL ERGONOMICS: CUSTOMIZING GOD'S IMPRINT ON OUR LIVES

First things first. If there ever was an easy place to get sidetracked from the role of spiritual formation, it's in ministry. Ironic as this may seem, the frequency and consistency with which Sunday arrives places the average leadership team and point leader in an interesting and even unique place. How do we keep our personal lives fresh, vital, and full, while at the same time producing the weekly "product" of multiple worship experiences and messages? Clarity on the front end of all this is important.

God is more interested in customizing his imprint on our souls than he is in building a ministry through us. Waters get easily muddied on this one. Building a heart is primary; seeing a ministry flourish is secondary. Personal spiritual wholeness and health are foundational to building any local ministry. Jesus said he would build his church and the gates of hell would not prevail against it. Jesus builds individual churches through building individuals and customizing his imprint on the soul lives of leaders.

Ergonomics is the study of how customizing our environment can increase our overall wholeness, performance, and effectiveness. Having a keyboard on top of a desk isn't very comfortable, and in the long term, it hurts your hands and wrists. A more ergonomic arrangement is to have the keyboard in a sliding keyboard tray directly under the desktop. Positioning the keyboard at **God is more interested in customizing his imprint on our souls than he is in building a ministry through us.** a height at which our wrists are in a straight line with our forearms is much more ergonomic and allows typing to go on almost indefinitely without fatigue. Of course, the very core of ergonomics is customization. The reason high-end desk chairs have as many buttons, levers, and switches as a stealth fighter is so all different shapes and sizes of bodies can customize the chair for the greatest comfort and ease of work.

I think God has a kind of soul ergonomics in mind for each of us. Most of us are simply not creative enough to see the variety of positions and postures we could be in for spiritual formation to become optimal. Several years into my ministry stint, I realized the expected and prescribed devotional life I had inherited from my seminary days was too much a one-size-fits-all approach. One-size-fits-all is simply a nice way of saying, "Our size fits no one, but we didn't have time to customize our sizing plan enough, so we just have one...Hope it fits!" I needed a life-giving, "customized for me" plan of experiencing the life of God.

Soul ergonomics is positioning our soul for the greatest imprint of God's life and power. Service and ministry from this posture enable flow from a reservoir of fullness and strength instead of dryness and lack. Ministry from this ergonomic position is far more comfortable and sustainable. If the truth were known, this is the only way healthy ministry can be done.

Spiritual Sculptures

The very core of all leadership and personal development is spiritual sculpting by God. Early in our Christian lives, we learn about the need for devotions, prayer, Bible study, memorization, and, depending upon your tradition, a host of other "musts." Vigilance in keeping those patterns and practices fresh takes monumental effort. Over and over again in my life, I've struggled to keep these intended life-giving practices fresh. When I released myself from the inherited "I must do these things this often to be spiritual," I started on a whole new course. I realized there were days I really wanted to read God's Word and days I really didn't want to. There were times I was motivated to memorize a chunk of Scripture and times I wasn't. Early in my ministry, I would have never given myself the permission to not read the Bible daily. But I have surely learned that the days I feel I want solitude or don't want to journal are totally fine with God. None of us wants T-bone steaks and baked potatoes every night for dinner. There is too much variety available to get stuck in that rut, and there are too many nutrients you can only get from other foods. Spiritual ergonomics says customize, vary, and fight rut-making practices with a vengeance.

Allowing spiritual disciplines to degenerate into oughts, musts, and shoulds voids our lives of the very power those practices are to infuse.

A quick word is probably in order about rut formation. I am not saying in all of this that we don't need consistent or relatively consistent routines. I would never think of going a month without reading God's Word or talking to God. I am not advocating nonsense here, only that routine plus a little monotony can lead to a seriously rutted spiritual life. Routines can be healthy; ruts are simply boring and unproductive. Routines have a healthy rhythmic variation; ruts have no deviation at all. Allowing spiritual disciplines to degenerate into oughts, musts, and shoulds voids our lives of the very power those practices are to infuse.

Paul calls us God's workmanship created in Christ to do good works which he has prepared for us in advance (Ephesians 2:10). We must grapple with this and what it means for our spiritual formation. We are God's handiwork, his artwork. We're a piece in progress; the canvas is still being painted on, the marble chiseled with holy finesse, the clay imprinted with divine pressure. This is what it means to be his workmanship. The degree to which we are unique pieces of work made by God is the degree to which he has customized plans for making those imprints and brushstrokes in our spiritual lives.

As God's workmanship—his divine art piece—Paul says we're being created, literally experiencing his transforming activity in our inner lives.[1] The creative, transforming power in this verse directly connects his *work on or in us* to his *work through us*. Here's the reason that the discovery of our God-designed destiny from the last chapter is so critical.

God is designing our lives, and he wants to bring about transformation so we can be better suited and shaped for the role ahead. What a sad state to meander through life with God attempting to shape us, but having no idea of God's intended destination for us. Soul ergonomics is the customization of God's life and imprint on us, and by intention it's as unique as our destiny.

Some may say we're all being shaped into the image of Christ for an eternity with God. This is a true statement, but it's only a statement about the finale, not any of the musical movements leading up to it. The route to our final destination is as variegated and unique as our fingerprints.

God is a molder, a shaper, a soul artist, a life sculptor. He does his creative work in a variety of ways, and as leaders we must be familiar with a host of them. The oughts, musts, and shoulds of which I spoke earlier were on one hand a well-intentioned effort to keep soul silt at a minimum. Unfortunately, I was actually contributing to a grainy buildup in my life. Intention isn't ever enough to bring God's life into a soul caught in a rut.

Through classes with men like Dallas Willard[2] and Eugene Peterson[3], I came to acknowledge my faulty view of discipline and the need to pursue God. While I was at Fuller, Dallas Willard challenged my conception of spiritual formation as a list

of practices in which I must engage. He was so relational in how he saw his life with God. When I really
stopped and thought about it, I would never consider
operating in any other relationship the way I did with
God. My wife, my kids, my friends would be bored silly
if I treated them with the predictability and mechani-
cal feel of the way I related to God. I needed to let him shape my soul instead of
attempting to impress him with my slavish regimen.

I needed to let him shape my soul instead of attempting to impress him with my slavish regimen.

Life Infusions

Soul ergonomics means you and I coming to the place where we see a variety
of patterns and practices available as vehicles of divine life infusion. Patterns and
practices are simply the steamy hot water in the mug, the medium through which
the presence of tea will fully infuse with some steeping time. We're looking for the
presence of God to be fully infused into our lives. In fact, that's the best definition
of spiritual formation I know—the daily acquisition of the life of God.

The importance of this for Christian leaders can't be overstated. Genuine morphic life is the first and foremost priority of every point leader, team member, and
unpaid servant leader in the church. The point of every pattern and practice in
which we engage is the download of that life—nothing more. If this isn't in place,
everything else is posturing. We need to root out our informational and performance approaches to God and reorient our approach around relational and transformational experiences.

Earlier we noted how we've been trained in information assimilation. From
early in our schooling, we learn to ingest information and spit it out on exam pages
or blue book essays. The gap between what we "know" and what we actually have
absorbed or really learned is usually quite high. Tremendous amounts of information are going in, but a nearly inverse proportion of life change is going on—information but no transformation; vast amounts of material but no morphing to show
for it.

The modernist project has reared its ugly head. We want information...lots of
it. And we assume that once we get it, we're educated, wise, and equipped.
Between Web sites, e-newsletters, periodicals, and other sources of buzzing material, we feel that we could become experts on almost anything. But "expert" as
defined by what? Amounts of information ingested, *or* the competencies, changes,
and actual morphing that can result from information intake?

Take this problem and migrate it into the spiritual arena. The complexity of
this problem is practical *and* spiritual. On one hand we live in a world of explod-
ing information. Some of it is necessary for us to continue to learn, grow, and
remain healthy. Of all the information available and streaming across the chasm
between our ears, how do we filter the important from the fluffy, wasteful, or

We want informa-tion...lots of it. And we assume that once we get it, we're educated, wise, and equipped. redundant? And in the midst of trying to navigate all that information, how do we do the work of soul for-mation? On the practical side, we want to capture the information that will serve our ministry ends, but on the other hand, the shaping of our inner lives is what God is most concerned about. Definitions and avenues are both important here. If the goal of the spiritual life is daily experience of the very life of God[4], then we need to do the kinds of things we'd do in all relationships. Relationships are pred-icated on variety, dialogue, activities, a change in settings, and a balance of some established patterns but with a large field of options that keep things interesting.

Think about interaction with your spouse, kids, or best friend. Picture your current practices of interacting with God as the only way you can interact with this person you have in mind. This was a sad and eye-opening experience for me. My wife would be bored silly with the typical perfunctory and regimented way I used to relate to God—calculated, predictable, zero variety, largely obligatory. Can you imagine saying to your spouse, "This is the way we're going to keep the marriage fires stoked. We're going to do everything the same every day, and we're going to do it for the same amount of time every day. Then we'll check it off our list. Cool, honey?" Oh, my wife is excited.

Relating Relationally

Could your current practices of relating to God function in healthy ways with any other person in your life? Chances are slim to none the answer is yes. Most of us simply don't see our relationship with God in relational categories. This not only impacts our personal lives, but it also has implications for the way we disciple peo-ple and help them shape their lives with God.

The reality is that we only pass on to others what we do. We may teach what we know, but we reproduce who we are. What does that mean? If our relationship with God is essentially informational, nonrelational, and not morphic, then how can we pass on anything other than that? This may be the single most difficult issue for the church to overcome.

Call me an iconoclast, but it seems to me that we've put in concrete and canonized methods that aren't biblically rooted or life-giving. This is a common problem in evangelicalism. Where is the thirty-minute "devotional" taught in Scripture? Even the word *devotional* rings legalistically, like we can somehow abbreviate devotion to God into something a bit more manageable like "devotional."

I recently reviewed over twenty different discipleship programs, and not one sounds, feels, or looks relational. Is it at all troubling to you that the most systematic training we have recorded of Jesus' training the disciples is not all that systematic?

Look at the Sermon on the Mount. I find no lecture, drill, test, or fill-in-the-blank booklets. Now one simple question: Why are we convinced that's the best way to grow people in relationship with God? Are we not unwitting victims of our years of inhabiting a modernist world? Linear information transmission was equal to knowledge in the old world; knowledge gained is life change made, or at least that is how it was supposed to work. Some will be quick to say, "But one-on-one discipleship *is* relational." Not in our modernist, fill-in-the-blank model, it isn't. The average one-on-one discipleship model is simply the lecture-drill-test method put into a new context. Instead of one teacher, one classroom, and twenty-five students, we have one teacher, one classroom, and one student. The methodology is identical.

Getting this foundational part right is pretty important if we hope to model what we're inviting others to experience. Let's start with what's familiar to all of us: information. Relationship with God starts by us coming to know him, and that knowing is mediated through his Word. The information of God's Word is the starting point, but only the starting point.

Look at the Sermon on the Mount. I find no lecture, drill, test, or fill-in-the-blank booklets.

Aerating our minds and hearts with God's Word can happen in a variety of ways: large blocks of reading, small atoms of a verse at a time, orally through Bible on CDs or cassettes, or reading aloud to have the double input of visual and oral. This is the easy part and rather apparent. Paul encourages this in Romans 12:1-2 when he says to be metamorphed by the renewing of your mind.

This is much like our human relationships. Conversation starts the ball moving, and that's typically information exchange of some sort. Morphing starts with the right stuff going in. Soul ergonomics gets interesting right at this point, because it's here that interesting customization begins with who you are at this moment, in your current context, with your current needs.

The Missing Step

Information without this next step of incubation is useless. And yet I contend that's often what happens. How else can we explain the inverse relationship between the vast amount of information taken in by the average Christian and the comparatively little life change? Think about the average week in a Christ follower's life: Sunday morning services (and Sunday night for some), Wednesday night services, a Bible study or small group meeting, men's accountability group, personal study, tapes in the car or Christian radio, night stand Christian reading, not to mention private devotions. Where is all the change if information is what does it?

So what do we do? We create more programs and more fill-in-the-blank booklets. This learning style taps a rather small percentage of people. Where are the hands-on, kinesthetic discipleship programs? Where are the discipleship programs based on storytelling? Certainly these options are a bit more primal and biblically defensible. Our love affair with Gutenberg and the printed word may work against us when it comes to thinking creatively about soul ergonomics. When we come up with something different for discipleship, it's always something new and different to print. Print is linear. It only hits one of the senses and is almost always left-brained.

None of us in our right mind (pun intended) would assume that because we read a passage of Scripture, somehow our lives have been changed. However, in the subtleties of our own private world, this is what often happens in practice. I remember a distinct sense of accomplishment when spiritual obligations were completed, and I felt a sense of relief that I had done what had been requested. When I read thirty minutes each day, prayed through my prayer list (and it was a list), and had done several verses of memorization that week, I felt I had done what God had asked, like I had gotten one more thing off my list of to-dos and could now move on to the real ministry stuff. I know that seems infantile and superficial, but I really operated out of obligation a good deal of the time, not out of relational interest or desire.

Information is where it begins, but it is incubation that brings to fruition and development the full imprint and weight of the information. I remember in kindergarten walking in one morning and having what looked like an overgrown aquarium full of eggs with a bright light in it. In the words of Mrs. Minor, my kindergarten teacher, this was an incubator. In kindergarten language we were told that "information" saying, "You are going to become a little baby chick," had been placed into these eggs. She went on, "We can't simply crack open the eggs and look inside right now; first we need to let that information mature, warm up, incubate. And one of these days after the incubator has done the job the mother usually would do in keeping the eggs warm, the chicks will crack their way out of their egg house." Incubation is being placed in the right climate, temperature, and surroundings to let the information warm up and mature inside us.

What does the incubation process look like? The first and obvious step is engaging in concrete practices to allow the information to "mature." In the history of our Christian tradition, we have lots of incubative practices. Meditation, memorization, journaling, study—all of these are ways we can use to get the truth of the information rolling around inside of us. While not seen as traditional practices, other things come to mind that are equally beneficial. One-on-one discussions, small group meetings, painting, drawing, doing digital art, cooking, long walks, sitting outside—all of these can have an incubating, marinating effect.

> Information is where it begins, but it is incubation that brings to fruition and development the full imprint and weight of the information.

An Earthed Spirituality

Morphing at its most fundamental level is allowing God's Word to move around inside us long enough for some of it to rub off on our behavior. We need to remember to be intimate with this process. It's the fundamental thing we're to model and invite others to experience. We are pleading here for nothing short of a fully earthed spirituality—an interaction with God that actually brings an impact in the way we look, think, and live.

We can engage a literally endless variety of patterns and practices to incubate God's Word or some truth he's trying to teach us or some character fissure he's working on. This is the creativity of relationship. We do this in other relationships we're engaged in, yet when it comes to God, we're often unimaginative, stale, and boring.

I think many people have been so concerned about being biblical that patterns and practices we don't find in Scripture become suspect. Nowhere are we commanded "do nothing to deepen your relationship with God except these three things listed in the Bible." However, that's often what we do. For me to bring up digital art, cooking, or pottery making as potential incubative processes before God is to cause some to raise their eyebrows. I contend that's simply our inability to view God relationally. We have no problem doing this with others in our lives but have a terrible struggle when it comes to God. Many of these activities are prayer venues—ways to communicate with God, incubate his truth, and gear down the RPM gauge so something other than a revving engine can be heard. It's why we have date nights with our spouses, times to let the revving quiet enough to really hear each other.

Customization and variety on this front will be guided and geared to our preferences, interests, and temperament. Incubation is a process, and the only limit to the variety of options is the imagination.

Reflecting on a Death Date

Let's get concrete. Take an incubation practice from Ephesians 5:15-16 that says we should live wisely and make the most of every opportunity. Or how about Psalm 39:4 that says, "Teach us to number our days, God." How about a practice called "Death in Outlook"? The double-entendre is coincidental but quite helpful.

I don't know about you, but I use Microsoft Outlook for my personal planner. This synchs nicely with my iPAQ Pocket PC so that I always have my key data with me. What if you put an arbitrary date for your death in Outlook (maybe for you it's a Franklin-Covey Planner)? How about opening to that page on the calendar and reflecting on the number of days you have left? Will that affect how you seize each opportunity? How will your actions change? Who will you call to set things straight before your death? To whom will you say, "I love you," more frequently in the interim? How will kingdom activity change in your life? Will priorities change, habits morph, spending alter? And here's a powerful incubation exercise: Does changing the date change any of your responses?

In our postmodern culture, people are looking for experiences to bring them closer to God. Why have we been so unimaginative? Postmoderns aren't looking for principles to die for; they're looking for practices to live by.[5] We need a whole new ministry description where a new brand of creatives dream up new, improved, contextual, and life-giving patterns and practices for soul ergonomy. Nothing short of this will reach a culture tired of what appears to them to be rules and regulations leading to dull, monochrome lives. How can we point the way to a path we do not travel? While the process of life change is hard and full of challenge, the process is not difficult to understand.

Information coupled with incubation sets the stage for the hard work of application or what I prefer to call re-habituation. This is the real work of morphing—God working in all sorts of situations to see if what has been incubated is ready to be birthed into a new kind of living. So what is re-habitutation? It is the simple re-patterning of the way we do things.

In our post-modern culture, people are looking for experiences to bring them closer to God.

We have rarely taken seriously our embodied existence. Much of Christianity in the West is closer to gnostic dualism than a biblical life-view. For many Christ followers, the body is something to be endured and put up with until the great escape of eternity. What many forget is that we'll also have a body in eternity; a body of a different substance and order to be sure, but a body nonetheless.

Soul ergonomics takes seriously our embodied existence. Real morphing is the shaping of the soul as the basis for the shaping of our bodily existence. Kneeling, raising hands, lying prostrate, and fasting are all physical activities—engagements of the body that we believe impact our inner selves. Inner life change that doesn't produce change in "our members" (to use Paul's term) would be considered incomplete and would fall short of God's goal of transformation. He invites transformed existence starting on the inside and leaking to the outside.

Deep Habit Reformation

What does our embodied existence have to do with leadership and spiritual formation? The body is the domain of habits and activities, the arena of transformed existence. If our incubation practices don't eventually issue forth in changed bodily habits, our shaping by God is not full-orbed.

Paul makes it clear that evidence of the activity of the Holy Spirit in the life of a Christ follower is not doctrinal recitation but evidence of a certain kind of fruit. Love, joy, peace, and a full complement of other such fruit are clear indications of God's work in our lives. These are much more tangible but so much harder to measure. This is where we often prefer the more pious-sounding, though legalistic, measurements of minutes spent reading the Bible, hours spent using our spiritual gifts in service or church services, or potlucks attended. But all of those may or may not contribute to deeper movement into the kingdom of God. Few would argue that clear movement is evidenced by an increase in patience with my children this last six months over the previous six, or an increase in self-control as evidenced by the evaporation of my anger flare-ups. These are the outward indicators of incubation coming habit-ward.

Every time I have the opportunity to sin, I have the opportunity to bear fruit of the Spirit as well. In a momentary flash, I can choose self-control or allow my eyes to wander. I can choose kindness or let a bit of vindictiveness leak out. What determines which one wins? In my life it's largely the level of incubation. When I'm incubating God's Word in my life, when I'm meditating on the book of the law day and night[6], I have in the forefront of my heart and head the preferred directional heading.

When a situation arises, without fail the Holy Spirit prompts us. When we head down the wrong path, rarely, if ever, is it due to ignorance that the path is wrong. It's almost exclusively a simple disregard for the Spirit's prompting. Incubation is the antidote. When faced with a prompting to do what's right, I can choose the way of the Spirit. I'm morphing and setting in motion a brand-new track of behavior.

> **Every time I have the opportunity to sin, I have the opportunity to bear fruit of the Spirit as well.**

This area of habit formation is where a whole different set of traditional and nontraditional patterns and practices can be used. Fasting to break food addictions, solitude to quell the feeling of being mentally online 24/7, and taking a walk in the part of town where street people hang out expressly to talk with them and crawl for a moment into their world are all practices aiding the breakdown of old habits. When coupled with incubation and the promptings of the Holy Spirit, these breakdown practices set the stage for soul morphing. Again, creativity and sky-is-the-limit thinking are the most helpful skills in designing life-changing patterns and practices.

Urban Experience as Formation Practice

My friend Alan grew up in inner city New York. When we were in seminary in Chicago, he felt that my white, middle-class upbringing needed some augmenting. As a soul formation practice, Al went down into the city and visited with street people. Almost every Friday afternoon, he would take off, grab a burger en route, and then spend the next several hours visiting Jim, who lived in a doorway, or Harry, who lived on a warming grate, or a prostitute named Linda, who always worked the same area. Al dragged me on a couple of these trips. I could list the vivid faces of these and others to whom he introduced me. The impact these experiences had on me made it clear that this was as important to my spiritual formation and God's imprint on my soul as prayer. My inner city experience gave me a heart for people who were essentially just like me, except in a slightly different location. They, too, wanted their lives to mean something. They also had dreams. They, too, were loved by God. Here was a pattern not recorded in Scripture but profoundly shaping.

This new behavior is the start of a new pattern of habits. Remember, this is the third stage resulting in transformation. Information → incubation → application (re-habituation) → transformation. Just as with physical fitness, when going to the gym or running the first time is the hardest, the second time seems less difficult, and the third even easier. In no way am I suggesting this is simply a linear process moving smoothly to culmination. There will be fits and starts along the way, a slip here or setback there. However, clarity on the transformation process has removed the mystery from it and has helped my spiritual life and my coaching of others.

This approach takes seriously every moment of every day as an opportunity to live the life Jesus would live if he were in my body. Driving, shopping, being at the office or school, and dealing with a difficult associate are simply a variety of training grounds where I get to see if my incubation can position me to respond to the promptings of the Holy Spirit. This is an earthed spirituality, one taking seriously our embodied existence and seriously concerned about inside-out change.

Soul-shaping, spiritual formation, and habit transformation are the foundations for closing the gap between what we know and what we do. Soul-shaping, spiritual formation, and habit transformation are the foundations for closing the gap between what we know and what we do. Knowledge is generally not the Christ follower's problem. Responding to and acting on what's right is the challenge. Our very credibility as leaders is wrapped up in this area of self-leadership. If we can't become proficient here, if we can't creatively incubate, then why would anyone want to follow us on the journey?

I've learned over and over again that my staff team is encouraged when I share my challenge to love an unlovable, or the challenge to be genuinely interested in yet the fifty-eighth person trying to bend my ear after one of our Fusion services.[7] There are certain things I have to do to be open to the Holy Spirit's promptings. My team feels encouraged that I'm in process like they are. They feel encouraged when I blow it like they do. They feel encouraged that over time there is genuine progress and movement deeper into the kingdom in my life. Here's the leadership leak: What is going on inside of me is flowing out into the "space" around me and impacting others. This is the creation of the ethos of church culture.

morph!

Fellow Traveler as Guide

People want to follow those who are in process, not those who have an air of perfection. People today want to share a path with fellow travelers, not be preached at with rules and regulations. If we genuinely believe Christianity is about relationship, not rules, then we ought to understand and model the relational process.

Dynamic morphing is the stage-setter for living the intriguing lives others are looking for. The typical nonchurched person coming to Westwinds these days is not looking for answers as to why we think the Bible is a reliable document or how to prove the existence of God. We don't typically have problems helping people believe in God. The real issue is which god? Most of the time, they're well into a process that started with them watching someone else's life from a distance. Maybe these people have a need, or they come to the realization that they have some core yearnings not being satisfied. They begin the hunt for a possible answer, perhaps with Oprah, the self-help section at Border's, a work associate, or a close friend. All are potential options for satisfying this hunt.

The person who shows up at Westwinds has been watching a Christ follower's life and has become intrigued. Intrigue turns to question asking. As story is shared both directions, nuggets about life in the kingdom begin to lodge and provide grist for further consideration by the questioner. Take a time out here. Without leaders deeply in touch with the customized process of soul ergonomics, how will we ever produce an environment and church culture in which Christ followers learn this process themselves? The importance of visible, clear, decisive life change is obviously catalytic in the process of others coming to Christ.

The life observation by the questioner moves him or her to story sharing and then into the marinade of community. What's happening here? The investigator wonders if this person he or she is observing is for real. So the investigator decides to check out a church service or small group. He or she has been assured over and over again that this isn't typical church. The person won't be bored, put on the spot, or talked down to. Once in a community context of other people also living these intriguing, genuinely changing, authentic lives, serious head scratching begins.

Shane and His Friend Jason

Let me quote from an e-mail that literally came in as I was typing this chapter. It was hard not to think it was made for this section. It comes from a nineteen-year-old guy named Shane who caught the vision for how the process of life change can impact a life.

"I invited my best friend, Jason, to church like two years ago, and he was totally against it. He had never stepped foot in a church and was doing just fine in life. He didn't need someone telling him why he was going to hell or to give him a bunch of rules. It was hard for him to go to church because he looks up to his dad a lot, and his dad is very successful and has never had a thing to do with church. I prayed about it a lot and asked him a few months later to go to church, and he said he would...surprisingly. He started going, and he liked it. He has been going about every Sunday with me for a year and a half. He had a lot of questions, and he seemed interested. But I didn't want to push the God thing on him, so I let him do it at his own pace. Anyway, I have been praying about Jason. And today at church we were sitting there, and I felt God kind of letting me know that I needed to pray for Jason. So almost the whole service I was praying. Finally, you said if anyone wants to surrender their life to God, please raise your hand. I felt God working, and Jason raised his hand. It was an amazing feeling to see Jason raise his hand. It has been amazing watching Jason go through the process from not wanting anything to do with God to getting saved. It took a year and a half of investigating, but he finally surrendered his life to God. It is one of the happiest days of my life."

Genuine transformation is what creates a compelling ethos in the church, a place people can come investigate and really see something happen in human lives. We can't lead where we haven't traveled. If all we do flows from who we are, then this is the starting point for ministry concerned with life change.

Inner Action

1. Could your current practices of relating to God function in healthy ways with any other person in your life?

2. Would you characterize your life as more informational or relational toward God? Be honest here. How about the ethos of the church? Would you say people are experiencing morphic dynamic or information and doctrinal overload? How can you tell? How can you be sure?

3. If the average person you were inviting into the Christian life were to experience the actual morphing and acquisition of God's life you are currently experiencing, would they want it? Could they see or feel anything different from their current lives? Would they find it compelling?

4. How have you gotten creative in designing patterns or processes to aid incubation? What about habit formation? Any unique pieces of your journey you can pass on or build upon?

Endnotes

1. *Create, call into being*; in the New Testament only of God's creative activity (1 Timothy 4:3); (2) of God's transforming activity in one's inner life *create, renew, change completely* (Ephesians 2:10), Friberg lexicon from BibleWorks.

2. Any of Dallas Willard's four books have the potential to rock your world. *The Spirit of the Disciplines* changed my life and is one of the top ten books I have ever read. Dallas Willard, *The Divine Conspiracy: Rediscovering Our Hidden Life in God* (New York, NY: Harper Collins Publishers, 1998). Dallas Willard, *In Search of Guidance: Developing a Conversational Relationship with God* (New York, NY: HarperCollins Publishers, 1993). Dallas Willard, *The Spirit of the Disciplines: Understanding How God Changes Lives* (New York, NY: Harper & Row, Publishers, Inc., 1988). His most recent is vintage Willard: *Renovation of the Heart: Putting on the Character of Christ* (Colorado Springs, CO: NavPress Publishing Group, 2002).

3. Eugene H. Peterson, *Working the Angles: The Shape of Pastoral Integrity* (Grand Rapids, MI: Wm. B. Eerdmans Publishing Co., 1987). Eugene H. Peterson, *Five Smooth Stones for Pastoral Work* (Grand Rapids, MI: Wm. B. Eerdmans Publishing Co., 1980). Eugene H. Peterson, *Under the Unpredictable Plant: An Explanation in Vocational Holiness* (Grand Rapids, MI: Wm. B. Eerdmans Publishing Co., 1992). Eugene H. Peterson, *The Contemplative Pastor: Returning to the Art of Spiritual Direction* (Grand Rapids, MI: Wm. B. Eerdmans Publishing Co., 1989).

4. A passage like 2 Peter 1:3-4 comes to mind: "His divine power has given us everything we need for life and godliness through our knowledge of him who called us by his own glory and goodness. Through these he has given us his very great and precious promises, so that through them you may participate in the divine nature and escape the corruption in the world caused by evil desires."

5. Leonard I. Sweet, *SoulSalsa* (Grand Rapids, MI: Zondervan Publishing House, 2000), 12.

6. Joshua 1:8-9; Psalm 1.

7. This is the name of our three weekend services. We also have weekly DEEP, which is verse-by-verse, in-depth Bible study, and a monthly ENCOUNTER, which is an aesthetic, laminated worship experience using all the senses, art, scent, inter-actives, and so on. Chapter 10 will detail this.

TECHNIQUE
OR
AUTHENTIQUE

The charge against the church used to be that it was "full of hypocrites." The charge today is subtler but no less indicting. Now we're just called "plastic and fake." This was found in the mouth of a nonchurched friend of mine at the golf course one bright afternoon: "Ron, people who go to church just aren't real. I don't think they're trying to be deceptive; they just seem fake and act like their lives are better than I know they really are."

I had to agree with Mark. He was right. We *do* come off as plastic a good deal of the time. Let's leave behind hanging this on TV evangelists and really hear the criticism. Mark had great insight into the reality of many churched people's lives; he could clearly see what they were usually downplaying or concealing. In short, Mark came to see church people as image-management experts.

What is image management except an effort to control the thoughts and perceptions others have of you and to paint yourself in a slightly brighter light than your portrait warrants? At root, image-management is a control issue. Of course, this doesn't just have implications for how those outside the church view people in the church. It also has profound ramifications for community. If I'm constantly putting forth a picture of myself that is incongruent with who I really am, the ability to enter into genuine community is compromised to that degree.

When we enter into the image-management game, we're splitting our lives. We live a plastic, molded-for-public-consumption version, and we also live a private, quite different version—one that reflects our true hearts and lives. The living of two lives, the wearing of two masks, and the painting of two different images are the exact opposite of integrity. Integrity in its dictionary definition means undivided.

We need to learn how integrity, authenticity, and credibility all fit together.

What is authenticity? What is this nebulous, touchy-feely thing? Quite simply, it's the ability to be honest and upfront about strengths and weaknesses, peaks and valleys, victories and struggles—both sides of the coin bring authenticity. The seeds of credibility start with humble acknowledgement of humble strengths, gifts, and abilities, as well as honest identification of shortcomings, weaknesses, and areas needing work.

Heightened Self-Awareness

Tremendous self-leadership is needed on this front. The ability to acknowledge and appropriately disclose strength and weakness assumes self-awareness of both. Peter Senge and others call it personal mastery: "People with a high level of personal mastery are acutely aware of their ignorance, their incompetence, their growth areas. And they are deeply self-confident. Paradoxical? Only for those who do not see that 'the journey is the reward'."[1]

Several things accrue to the leader willing to do morphic work here. First, self-awareness skyrockets, and the fruit of an integrated life results. Note the connection between the word integrated and integrity. When I couple my leadership DNA, my definition of leadership, my sense of personal destiny, and my principles of passion with a deep understanding of who I really am, I'm slowly going to more fully leverage who I am and live a more genuine life. Authenticity is the very opposite of living a fake, plastic life. It's learning to integrate the full picture of who I am into my conscious life, thereby leaving duplicity and image management behind.

We mentioned earlier the adage, "Build on islands of health and strength." But profundity will escape us if we're not careful. Inherent in this adage is a deep insight: The owning of strengths can only occur if we're clear what those are. The natural result is that we come to understand, see, and own more clearly our weaknesses. Far from being a downer, we have a much deeper and clearer understanding of who we are. Instead of hiding it, managing it, concealing it, or denying it, we can be honest about it and embrace it. In this way we celebrate our strengths and own the fact that we also have weaknesses (which everyone already knows).

Dr. Cavendar on Mediocrity

When I was a drum major in the band in high school, I had the honor of studying with one of the most celebrated marching band conductors of all time: George Cavendar from the University of Michigan. He said something on the opening day of our leadership camp that hit me with indelible force: "Mediocrity is the standard of excellence for the incompetent."

Dr. Cavendar hit on what is a biblical principle. No one is created mediocre. Everyone is a ten somewhere. We all have strengths and gifts. To not spend time seeing those soar is to rob others of the best we have to offer them.

Paul said essentially the same thing. We're never taught in Scripture to try becoming a nose because we think a nose is more valuable than an eye, or to covet being a hand when we're actually an elbow.

Paul's whole illustration for the Corinthians was that we all need the unique gifts we each bring to the table. Don't try to be who you aren't. Instead spend time developing and becoming the best eye, elbow, or hand you can be. This requires laying aside our techniques for keeping people in the dark about what we aren't good at; what flaws we have; and what weaknesses, screw-ups, or shortcomings we have.

This seems to be at the heart of Mark's complaint. Everyone has weaknesses. So why does it seem that once many people become churchgoers, they contract a horrific case of amnesia, coyly ignoring their downsides and presenting a picture that doesn't even exist?

This is the heart of image management and control, and is precisely why Jesus challenged the Pharisees.[2] Jesus called the Pharisees hypocrites because they washed the outside of the dish but inside were full of greed and self-indulgence. They were two-faced, living publicly as if things were one way while privately knowing they were another. The Pharisees were deeply into control—control of what others saw, perceived, and believed about them.

The Fruit of Integration

Jesus invites you and me into a fully integrated life, one in which we are not perfecting techniques to hide the real us, but developing authenticity to affirm we are the work-in-progress that we really are. The first necessity is to live more integrated lives.

A life of integration naturally develops authentic teams. If we get what we model, then we'll be creating an environment for our teams in which they are granted permission to be imperfect, to work on strengths, and to be honest about weaknesses. What would the implications be for an entire staff team to be honest? That's almost laughable to ask the question of a church staff, isn't it? But if we emit the myth of perfection, which no one believes anyway, we simply lose credibility.

A life lived authentically will produce compelling community where people far from God or the church see real, genuine people struggling in the process just like they are. This is one of the most critical components for outreach. None of this is an effort to go easy on sin or wrongdoing, to wink at moral transgression or what is outright wrong. But for far too long, the Christian community has modeled that once you're in Christ, you better get the nasty nine and dirty dozen cleaned up in your life and pretty quickly move on to the fine-tuning that leads to perfection. This is bogus plasticity.

The issues facing those inside and outside the church are in every way nearly identical. Everyone has trouble trying not to blow their cool with their kids and become the screaming parent. Every man struggles with lust, and so do a lot of women. Everyone struggles with loving the unlovable who may be marginalized people or upper-middle-class, white-collar male oppressors. Everyone struggles with materialism, power, title, or visual image and how they think people see them. These issues are endemic to the human condition. Why do we act like, in one fell swoop, Christ followers are somehow elevated to another plane of existence? Sure, we've been translated into a new kingdom, but these issues didn't vaporize on that day.

A life lived authentically will produce compelling community where people far from God or the church see real, genuine people struggling in the process just like they are.

So how do we become more authentic? What does it have to do with leadership credibility? In what areas do we need to see the leak of authenticity into the life of the church? We've already done preliminary work on the first question. We've started to get in touch with our strengths, how we've been made, and what we will build on for the long haul. Seeing some weaknesses in this process would have been unavoidable. I certainly found some in myself. And if you're married and have children? Let's face it, your spouse and kids have built-in apparatus at being honest with your areas needing improvement. A couple of times, Valerie has said to me (I am sure it was no more than a couple of times as I am a swift learner), "Ron, go easy, have a little compassion." Think about how that might play in a ministry context.

Will I Still Be Needed?

Early on in my personal discovery, I learned that shepherding and compassion were not high in my gift mix. While I had to learn it, Valerie already knew it, and my kids over time would experience it. On both the family and ministry fronts, I have had to work hard in this area. An observation like this doesn't give me warrant to blow people off, be unkind, and act like I don't care. But insights like these have led me to organize, enlist, and release people into those ministry areas in which I was weak but they were strong. For some leaders this can raise a whole new emotional issue: "What happens if those people come to be needed more than I'm needed?"

I don't ask those questions in a vacuum. I'm in the process of hiring two full-time and two part-time staff members. One of the full-time staff members will be a speaking pastor who does leadership development. I'm actually in dialogue right now with a guy who is so far ahead of me that it makes my head spin. He has forgotten more about staff development than I've learned. It would be very accurate to say I'm a bit intimidated at the thought of him on staff; intimidated not in the sense of my job being secure, but in the sense of him being so far ahead of me that I may look like quite a fool at times. Yet the learning and synergy he would bring are absolutely incredible. These are discussions in the arena of personal beliefs and are at the heart of where authenticity begins. Every leader has thoughts like this at some time or another. Maybe it's not about releasing those with shepherding gifts, but maybe it's about the next hire. Will you hire someone more gifted than you as a speaker? Would you bring on staff someone more culturally tuned in or a better motivator? What are the feelings going on inside as you process those questions? Feelings of insecurity, the desire to be needed by others, the desire to be seen as the top dog expert—all of these rear their ugly heads when we start asking the hard questions. On one hand we feel these are infantile thoughts, and we want to dismiss them as irrelevant. The truth is that they're very real and operate in subtle and undermining ways. We're in the realm of what Kevin Cashman calls "Shadow Beliefs."[3]

From the Shadows

We all have two kinds of beliefs. The first one is conscious beliefs, which we are readily aware of and can articulate. These may be beliefs about ourselves, others, or life in general. Shadow beliefs are subtler; less apparent to us; and usually the manifestations of hidden, unresolved, or unexplored dynamics in our lives.[4]

Heading home after church on Sundays is usually a good experience. But doing an exercise a few years ago to uncover shadow beliefs, I came to see some things about me that I didn't particularly like. This took some probing, some discussion with my wife, and then simple admission of the ugly. The tenor of each Sunday afternoon was essentially determined by the kinds and amount of feedback I'd get about my message and our church service. Sounds like an easy admission, but it wasn't. Denial was present for quite a while. Dismissal with "this isn't that big a deal" persisted for some time. Rationale and justification for why I had these feelings surfaced. But to finally admit I had this subtle, secret belief that my value and worth were wrapped up in a few comments on a Sunday morning was no small task. There's obviously a lot to be explored here. Why did I feel that way? What was spiritually going on? Where was there pride involved? All of these questions were part of the process.

When we can own these issues and admit them to others, those natural outcomes we mentioned begin to flow. I become more whole, the community I'm in is

But to finally admit I had this subtle, secret belief that my value and worth were wrapped up in a few comments on a Sunday morning was no small task.

granted permission to be real as they hear me being real, and we leak the same authenticity to the larger body of the church community, creating a more real place for those outside the church to find a home. Authenticity is about exploring our shadow beliefs, bringing them to the surface, and transforming them into conscious beliefs.

This is the hard but profoundly morphic work of self-leadership. If we as leaders can't model the way on this front, we'll end up creating inauthentic communities where anything but the genuine issues can be freely discussed. We lead out of our conscious beliefs that make sense. What's less obvious, but no less true, is that we lead out of our shadow beliefs as well.

What does authenticity have to do with leadership credibility? The answer may be transparently obvious: everything! There's a temptation to think credibility is essentially about creating a track record of "good calls" and successful initiatives. Of course, there's a dimension where these are important for credibility. This is, however, a glance to the outside before we look at the deeper and more significant and personal inside issues. If authenticity is about us being honest about who we are, credibility is about the resultant understandings people have about us in light of that honesty. Credibility is essential to building community.

WYSIWYG (What You See Is What You Get)

Credibility brings us to the heart of leadership reciprocity. You and I lead, but without followers, we're merely taking a stroll. Leaders lead because followers follow, and followers follow first because of credibility and then because of a growing track record. Parker Palmer, who always writes with such profound wisdom, said in a recent interview, "I know from experience inside corporations and large-scale organizations that everybody is sizing up the leader and asking, 'Is this a divided person or a person of integrity? Is what we see what we get? Is he or she the same on the inside as on the outside?' "[5]

When followers follow, we enter into community where we get to learn how to be the same on the outside as we are on the inside. Clearly this should be happening in the church. A new community is what Jesus came to start—a community based on new metaphors, values, priorities, goals, and ethos.

Authenticity serves as a base and springboard for credibility. Some of the leading experts on the topic of credibility are James Kouzes and Barry Posner. Their book details several factors contributing to the development of credibility. In their research, *honest, forward-looking, inspiring,* and *competent* are the four bedrock qualities indispensable for leadership.[6] They spent an entire volume detailing the role each of these plays in the leadership arena. Three of them, however—honest, inspiring, and competent—are what communications researchers refer to as source credibility.[7]

The implications here are rather clear. Leadership credibility is, across the board, an important quality; and honesty stands at the head of the list for fostering it. This is simply another way of saying authenticity—the ability to be honest—brings the reciprocation of followership.

Early in ministry I had some people challenge the lack of personal illustrations in my speaking, particularly my weaknesses or shortcomings. I came from a rather functional family, generally very healthy, both birth parents still married, no abuse of any sort. Compared to many of my friends, my upbringing seemed like utopia. Returning to plant a church in my hometown brought with it the challenge of relating to people who were convinced I couldn't relate to them. My life was perfect in the minds of some. I had it easy. I was whole. This outlook had an obvious outcome: my inability to connect with them in my speaking.

Using a Sieve on Criticism

Unfortunately, I didn't understand how to change this situation. I simply apologized that I couldn't change my past and dismissed further criticism until it popped up again. I came to learn some valuable lessons at this junction of ministry. Criticism usually has a kernel of truth in it if you can get past the often-inflammatory front end with which the criticism is usually leveled.

Further exploration of this topic simply showed some real immaturity in my speaking. People weren't begrudging me my past as much as they were saying, "Show us you're real. Be authentic with us. Your life can't be that perfect." People simply needed me to share out of my life that, while I didn't struggle with alcoholic coping mechanisms or verbal abuse or come from a home void of love, I did have my own issues. I had insecurities. I fretted about how people perceived me. I had messed-up priorities at times. I struggled with materialism.

Criticism usually has a kernel of truth in it if you can get past the often-inflammatory front end with which the criticism is usually leveled.

Honest admissions in the course of weekend talks are what brought people into connection with my messages and me, God's presence, and the Westwinds community. Visitors came to conclude that if openness at that level can happen from the platform, then people in this community are probably open about their issues.

All of us connect at our points of failure, struggle, or need. Early on I simply didn't talk about the hard stuff because most of my life wasn't about hard stuff. I learned that simply sharing my life and struggles could easily provide the touch point most people needed in order to see that I was a real person with real warts.

My wife, Valerie, and our neighbor were down getting the mail at the same time one day. Valerie mentioned something boneheaded I'd done, how mad I made her, and that a blowout had ensued. Our neighbor was flabbergasted. She couldn't believe we would ever fight or have a problem.

Two things surfaced in this event. Had we lived lives in front of her that appeared that inauthentic? Was the dominant assumption of the typical unchurched person that church leaders should not or do not have marriage bumps and other difficulties? Those little indicators helped me realize how sharing even the obvious with people is often helpful in keeping the myth of the omni-competent, problem-free leader at bay.

Another way of saying this is that we need to learn to lead out loud. To motivate the staff to see the vision for a building campaign is the job of leading. But to conveniently omit your concerns as they are sharing theirs and to motivate them to charge full steam ahead is to miss an opportunity to lead out loud, make an authenticity deposit, and gain credibility.

Credibility and Reciprocity

Morphic leadership sees the hard work of authenticity and personal beliefs to be the necessary prerequisite for garnering credibility. Only credibility can birth the reciprocity of followership. We have essentially said the way this is garnered is through personal storytelling. Much more will be said later about storytelling and its importance in our emerging post-Gutenberg age. But several things now warrant our connecting of story with authenticity and how that creates a certain kind of community—a community of process; one less concerned with legalistic definitions of holiness and more concerned about the impact of how being in Jesus' presence eventually changes a human life.

On any given weekend, scores of unchurched people walk into churches, listening for the opportunity to connect their stories with a large whole. On a weekly basis, we have a couple hundred doing just that. They're listening for someone who can honestly admit to having struggles, problems, and unresolved issues. *But* they will also see that the God that someone claims to serve has met that someone in those issues. Notice I didn't say "solved" all those issues.

Now we can say, as some have, that the gospel isn't essentially about the masses having their needs met and thereby further propagating our narcissistic culture. Of course, there's truth to that. However, Jesus repeatedly met people at exactly the juncture of their hurt, pain, and need and connected them to the possibility of God moving in their lives. The New Testament is replete with this model of reaching people.

The story we tell and invite others into creates a certain kind of ethos. We decide whether it will be an ethos of acceptance, love, and life-changing challenge, or whether it will be judgmental, condemning, and ultimately guaranteeing that the church will never get another hearing with that person. I'm afraid the latter is more normative than the former and may be a good deal of the reason why the

Jesus repeatedly met people at exactly the juncture of their hurt, pain, and need and connected them to the possibility of God moving in their lives.

church is perceived as so *in*credible. The connection here cannot be missed. The inner morphing of leaders who are genuine and honest about their own growth can't help but create an ethos that becomes the dominant environment in which people can tell their story.

Let's try to climb into the mind of the typical church visitor. Often we preach down to the congregation. They're told all the things they should be doing but aren't and all the things they shouldn't do but are doing. We then conclude with the pious line "Christianity isn't about rules but about relationship." Does it take a genius to see "disingenuous" emblazoned all over this?

As much as I'd like to say I think that's merely a characterization of how things really are, it simply isn't the case. My Bible school professor mentioned in Chapter 1 certainly confirmed this as his concern about the kind of "pastoral product" his institution is developing. Sadly, his situation is not unique. A good deal of Bible-believing Christianity is exactly this way. And we wonder why we're having trouble connecting to those outside the church. The issue of authenticity just screams to be noticed.

Moving Beyond "Us Versus Them"

The "us versus them" dichotomy is a classic Christian challenge. We have all the answers; they don't. We have the inside track they're looking for. We know the truth; they're mistaken. This "who is in and who is out" mentality was exactly what Jesus constantly challenged with the Pharisees. More often than not, Jesus was including those who thought they were "out" and excluding those who thought they were "in."

If we have majored on minors and the majors have slipped into oblivion, then our leadership task is monumental.

On careful analysis, it appears we've made nonissues the main issue and let the main issue slip from view. How can we have churches replete with rules and regulations about what movies you can and cannot attend, alcohol consumption, distinctive jewelry prohibitions depending on gender, and who you boycott this month—and then turn around and say religion is about rules and Jesus is about relationship?

I've consulted in a church where if a member was caught smoking a cigar on the golf course, he would have been kicked out of the church. But the pastor was seventy pounds overweight (and not because of a metabolism problem). Scripture is crystal clear on the gluttony issue, but I'm still searching for a cigar reference. How can people connect with our story if this is the kind of thing we have to tell? If we have majored on minors and the majors have slipped into oblivion, then our leadership task is monumental.

This raises the issue of how we define holiness. I want to suggest that this is core to the issue of our personal authenticity and the ethos of the church. If we define holiness as a whole list of external do's and don'ts, then it's no wonder we don't get authentic storytelling from the pulpit. If holiness is construed as an external standard, then there is absolutely no safety in the sharing of genuine struggle. If that's the church ethos being created, it's no wonder those outside the church feel so distant, unable to connect, and unworthy to be a part of the community.

One of the most compelling things we can do is to be on the same path we invited others to journey. They're looking to see if we, too, are fellow travelers, if it really "works" for us, if we believe and experience that into which we are inviting them. Only this kind of authenticity will be believable to a world skeptical of what the church has to offer. We need to admit that we're with them on the trek or they'll find others more interested in them as traveling companions.

Terry Gets Authentic

Terry came to Westwinds a couple of years ago. He's a teddy bear of a guy, is married, has three kids, and has an incredible servant's heart. Many months after they had first attended, Terry's wife, Lori, confided in me about Terry's marijuana addiction. She was tipping me off because she felt if I was around Terry long enough, some Sunday morning he'd drag me aside and tell me. He really wanted me to be aware of it and wanted to get help, but his shame and guilt had prevented him from being forthright so far. He had been in one other church in the past but, after being there a while, came to realize that if he and his family wanted to stay in the church, he would have to make sure his secret never became known. In that church you could be thrown out for tobacco use of any kind, so where did that leave him with pot?

The healing organism of that body of Christ failed Terry and his family because the story told was that addictions like his were intolerable. Therefore, Terry pushed it underground; never got help; and lived with the guilt, shame, and addiction longer than he needed to. I ran into Terry this last Sunday. Post-rehabilitation Terry is ninety days clean. During the whole thing, he has remained an active part of the community, served using his spiritual gifts, and learned what real community and holiness are about.

Jesus didn't describe holiness as an externally defined set of boundary markers, and he certainly didn't live within those either. The cultural triad again bubbles to the surface: We need to be in the world, not of the world, but not out of it either. Jesus hung around "sinners" and questionable people. He was at so many of their parties and apparently ate enough food and drank

We must seriously reconsider the level of authenticity we model in our churches.

enough wine that the charge that he was a glutton and a drunkard, though false, could have some remote foundation. If Jesus didn't party, wasn't in those contexts, and didn't feast and drink, then the charge would have been patently a lie. This isn't to suggest Jesus ever over-imbibed or was a glutton or a drunkard. Interestingly though, Jesus never denies the charge of hanging out with sinners, partying with them, or trying to reach their friends. In fact he directly affirms he has come for them and not for those convinced they have no need of Jesus.

We must seriously reconsider the level of authenticity we model in our churches. This whole issue starts with how serious we, as leaders, are with the hard work of morphing our inner selves. How willing we are to get honest about our "stuff"? How open will we be with those around us about our own process?

Up to this point, I haven't made distinctions between what are appropriate things to disclose and what are inappropriate. I also haven't addressed what the appropriate limits and boundaries are of our public lives and our private lives. I don't feel I should disclose it every time I'm struggling with something or every time I have a marriage hiccup. This chapter is in no way a plea for a lack of boundaries. I am not suggesting that there is no line between the public and private lives of public servants of God's Word. However, this is an effort to challenge us all not to hide behind the pulpit and pontificate truths that appear to have no impact on our lives.

Saran Wrap or Realness?

We also haven't identified the difference between transparency and authenticity, and there is a difference. We aren't arguing for a Saran Wrap see-through-ness but only appropriate disclosure of struggles and the process we're in. How many Terrys are out there crying for help, but no one can hear them amidst the roar of our detailed rule-citing?

If we could get down into our own hearts (the heart *is* the wellspring of life, you know) and begin asking the questions that will expose our shadow beliefs, I think we might find hope for the church. As we find ourselves in process, we experience the tremendous exhilaration that comes from fresh encounters with the Holy Spirit. When we share those encounters, the setbacks, and the progressions, we are powerfully granting permission—permission that process is acceptable, perfection not expected. In fact, perfection claimed is suspect. When our deep morphing yields authenticity, which, in turn, brings credibility and the reciprocity of followership, we create compelling communities that people want to be a part of and a place to which people want to invite others. Let's lay aside image-management techniques and control and, instead, plunge deep into the well of life God opens to us. May the morphing bring life.

InnerAction

1. How would you rate your overall authenticity quotient with your team, your close friends, your church?

2. How helpful is the distinction between conscious and shadow beliefs for you? Do you have any shadow beliefs you can identify?

3. What are ways we elevate the authenticity value in our churches?

4. What can you do to be more authentic in your storytelling of personal struggles and difficult issues?

Endnotes

1. Peter Senge, *The Fifth Discipline: The Art and Practice of the Learning Organization* (New York, NY: Doubleday, 1990), 142.

2. Matthew 23:25

3. Kevin Cashman, *Leadership from the Inside Out: Seven Pathways to Mastery* (Provo, UT: Executive Excellence Publishing, 1998), 36.

4. Cashman, *Leadership from the Inside Out*, 36-37.

5. Parker Palmer, "Leadership and the Inner Journey," Interview with L.J. Rittenhouse, Leader to Leader (Number 22, Fall 2001), 27.

6. James M. Kouzes and Barry Z. Posner, *Credibility: How Leaders Gain and Lose It, Why People Demand It* (San Francisco, CA: Jossey-Bass Publishers, 1993), 14.

7. Kouzes and Posner, *Credibility*, 21.

CHAPTER SIX

LOGIN FOR L³ (LIFELONG LEARNING)

You can hear it echoed at seminars, from the lips of mentors, and from high performing leaders: Leaders are learners. You cease learning, you cease leading. While this has always been true, the explosion of issues surrounding most ministry today requires fluency in a vast array of areas. From blended families to biotech, we need a working knowledge in a host of arenas just to intelligently speak and connect with the diversity in our congregations.

And that's only the beginning. If you and I are to do our job as leaders, our goal is not only connecting in our talks, but also connecting others with resources. Leaders at their finest aren't primarily answer repositories; they're resources brokers.

Not long ago the pastor was considered one of the leading intellectuals in the community. As a group, we're not that well-read anymore, and we're usually not the leading intellectuals in our communities, either. On the contrary, Christianity in general and the pastoral office in particular are often demeaned, caricatured, and sketched as out of touch, on the fringe, socially inept, and intellectually sub par. Unfortunately, we can't rise up and say that's an entirely false sketch. We need to ask if we're in a place to dialogue as Paul did with the leading Epicurean and Stoic philosophers of our day.

Learning is morphic bedrock. The very nature of growth makes this quite self-evident. Growth requires change; need for change comes through learning. This is an area close to my heart and a deep value in my personal leadership DNA. But that's not the only reason we're devoting a whole section to this topic. The church built by Jesus, against which the gates of hell will not prevail, requires growing-edge, laser-sharp leaders. Effective leadership in this new millennium requires tremendous facility with a host of skills not always resident in the leadership toolbox.

Consider this: Who taught you how to assess where you are in your skill-set development, and what next steps will help you arrive at your desired destination? What is your desired destination? How does personal growth happen, and what are the things you should be thinking about for long-term interior growth? What is the shape of personal emotional health?

My Dark Cycles

Credit goes to my wife, who several years ago pointed out cycles of unexplainable melancholy and mild depression in my life. I would arrive home from the office, and Valerie would notice my typical verbal flow would be a mere trickle. Initially, I thought I was simply living a little too much at the office, unable to be fully present at home. But there seemed to be a pattern. When I was faced with a difficult decision, one that impacted how others thought about me, I went into a dark reclusive brooding. This was not an easy admission. I took no classes to prep me for this realization. Discoveries like this invite us into a whole new sphere of personal growth. When we say personal growth, I think we're often looking to acquire new knowledge to help the church get healthier, assimilate people better, or launch a better small group ministry. And surely that is part of what we need to talk about.

But morphic leaders take a look at self, not first as a repository of skill accumulation for the success of the church enterprise, but as the locus of God's activity to bring about interior maturity. Self is looked at so we can see deeper surrender within ourselves. Deep down, inner-life work is where we confront our fears, identify the sources of depression, understand our emotional wiring, come to grips with control issues, confront obsessive patterns, and ask God to grow us up. This is the growth, when leaked into a team context, that sends a clear signal. Personal growth is the basis for your leadership life.

Every time you and I come to a snag in our personal lives, marriages, parenting, or leadership, we come to a critical junction. Any snag tells us our skill-set has reached exhaustion. We have hit a plateau in what is available in our arsenal to deal with the current issue. Whether we're looking at cyclical depression, as I was, or repeated staff conflict over the same issue, snags are invitations to morph.

At every offered invitation, we have only two options: rest and recede or morph and proceed. For many, the work of morphing is just too hard. Letting go of deeply ingrained patterns, asking incessant "why" questions until an answer emerges, or seeking help

There's no standing still with God or his church.

from somebody who is down the trail a bit further is simply too painful for some. In those cases, the plateau will only last so long before a recession leads to decline. There's no standing still with God or his church.

The other option is to seek help, resources, or mentors; confront inner monsters; and adopt new skills. This option leads to morphic movement deep down inside and the opportunity to proceed further down the path.

Here's the fundamental reason change must start with you and me as leaders. The way we see the world, interact with the world, and view the world is a cumulative result of all our experiences and learning. From our upbringing to our schooling, from our friends to our life experiences, from our geography to our religious formation—every factor of our life experience molds and shapes how we view everything around us. There's nothing particularly insightful about that observation until we stop and think about the implications it has for leadership.

Differences Can Be Radical Though Invisible

Possibly the most dramatic way of getting at this is to think of someone from a tribal village in India. I worked among many of them and trained lots of pastors who have small churches in these remote parts of the world. How different is their view of the world? For them politics, social caste, and religion are all viewed as intimately interrelated. Their view of life is one of day-to-day survival. Or think about a hovel village of 800,000 in Irkutsk, Siberia, one of the first hard labor camps under the old communist regime. I've witnessed their day-to-day life. The differences are graphic and radical. Dramatic differences exist between our typical American life and their way of life. The cross-cultural differences are readily identified with some reflection. Here is our problem though: We tend to view "our typical American life" as some sort of consistent and monolithic existence everyone in America experiences. The reality is that the differences among you and me are just about as cross-cultural.

We may be a dominantly English-speaking country, but the similarity ends there. The geographic location of our upbringing, the type of schooling we've been through, and the socioeconomic context of our formative years all have profound impacts on how we see the world and who we are. Couple those factors with well-documented changes in how different generations form values, process information, experience relationships and community, and it is not an overstatement to say the church in North America is ministering in a cross-cultural age. Simply walking across the street may put you into a new culture, with new values, expectations, and assumptions. In short, maybe the cross-cultural context of Siberia or India doesn't have any more variables to consider than the crosstown context in which I daily work and minister.

When we begin seeing the church as a ministry beach-head in a foreign land, we will begin taking more seriously the need to understand and study our culture, faithfully translate our message, and see people respond to the incredible headlines that they are loved and are invited into life with Jesus. A mental shift of this magnitude will not be easy but is necessary if the message is to be understood. Our need for wide learning should emerge as rather obvious.

Simply walking across the street may put you into a new culture, with new values, expectations, and assumptions.

Learning expands our field of reference and, therefore, how we view life and each other. Learning reshapes the way we view people, ministry, God, and life. Learning lifts us out of our cloistered enclave where we operate with a relative confidence that our view of the world is about 99 percent accurate. Learning helps us get in touch with our deeply held mental models and assumptions and allows us to question what might have been considered sacred. Learning at this level is where the real adventure takes place.

When we take in deep-level learning, it causes pervasive changes at the structural level of our self-understanding. Deep changes of this nature cannot help but leak. More than that, modeling this kind of interior work invites a team, and then the larger whole of the church, to also drill deep into the kind of life God offers. This is genuine morphic work. When we begin to recognize that all we know is only partial, incomplete, and at times even incorrect, we're opening ourselves to the possibility of God doing really big things.

What happens when someone grows up in a context where no matter what, Mom and Dad never seem to get any "breaks"? The ethos is that of giving in to what life may bring. Over time the dominant flavor and feel of life is "fate rules." What chance do children growing up in that kind of environment have for charging into life, expecting the best, shooting for the stars, and genuinely pursuing life as an adventure? This is no argument for a sociological determinism; only a challenge that the mental models we hold, the deeply held internal images of how the world works, rule every human life. Such internal images are quite changeable and more malleable than we think, but you have to be in touch with what they are before they can be offered to God for his reshaping.

The more aware we as leaders are of our own mental models, the better we'll lead. We need to learn how to augment or even shed some of these deeply held paradigms and replace them. I think this strikes at the heart of Jesus' statement, "You will know the truth, and the truth will set you free" (John 8:32). To know Jesus is to know truth. Embodied truth in Jesus opens us to new possibilities that we might have thought to be impossible before. Think of a leper being cleansed and for the first time being mainstreamed into society. There's a shift in life, a shift in thinking, and a shift in self-understanding.

Intellectual Humility

Lifelong learning is much more than just reading a lot of books and staying current on the newest leadership releases. That's an assumed necessity. But all that reading and informational intake must incubate and then challenge our deeply held views of the world, humanity, God, and each other. I'm surprised how convinced I am that my view of God, doctrine, and the Bible is close to 100 percent accurate. Think about that. Have you ever met anyone who said, "I hold to the basics that are clear, but I'm pretty tentative on a lot. I'm pretty sure some of what I think is certain right now will probably prove incorrect"?

If church history has taught us anything, it ought to be intellectual humility. The modernist project of knowing everything with absolute certainty works against our learning. We have a "once you have learned it, don't ever revisit it" mentality. In areas like math and mechanical engineering, it's probably fine to never ask questions about "settled truth." But in the ministry areas of relationships, motives, and beliefs, a lot more mystery, uncertainty, and fluidity prevail. As learning ignites at this level, we can then move to the skill development area.

> **If church history has taught us anything, it ought to be intellectual humility.**

Think about this for a moment. When you landed at your first ministry post, how much formal training in leadership did you have under your belt? How much did you know about systems thinking? I'd never heard of it. How much training did you have in cultivating a team? How about training on reading the cultural signs and designing ministry with those signs taken into consideration?

The list of questions like this could fill a book. There's tension in even raising the learning question. Most of us are so busy with the day-in, day-out hustle that learning gets leftover time. And since there's no leftover time in ministry, learning is often a perchance enterprise.

Morphic leaders take a different tack on this issue. They know that unless they carve out of their weekly calendar priority slots for learning, they will simply be unable to grow and move forward. And since the leadership leak applies to the good, the bad, and the ugly, a "learning is a low priority" posture eventually hurts the team and the church at large. The "calendar" issue is addressed in the next chapter. Let's look now at inner-life maturity issues.

Inner-life Maturity

Few tools could better serve us here than learning to ask good questions, coupled with reflection time. This can't be overestimated. Socrates is credited with saying the unexamined life is a life not worth living. Parker Palmer expands on this and says, "If you must live an unexamined life, please don't inflict it on others."[1] If you can't take time to reflect, you have misaligned priorities.

Let's start with these questions: What are the next steps in my emotional growth? What emotional areas need the most work, or what areas would pay huge dividends to go to the next level?

We must fight the tendency to say this doesn't really impact our leadership simply because it is personal. By paying attention to your own growth, you become a better person and, therefore, a better leader. What we do flows from who we are. We model for others the process of growth. This is the leadership leak. As you come in touch more deeply with the process of morphing, your empathy rises as well. We will find out later that empathy—the ability to enter into someone else's world—is a key indicator of emotional intelligence and maturity.

Emotions Have Intelligence?

I tend to be a "rational mind" guy, not an "emotional mind" guy. We all have two minds, and knowing which dominates your life experience is a first step in moving forward.[2] In fact, Daniel Goleman tells us that an accurate view of full intelligence "puts emotions at the center of aptitudes for living."[3] Learning the language of emotional intelligence (EI) gave me a place to begin reflecting on things like the fruit of the Spirit mentioned in Galatians. For instance, the first tool of EI is self-awareness—really becoming aware of your current internal state, the emotions swirling around, how they got there, and what is stirring them. Self-awareness is an intuitive skill everyone has, right? Not all of us. Self-awareness exercises are what finally uncovered the cycles of dark brooding I was going through. Self-awareness was what tuned me in to my people-pleasing habits. Self-awareness was what enabled me to catch the slow emergence of tension when I felt paralyzed about a major decision but totally untooled as to how I should proceed. Strengthening this emotional muscle was powerful help in my own growing up on the inside. How does it work?

If self-awareness is the starting point, then here are some quick diagnostic questions: Are you able to sense the slow broil of emotions like anger, irritation, frustration, and the dark cloud of depression? Can you sense when you are feeling out of control, when a flight/fight response is kicking in, or when despair hits and you want to hide? The ability to sense the slow rise of these is the first step toward emotional maturity and health. In short, self-awareness is being conscious of our moods and even our thoughts about those moods.[4]

Without self-awareness, there can't be any fruit-bearing because, before we know it, the emotion will have sneaked up and overpowered us.

Without self-awareness, there can't be any fruit-bearing because, before we know it, the emotion will have sneaked up and overpowered us. The ability to take awareness to the next stage of self-management is another tool in emotional development.

My melancholy was also catalyzed by another factor; when I had nonstop people interaction and little solitude, I felt the slow strangle. This is where self-management came into play. Again, a rather lengthy period of time was necessary to get this sorted out, along with some counsel from a close friend who was emotionally well ahead of me. I discovered that I was quite an introvert as defined by how I receive strength and energy from alone time. This was obvious once I discovered it, and now solitude is a part of my normal daily rhythm. But early on in my leadership experience, it wasn't so transparent. I'm outgoing, gregarious (nice way of saying bigmouth), and enjoy interaction. The truth is that all of that is extremely exhausting to me. I can enjoy it, but it doesn't energize me.

These types of insights are only the beginning. By just using this as an example, I hope you'll be encouraged to dig deep. Think of the inner freedom, the family health, your leadership team, and the tremendous morphing just around the corner. Lifelong learning starts with inner-life morphing.

Skill Set and Ministry Development

When we think of lifelong learning, what comes to mind is knowledge acquisition and developing the enterprise we lead. For many, however, this is not a natural pursuit. I know for many of my colleagues, reading ministry books, let alone other areas outside of ministry, is a very infrequent happening.

Let's state what should be obvious by now. Ministry in 21C is impossible without a growing knowledge and skill-set base. The responsibility for growing is yours, and the knowledge you have or don't have is entirely your baby. So let's just decide that we will give weekly calendar time to learning, moving toward greater health, and acquiring new skills. This will have to become a lifelong endeavor if we want to remain fresh and moving forward. If you want to lead a vibrant, life-nurturing organism, whatever that may be, then you have no other options available but to lead a vibrant, deeply morphing life.

Ministry in 21C is impossible without a growing knowledge and skill-set base.

Before exploring lifelong learning principles, we need to keep a couple things in mind. First, learning doesn't always imply reading. Reading *is* clearly indispensable. There's no possible way you can lead to your potential if you're not a reader—a voracious reader. I read a hundred and fifty books a year, three hundred or more book reviews, and the number of articles is easily in the hundreds.

I think reading is so important that I built it right into my kids' lives with certain payout. I wanted them to learn the value of reading and goal setting. My wife,

Valerie, and I adopted a practice my parents had used with me that added to our reading value. They always bought us all our "firsts": our first bike, our first set of golf clubs. You get the picture. But when we wanted the high-end version, we were invited to set a goal and save our allowance, do odd jobs, and eventually pay half of the new ten-speed or set of Ping golf clubs. We decided to do the same arrangement, except they could pay half *or* "read off" their half. The reading deal looked like this: I would develop the book list, and we could negotiate some of it. Then they could begin the reading project.

My two sons are now fifteen and twelve. Since the time they were seven, they have read for nice mountain bikes, extreme sports gear, golf clubs, and other big-ticket items. Part of their reading included leadership volumes. When John Maxwell found this out, he took time at his conferences to meet them and sign their books. They've read classics, creativity pieces, mysteries...you name it. So you can see that I believe the reading issue is insurmountable—a leader must be a reader.

Beyond Reading

But there are other input channels. Remember, information is simply the first step in the morphing process. There are a variety of ways to get the information in. Audio books are a great way to assist you if reading isn't your strong suit. Seminars are offered on almost everything under the sun. Personal mentoring relationships with someone ahead of you in an area are also another avenue. These mentors could be local or long distance. With the Internet, long-distance mentoring is no longer long distance.

Obviously you must come to grips with your learning style. Are you aural? Get tapes. Visual? Get books and articles. Need more interaction? Find a mentor. So as we talk of learning, we aren't saying reading is the only method, though it's the dominant one.

Also, don't let the most ubiquitous resource go unnoticed—the Internet. Free e-mails can keep you abreast of books coming out, trends going on, ministry ideas—and the beat goes on. All this illustrates that there are also easy, low- to no-cost ways to learn.

L³ #1: Identify Survival Learning Areas

Every ministry context has certain things you simply must know and continue to grow in. Given your situation, what are those things? A couple of hints will be helpful here. The intersection of your personal mission, definition of leadership, and local ministry context bring about those "survival learning areas." Presenting Christ at Westwinds in credible and creative ways is written in our vision statement.

So for me, apologetics, philosophy, and creativity input are important. Other things come to mind for preaching, such as family issues, preaching and speaking technique, and relationship issues.

L³ #2: Learn Outside Your Frame

Most people are very focused in their knowledge base. By learning outside your frame, I mean learning about things outside of direct ministry knowledge or your area of expertise. Talk to people, and begin quizzing them on anything outside their direct vocational area. You'll find few people who have broad knowledge. Most of us just couldn't survive long on *Jeopardy*.

Now there are a couple of reasons for this principle. Learning outside your frame makes you a much more interesting person, speaker, and leader. A more important reason is that you begin making connections you would have never seen before. In other words, it's the most powerful catalyst to creativity. In the "ideagrapher" chapter, we'll talk about this at length.

Recent reading outside my frame is in the abstract art approach and technique of Mark Rothko (with whom I am obsessed), Frank Gehry and Peter Forbes' volumes on architecture, *A Theory of Everything* by Ken Wilber[5], color theory, chaos and complexity theory, brain science, biotech, robotics and cloning. In some ways these have absolutely nothing to do with ministry, and in some ways every one of these is integral to ministry. The more you read outside your frame, the more cohesive is knowledge as a whole, and the more relevant and transparent are the connections. How do you start on this? Pick up a volume in an area in which you are interested that isn't ministry-related, and begin. You'll be surprised.

L³ #3 Ask Every Leader You Respect for the Best Web Sites and Periodicals They Read

This is a no-brainer, and yet I am surprised how many people don't do it. One of the first questions I ask any leader is "What are your best reads these days, or what magazines or Web sites do you tap?" There are obvious things every leader should be checking on. How can you not take the free e-newsletters of George Barna on trends, or the Gallup organization's "Tuesday Morning Briefing"? These are free, gang. Every leader who asks for some picks, I tell about Wired magazine and Fast Company. In 1996, right after Fast Company was released, I was in a discussion with Carol Childress of Leadership Network and she turned me on to both.[6]

L³ #4: Make Lifelong Learning a Church Value

There's simply no substitute for the whole church owning the value that learning has to be a priority. To not learn and grow is totally incompatible with a Christian world and life view. Granted, I started in a church plant, so I had a tremendous amount of influence in sculpting the values of Westwinds. From the very beginning, we simply made it clear that continuing education seminars and subscriptions to periodicals would have to be line items in the budget.

Create in your ministry a craving for brokered resources. Give people the values added of having recommended ideal resources for message series follow-up. Print in the bulletin or in pre-service projected art ideas for "next reads." This creates a certain kind of environment in which people come to expect "this is a place that gives me the next steps in my development." I realize I have a high value on this because "full life development in Christ" is our mission. But I'm simply naïve enough to ask why everyone doesn't also have this as a high value. At the end of every series of weekend talks, we suggest three or four volumes we think will reinforce the last several weeks of messages. People have come to expect it.

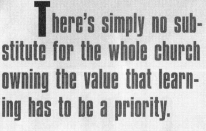

There's simply no substitute for the whole church owning the value that learning has to be a priority.

Given the above pointers, here are the top areas in which I learn and some of the rationale as to why. In the next chapter, we'll talk about how to make this learning a calendar priority.

Area #1: Biblical Studies

Much rationale here is unnecessary. The message we speak is a biblical one. We simply cannot rest on our laurels and act as if we've learned all there is to learn. Under this area, I read widely in hermeneutics and literary theory. Why? Did you know postmodernism is simply the name we use for a movement that started largely in literary theory? Post-structuralism and some of the French postmodernists are responsible for questioning the idea that there is inherent meaning in a text. For us to be ignorant of this discussion when our message comes in the form of a text is dangerous. Cultural awareness of what could be a significant assault on our message and potential dent to Christianity is not optional but our obligation. Here's where philosophy, culture, and biblical hermeneutics converge.

Area #2: Cultural Contours[7]

Since ministry is about the intersection of biblical context with cultural context, no ministry leader can afford to be culturally uninformed. Of course, many are. What are the demographic, psychographic, and generational trends? What are the current religious interests, and what's so captivating about them? What do people say they want and need, and why? You have to be aware of these things to be able to make relevant application. We can give biblical answers all day, but if they aren't to questions being asked, then we've been unfaithful in proclaiming the gospel. What about the whole area of biotech, nanotech, and robotics? These three areas will provide more ethical dilemmas for the church than anything in the past.

Area #3: Learning Styles and Multiple Intelligence

The work of men like Howard Gardner and Daniel Goleman is important to ministry effectiveness. How do you best communicate to culture where there are several dominant learning styles and eight diverse areas in which people have strong aptitudes for what they best assimilate?[8] I believe learning in these areas will change the way we do church services. Our post-enlightenment, talking-head model of doing church assumes that everyone learns through linear, deductive streams of information. This is a faulty assumption. I think at least minimal learning in this area is mandatory for every point leader.

For the record, it helps if you are a parent. Our IQ tests and college entrance exams only test two or three of the eight intelligences. This explains why many very successful people in life never went to school. Helping us identify our kids' dominant intelligences and how to foster and encourage those is very important. We need to help our children build on their islands of health and strength; it's the way God made them.

Area #4: Theological Trends and Apologetics

This is simply a must. This is very different from biblical studies and looks at currents out there impacting the trajectory of the biblical message. Right now debates are raging in our most conservative theological societies about inclusivism, particularism, whether or not God knows the future, free acts of human beings, whether evangelicalism is a bounded or centered set, and a host of other things that have immeasurable impact on Christianity. Many of us aren't even aware of the discussions, but they will eventually affect the average Christian.

Take for instance, the founding of the *Jesus Seminar* nearly twenty years ago. Who would have thought a few scholars meeting to discuss the authenticity of the gospels and sayings of Jesus would eventually have a publishing empire and entire prime time specials devoted to popularizing their findings? This is just the beginning of the kinds of issues we have to be conversant in. The cultural arena of ideas and theological trends are often found in the same pot these days. We remain ignorant to the peril of our people who will eventually be touched by these ideas.

Significant discussions rage in the theological world around pluralism, inclusivism, and the role of world religions. Debates over foundationalism and competing views of truth are hot topics in even conservative circles right now. The reality is that few pastors remain tuned to these frequencies. The day-to-day grind and regularity with which Sunday morning rolls around makes staying up-to-date very challenging. And yet these are the hot topics that threaten to encroach upon the very message we are trying to communicate.

The day-to-day grind and regularity with which Sunday morning rolls around makes staying up-to-date very challenging.

Area #5: The Self-Help Section

What is America buying in the single biggest revenue area in the bookstore? Every leader should spend one day a month in Borders or Barnes & Noble. Reading here tells you what America is reading and the questions they're asking. A few years ago, it was time and life management (which has seen a recent resurgence of interest). Then it was family and relationships. Men are from Jupiter and women from Neptune books were the rage (astronomy is not one of the areas I read in). Now spirituality is the spin. Everybody has some spiritual take on what will make life easier, better, or more prosperous. You have to read here or at least visit the bookstore and bullet-hole some books.

Bullet-holing a book raises a very important issue. Do you know how to get a thirty-minute overview on a book? do a one-hour read of any volume? scan a book for critical argument in two hours? These are skills you can survive without but not unless you have time to burn. Speed-reading classes are not expensive and pay for themselves in a couple of months.[9]

Area #6: Leadership

I'm sure you would expect and assume that this is one of the areas I would suggest. A lot is written on the area, but not a lot that's fresh. This is where talking to the leaders in your life who view reading as an extreme sport pays rich dividends. The leadership area includes related items such as team development, planning, motivation, and vision. Are you aware of the top ten must-read leadership volumes? What are the best resources for developing leaders? What about leadership spiritual formation? When answered, these questions create resource brokers to assist those we serve.

Area #7: Ministry Models and Paradigms

There are always new contributions on how to do ministry more effectively. New books come out annually that help us think better about small group ministry, spiritual-gift discovery and deployment, church systems, planning, vision development, worship service design, and just about every other major ministry area you can name. We are becoming increasingly familiar with the emerging churches in the country as they contribute their piece to the ongoing dialogue. These are helpful resources because at least in one place they've proven useful and effective. While we cannot expect to clone anyone's program, we can expect him or her to shed fresh light on some potential spots where we may be stuck.

Remember, your master areas do not need to be the same as mine. Of course, I have rationale as to why these are crucial for my context and me, but you needn't share my convictions. What you do need is some master areas of your own to go after, areas in which you can consistently grow and that will act as sources for your ministry. I'm certain a good deal of ministry could radically improve if point leaders simply became lifelong learners and developed the value in their teams.

Inner learning, emotional growing up, inside maturity—this is where it all begins. When that's coupled with a clear desire to expand horizons, improve the health of the church, adopt new skills, and understand better and more effective ways of doing ministry, the church can move toward health and have an even clearer message in our changing culture.

InnerAction

1. What repeated snags indicate an invitation to morph in your personal life, leadership life with your team, or the larger sphere of the church?

2. What are the dominant ways you best learn? What is your plan to have steady amounts of learning flow through that channel?

3. Have you identified the five or six areas in which you must constantly be growing and learning? What is your plan to stay on top of the best resources coming out? With whom can you network and pick his or her brain to uncover the best resources?

4. Is your lifelong learning plan balanced? What about marriage and family? time management? emotional health and balance? theological issues?

Endnotes

1. Parker Palmer, "Leadership and the Inner Journey," Interview with L. J. Rittenhouse, Leader to Leader (Number 22, Fall 2001), 27.

2. Daniel Goleman, *Emotional Intelligence* (New York, NY: Bantam Books, 1995), 8.

3. Goleman, *Emotional Intelligence*, introduction xiii.

4. Goleman, *Emotional Intelligence*, 47.

5. Ken Wilber will be an increasingly important figure in the 21C. Though clearly not a Christian, his effort to construct an exceedingly complex and yet plausible theory of how all of life fits together is an increasing craving in our culture. People are looking for cohesion; Wilber is trying to provide it. Ken Wilber, *A Theory of Everything: An Integral Vision for Business, Politics, Science, and Spirituality* (Boston, MA: Shambhala Publications, Inc., 2000).

6. If there is anyone on the planet that fits the title "resource broker," it is Carol Childress. She must have a photographic memory and more extra assimilative skills than anyone else.

7. *Carpe Mañana* is a good example. Leonard I. Sweet, *Carpe Mañana* (Grand Rapids, MI: Zondervan, 2001).

8. Cynthia Tobias' *The Way They Learn* is the best little volume that gets at the learning style issue in an easy and concise way. Cynthia Ulrich Tobias, *The Way They Learn* (Colorado Springs, CO: Focus on the Family Publication, 1998).

9. Every leader should have to read Mortimer Adler's *How to Read a Book.* I had to read this as a college freshman, and it literally changed my life. Mortimer Jerome Adler, *How to Read a Book* (New York, NY: Simon & Schuster, 1972).

LifeWare Design: Mapping a Sustainable Healthy Life

Computers take software to make them work. Software provides the means by which we, the humans, tell the hardware box called a computer what to do. Without software, we wouldn't have a way to communicate with all the different parts of the computer system. The software that really makes the computer experience seamless is the operating system (in the computer world, this is called the OS). Whether you are a Windows PC user or a Mac user, the operating system is what allows users to get all the programs to operate. The programs can operate one at a time, or you can have several open simultaneously and do multi-tasking. Without the OS, we would have no idea how to navigate around the hundreds of thousands of files resident on a computer.

We need a kind of OS for our lives; a software that would enable us to look at all of life's programs, organize them, and even juggle them simultaneously. We might call a software for our lives LifeWare. LifeWare would help us see, communicate, interact, goal set, and navigate all the parts of our lives with a better sense of the big picture. LifeWare would help us fight getting lost in all the detailed "files of our life" and instead keep the main things clear and the most important things central. Unless we have amazing gifts, without some LifeWare in place, we'll end up caught in a software snarl where our lives look like a jumbled mess of activity with no real purposeful orientation. We can't afford this in life or in our leadership. If you can figure out how to manage the wide-angle lens of life in general, then doing the zoom lens leadership portion is a lot easier.

We were on a family vacation in Colorado. Valerie's two siblings, their spouses, and kids were also there. We decided we would go on a mountain hike...kids and all. The goal was to head up the mountain to a particular lake, circle it, and then come back. That should have been my first indication that I may be in trouble: We had a goal. Well, we didn't actually have a stated goal. I heard the "circle the lake" plan, and in my type-A, driven, goal-oriented, and generally impatient disposition, I heard "Goal." Goals for me are always capital G. So picture this.

Seven kids from five to twelve years old on a hike, and we have a goal. I'm totally oblivious to the tension I'm about to experience. Call me stupid, blind, dumb, or simply totally out of touch, but when we decided we were going to reach the lake, I was on a mission. As I slowly experienced a smoldering frustration with our pace, I'm thinking two competing things, neither of them even remotely near where a balanced and healthy parent should be thinking. Thought #1: If we wanted to really hike, why didn't we leave the kids with Grandma and Grandpa? Thought #2: I am a leader. What can I do to move the troops along a little quicker? At the very least I can get near the front of this slow-moving mass and move people along. So that's what I do.

We're literally sauntering our way up this trail and calling it a hike. Then wisdom speaks and Valerie sends this question up the trail my way (of course she was behind me; leaders lead, don't they?), "Ron, the goal, what is the goal?" I felt that same disorientation that came over me in college when I saw the blue book exam question in humanities. "Do I know the answer to this? Is it a trick question? Am I missing something? Were we told to study this?" My less than lightening quick response was "We are trying to get to the lake, aren't we?" Then I uttered one of those "Uh, duh, I think it's pretty clear where we're heading, isn't it?" (in a singsong voice attitude). No blinding insight has dawned on me yet.

So Valerie throws one more decisive volley my way. "We're here as a family. Get off your focused pursuit, and enjoy life a little." Being incredibly perceptive, insight dawns. A life without LifeWare is what my life looked like right then. I had displayed the inability to balance the big picture. I was desirous to get to the lake but forgot the real point: to enjoy life, kids, foliage, sounds, and colors.

When we're so focused on one thing, it's easy to lose sight of the bigger picture.

When we're so focused on one thing, it's easy to lose sight of the bigger picture. Life is a lot like those photo mosaics you see in poster shops. A ton of little miniature photos are configured in such a way that they all combine to form a much larger image of something else. When you look up close at the individual miniatures, you can't possibly see the larger image created by the montage. Time with my kids and family was the larger image. I was going to miss the whole point of the hike if I wasn't careful. This little event also highlighted another issue of balance in my life. How quickly can I unplug from performance mode and just enjoy life? Not everything in life is about reaching the summit, or in my case, the lake.

I Need Rhythm

How could this experience have been different? What if I had been a bit more attentive to separating where goals and accomplishments were important and where simply "being" and enjoying was the primary point? Part of my challenge, and part of what my LifeWare helps me with (or is supposed to), is keeping the main things the main things.

Designing LifeWare is an effort to create a very simple way to navigate all the components of our lives. This is nuts and bolts...nothing fancy but abundantly useful. If we could just get clarity on who we are, who we are called to become, what we're called to do, and how to make it happen, we'd be further down the road than the average bear.

A careful reading of the Gospels yields a Jesus with rhythm, a healthy rhythm of "with-ness" and "away-ness." If anyone had a busy life, it was Jesus. Yet you never get that impression from the Gospel writers. On a number of occasions, Jesus walks right past the crowds and all their demands to fulfill what his LifeWare told him was appropriate and healthy. Frequently, he was found going to the mountain or the desert or a solitary place. Jesus had rhythm, and it kept him sane and healthy. I guess this is the rhythm I need to shoot for, because according to my friends, if I am looking for it on a dance floor, my search will be in vain.

If you're saying, "I really need this, but I simply don't have the time to ever implement this type of thing," you need to hear Solomon's words in Ecclesiastes. "If the ax is dull and its edge unsharpened, more strength is needed but skill will bring success" (Ecclesiastes 10:10).

A couple things bear pointing out. In Hebrew the word for *wisdom* literally means "skill" or "skillful living." Solomon says skill in living brings success, and to continue beating a tree with a blunt axe is not skillful or smart. A brief break to sharpen the axe will more than make up for the time it takes at the sharpening stone. Let me finish my mini-sermon with the parting shot of a college professor who uttered these words every time he wanted us to catch what was just said: "A word to the wise is sufficient."

Attitudinal Chiropractic

Let's head into this whole thing with the right attitude. My experience indicates that being caught up in thinking about events is even more germane to my feelings than the actual events themselves. Take for instance a potentially volatile meeting with a ministry leader or staff mate. My pre-meeting thoughts and ruminations are usually far more challenging than the actual meeting itself. There is a tendency to spin out worst-case scenarios, and before you know it, you are having a Maalox moment. Ministry is challenging. When things are on the smooth download, we think life may never get better. When we feel the snags of day-to-day headaches that grow into monumental fiascoes, we consider help-wanted signs at Kmart. That's simply the nature of the ministry beast. Feelings of being overwhelmed; of not having enough hours in the day; or of being caught in the chaos and confusion of "people issues," weekly preparation, personal life maintenance, and leadership complexities can leave our navigational equipment locked up. It's no wonder pastoral sidelining is high.

Let's be clear on one thing. Our attitude to the whole area of time is critical. We're trying to calendar our commitment to personal morphing. If who we are leaks and is the most important factor in church ethos, then our time investment in personal health is important.

32 Hours a Day, 8 Days a Week

What do we want our LifeWare to accomplish for us? Are we seeking a balanced life? What is balance, and is it our goal? Do we seek a life in which all the individual parts get airtime so we end up feeling guilt-free, knowing we've at least hit the high points? To many, that sounds so much better than the current situation. On the other hand, are we seeking a focused missional life in which we are becoming and accomplishing our God-design? Do balance and missional living converge, diverge, collide, or divide?

For those whose rackets are strung a little bit tighter than the rest, I know this is a burning question. Where do goals fit? And where do we factor in Palm Pilots; pagers; and five-pound, two-inch thick leather planners? Are we going to be list-focused and do the planner and time management thing, set goals, and reach them? Or are we going to be a "go with the flow" type, hoping the river goes through exciting jungles of relationships and spontaneity that can't be scheduled or managed? Are these options mutually exclusive or complementary? Is it possible to do it all, or will we have to resign ourselves to compromise somewhere along the way? With reflection, we quickly realize these questions hardly begin to frame the myriad of options before us.

Let's first acknowledge the obvious and get past our complaining. Everyone has the same amount of time. We have access to all the time available every single minute of every single day. The way we talk, however, you'd think most of us feel that we've been shorted on our daily

I'm like most people. I think the world would be a lot easier place if days were thirty-two hours long with an eight-day workweek.

ration. I'm like most people. I think the world would be a lot easier place if days were thirty-two hours long with an eight-day workweek. The reality, of course, is that the amount of time is not our problem. It's our conception of time, our relationship to time, and our approach to time.

Scripture enjoins us to number our days (Psalm 90:12; Ephesians 5:15). For instance, the Psalms passage provides us with some philosophical grist I don't think we reflect on very often. The psalmist is writing about our appointed time on this planet being seventy or eighty years. The writer says they are troublesome years for "they quickly pass, and we fly away" (Psalm 90:10b). Here's a tremendous insight we need to reflect on more, and it's in keeping with our mission statement exercises. Do we live our lives and spend our time as if death is right at our door? This isn't morbidity run wild; this is wisdom asking for a hearing.

On the heels of this statement, Psalm 90 is where we're encouraged to "number our days." We talked a bit about this earlier, but is it possible that by internalizing the fragility and transience of life and the immediacy and surprise of death, we might finally stop wasting time and act on "becoming" and "accomplishing" God's best for us? This may be one of the insights that prove more valuable than anything else said in this chapter. Do we need to reflect on death more and ask God to teach us to number our days?

Countdown

During a time-management series (a misnomer that should be struck from our vocabularies because time simply can't be managed) a few years ago, I realized after preparing a message dealing with this section of Psalm 90 that I was more interested in the teaching device of "numbering our days" in light of impending death than I was in actually practicing it myself. I confess that this little jolt has done my heart and life some good, and I have now woven into my quarterly routine a reflection around numbering my days.

Some of the ancients in our Christian heritage maintained the practice of death reflection by keeping real human skulls on their desks. A daily routine called for holding the skull and reflecting on this day being potentially the last and what that might mean for the day's activities. What is most important? Would God be pleased with the agenda? Were there any issues needing to be addressed in life? Were relationships whole and without regret? What a powerful tool!

I need to spend more reflection on time usage. It's the only resource at my disposal that cannot be recaptured or renewed after it's used. The reality is we deprive ourselves of a good deal of the time at our disposal through simple lack of attention or laziness. So much of what we do is on autopilot. In an airplane it may be called progress, but in the game of life it's called being a zombie. The goal isn't so much a mastery of time—it marches on untouched, unmastered, and unmarshalled by the vast majority of people. The goal is mastery of self to be employed for God's purposes in the time he has allotted. I am struck by what was said of David: When he had accomplished God's purposes for his generation, he died (Acts 13:36).

Binoculars and Microscopes

The mere fact that the biblical material never discusses balance may be an indicator that it is a wrongheaded entry into this challenge. Have you ever thought about that? Even the concept of the word *balance* doesn't seem to be anywhere on the pages of Scripture. Paul addresses the time issue to the church at Ephesus as "opportunity" (Ephesians 5:15-16). The word has interesting overtones. The word for opportunity in the original language of the New Testament has within it the idea of an appointed moment or divinely orchestrated time window. Paul encourages us to make the most of every opportunity because the days are evil. In light of the evil days, we are to live wisely, skillfully, and intentionally.

The question giving me pause is this: To what does the word *opportunity* refer? What is this divine window or appointment moment? For me this is a way through some of the time management impasse. Opportunity is "lens specific." Depending on the lenses through which you view your sense of destiny, mission, giftedness, philosophy of ministry, and life phase, opportunity looks and means something very different.

To say it concisely, opportunity is defined by your personal sense of destiny and mission. What is missional to me as a transformational architect may not be missional to you. What is core to being focused at fifty-six years of age with your children married and gone may be very different from what it looks like as a church planter at twenty-two and newly married or a single parent with three teenagers.

Our concept of time and opportunity ought to liberate us.

Our concept of time and opportunity ought to liberate us. I think moving toward a focused life seems so much more understandable and malleable than the simple linear goal-setting models that prevailed in the '90s. Life is curvilinear, not rectilinear—more about loops than lines. So is leadership. Learning to be focused seems to be critical to making the most of every opportunity and numbering our days.

Now lest balance get an entirely bum rap, let me say I do think there's a place for it. But I think it needs a slight redefining. We ought to constantly balance the ability to enjoy the moment while we're en route to accomplishing missional things. Living in the present while moving into the future is important. To live only in the future is to miss living life. You can't simply walk around peering into tomorrow with binoculars. To live only in the present is to enjoy the detail of the microscope but never choosing which slide to put under the scope. We want the magnified detail, beauty, and wonder of the microscope with the panoramic view of binoculars looking out over the upcoming terrain. Here's balance at its best.

I confess this is my trouble. I usually have the binoculars out but rarely pull out the microscope and gaze on the intricacies and nuances around me. Hence my goal to reach the lake, not gaze at foliage. When was the last time you really looked at the different shades of green in your grass or browns in your desert? When was the last time you really tasted food? I know food is fuel, but God didn't give us an intravenous bag of nutrients to pump into our systems each day. He gave us mouths with taste buds and foods with infinite flavor combinations. What does the seasonal air outside smell like these days?

So how do we make all this work in the life of a leader? How do we keep the binoculars in use and help our teams and families see the hoped-for outcome? At the same time, how do we enjoy the journey, community, and process of it all? Here are the nuts and bolts that have worked for me. You'll need to modify and tweak this to make it work for you. We want something that's simple and usable but sufficiently nuanced to account for seeing life as it really is. We want something that will move and morph as we go through various stages of maturity...both spiritually and chronologically.

Focus Through Three Lenses

I had to come to a place of asking how I will organize the entangled web of all the areas of my life as a husband/dad, a church leader, an individual. How can I see my life at a glance, keep the main things in focus, but also have a way to move into the future with some sort of direction? How can I balance the need to personally develop with the need to professionally accomplish? These are the types of questions informing my drive to design LifeWare.

The three categories I listed above were a great starting place for me. In fact, those lenses of self, vocation, and family are nearly universal in how we conceive ourselves. No matter our gender, age, station in life, or relationship with God, we tend to define our lives and existence through these three. I took a large piece of paper with my mind-mapping markers and started into my LifeWare design process.[1]

I drew three large circles and labeled them familial, vocational, and personal. The next step is where to customize and get creative. How do you define yourself in each of these three areas, and what do you need to keep track of? You can use no more than three or four labels to define yourself in each of the three lenses. Now, of course, this isn't a law tucked away in the annals of heaven that you can get prosecuted for. But there is a reason for minimizing your labels. We're going to eventually tie these into your mission statement, and the fewer you have to navigate, the easier it is to monitor and link them to values to see how they fit into your overall reason for being.

Identify your three or four words or phrases that describe the way you define your life in each of the three lenses *and* simultaneously define an area you need to monitor, then write them in their corresponding circle. In my vocational lens, I have written, "Strategic Designer," "Growth Catalyst," and "Team Architect." In my familial lens, I wrote, "Organic Gardener" (emotional health, love and nurture for my wife and kids), "Life Developer" (spiritual, intellectual, and life skills), and "Fun Injector" (sports, dance, stunt kites, chess and so on). In my personal lens, I have written, "da Vinci" (this is my creative outlet and areas of interest that energize me: digital art, painting, gourmet cooking, and so on), "Reflector" (double-entendre with spiritual and emotional growth focus), "L³" (lifelong learner), "Embodiment" (health, fitness, golf, biking, and so on). Note that these don't all have to be verbs or nouns or phrases. For those more anal in our midst, maybe consistency is necessary; again, no rules just clues.

What are these labels helping you monitor? Our effort is to move toward greater health and effectiveness in each of these three areas of our lives. We want to be healthier as individuals, as vocational participants, and as family members. What is health? Health has five different components: emotional, physical, relational, intellectual, and spiritual. Not all five equally apply to each of the three life lenses, but overall health requires movement in all five.

For the personal lens, you may opt for no descriptors, but as you can see from mine, I have four. You may decide that "fitness freak," "spiritual dynamo," and "Monet-in-waiting" best get at the three big areas of self-understanding. Be creative, inspiring, and descriptive with these labels. Leonardo da Vinci was one of my labels because he was one of the most incredibly diverse people in all of history. He is considered by some to be the greatest genius ever. His diversity among hard and soft science, his artistic sense, and his ability to be whole-brained are really inspiring to me. I have copies of his personal sketches and journals on my desk. The labels we pick may best be compared to color filters on these lenses. While we all have the lenses, the coloration is unique and specially mixed by each one of us.

Maybe Monet is not your artist of choice, but if art is one of your hobbies and one of the main things you need to cultivate to keep the self healthy, then come up with some creative label for your art interest. In the personal lens, we would include everything from our relationship with God to our physical fitness to hobbies to intellectual stimulation to creative outlets and so on.

Cleaning My Lenses

The vocational lens is the one we will puzzle over most as leaders. How do we define our life as leaders, and how do the color filters of our sub-areas relate to our sense of mission? As the point leader of Westwinds, I have very definite ways of understanding what I've been charged to do by God and our church board. Hopefully, those are one and the same. The primary shaper of my understanding of both of those is my personal mission, my unique sense of destiny. My personal metaphor of transformational architect has three distinct responsibilities or manifestations at Westwinds and a couple outside Westwinds.

All of them are in the vocational lens, but all are more defined by my sense of mission than where I get my paycheck. At Westwinds I'm a Strategic Designer, Growth Catalyst, and Team Developer. Every single thing I do at Westwinds fits within one of those three areas. Those three lens colors comprise a good chunk of my vocational lens, but not the whole picture. My writing, outside speaking, and international mission training of other pastors are all part of my transformational architect mission. They define who I am and are just as missional to what God has called me to do as my primary locus of activity, Westwinds.

Don't get discouraged with the process. Seeing through the three lenses and forcing yourself to be concise is a real clarity exercise. For me this exercise took several months of massaging labels, reflecting on my mission, and gaining an understanding of who I really was. While the lenses through which you view life never change, the color filters you use may. A change in ministry role would obviously change the vocational lens significantly. Age of children and family activities obviously change over time. Let this process work in you. Part of the experience is the morphing that comes from simply thinking long and hard about it.

Seeing through the three lenses and forcing yourself to be concise is a real clarity exercise.

Seeing Through (Rose) Colored Glasses

Once you've done this for all three lenses, you'll have nine to twelve total titles or descriptors. These color filters on your lenses are the short, creative phrases of how you see yourself. If you've been creative, they are probably motivating, bring a smile to your face, and have embedded in them all sorts of pregnant meaning and aspirations. Now the fun begins. Your LifeWare is starting to take shape. These various labels are the programs you have operating in your life, most of them operating simultaneously. We are getting an operating system in place that will allow us to see on the "computer desktop" of our lives the various programs we must keep track of. These labels are filters through which we view our familial, vocational, and personal lives.

Obtain a journal of some sort for the following exercises. You may opt for a typical planner and just have a section where you record this material. You may be using your computer so it synchs with a Palm or pocket PC. You may opt for an old world leather journal with handmade watercolor paper (my personal choice because I paint in my journal). In years to come, you'll look back at the exercises you're about to do and see what God has done. I remember doing this for the first time in 1990, and God has eclipsed those wild dreams. He has brought to pass in my life and ministry context Paul's prayer in Ephesians 3: God wants to exceed our expectations abundantly.

The phrases in my mission statement that I haven't shared so far are the whole purpose I have in being a transformational architect: "to coach people toward irresistible life change and influential life work." Or to say it slightly differently: I want to help people become and accomplish.

So here's your exercise for each of your lens filters. For each of your nine to twelve labels, list in two separate columns concrete traits you want to see woven into your life ("being" goals) and concrete accomplishments ("doing" goals) you want to pursue. Now before you balk, a couple qualifiers are necessary.

This exercise is only effective if you've developed your mission statement. If you are still in the place of really landing one, your vocational lens will be muddy. You'd be smarter to leave that lens alone until the mission statement has been brought in for a landing. Second, these being and doing goals need to flow in line with your sense of God's will. Remember, we are trying to create a LifeWare plan that will get us to focus on the most important stuff in our lives.

Let's say under the familial lens, you simply have the word *father*. Maybe one of your "being" goals is to become more patient. You recognize that this is one of the next things God wants you to work on. I think you can be quite assured that God will put you into situations in which patience will be tested and stretched. Why? Because one of God's desires is to see us grow in the fruit of the Spirit, and patience is one of those. You are smack dab in the middle of his will. If you need practice developing spiritual conversations with people far from God, you can be assured God will assist you in this pursuit.

When this exercise is completed, it paints the short- and long-term picture of the life and legacy you wish to leave behind on this earth. Will all of these things come to pass? Probably not, but maybe all of them will and then some. The point is get-**Who is God calling you to become, and what is he calling you to accomplish?** ting directed in our living. The entire process of prayer, reflection writing, massaging, and revising may take a couple days on a retreat or a couple weeks, depending on how much focused time it gets. The goal is not to come up with every character trait you can possibly identify and every possible accomplishment a leader like you could pull off. The issue is much deeper. Who is God calling you to become, and what is he calling you to accomplish? You will emerge with a picture here of where God's morphing will take you.

Divine and Human Intersection

Before continuing any further, I need to unravel my sense of how we interact with God to reach these aspirations. Some will be cautioning me under their breath, saying, "This sure sounds like we think we're in control, and we're the ones who bring this about." I hope I haven't communicated that. But I do think we need to note the synergistic view of "life work" Scripture paints for us. Isaiah 26:12 is an interesting commentary: "Lord, you establish peace for us; all that we have accomplished you have done for us." Are we doing it, or is God? Both are correct; we are doing it, and God is doing it.

Not far from the same idea is Solomon's comment in Proverbs 16:3: "Commit to the Lord whatever you do, and your plans will succeed." This is followed up a couple verses later in Proverbs 16:9: "In his heart a man plans his course, but the Lord determines his steps." The synergism, designing together, and bringing about in concert seems to me unmistakable. Our lens work is our part.

To wrestle with these questions and then to write them down is a tremendously self-disclosing process. I think many people struggle with this process because it genuinely brings to the surface what we really believe about why we're here. It shows us in black and white what our truest aspirations for God really are. Part of the morphing process is learning to get in touch with those deepest assumptions about who we think we are and who we think God wants us to be.

On the lists in front of you will be sacred thoughts, treasured learning, vulnerable ramblings and discoveries; they are for your eyes only. If you really do feel passionate about them, though, if God has really directed your steps on this endeavor, then they are worthy of being pursued and worked on.

So the next phase of the exercise is how you'll attempt to reach these being and doing aspirations. Will you need a support group, a book, some continuing education, or an online mentor? The aspiration without the avenue is wasted effort. Jot down the approach to pursue with each item. There should be three circles with three to four labels in each. Under each circle there should be a list of being and doing goals for each label. Some of these will be long-term, never actually accomplished character aspirations. Other will be time frame goals, such as publishing an article in 2004, that you will cross off the list and replace with something new. Once these labels or color filters and being and doing goals have solidified, it is time to start each label on a fresh page of paper so you can not only list the doing and being goals for each label, but also note any avenues you need to pursue to see that goal come about. These goals won't simply happen because we wrote them down; scheduled time and intermediate steps may be necessary.

From Color Lens to Concrete Attention

Obviously, many things on the list are items you'll work on in the course of life. Simply putting them on a list you're going to review periodically is a powerful reminder of what needs front and center attention. For instance, if patience is really a written goal, then you're probably not going to schedule a time on the calendar to work on patience. You'll have opportunities in the course of the daily grind to work on it. You may, however, need to schedule some time to get clarity on a chronic pattern of impatience with someone you work with or with one of

morph

your children. A chronic pattern is a good indication that some things going on need some reflection.

Other things on our list will definitely need scheduled time on our weekly calendar. Before our week gets going and out of control, we should sit down and schedule time to work on these items. If I realize I need to understand more about growing church ministry and all the systems that are necessary to expand as I go through certain growth markers, then unless I schedule some time for learning of some sort, this knowledge will never come. Identifying needs for learning is a great first step, but the learning doesn't come by osmosis.

> **Identifying needs for learning is a great first step, but the learning doesn't come by osmosis.**

I remember hitting certain plateaus in our church and not knowing what was going on until I stopped and looked at my colored lenses. As a Strategic Designer, it was my role to understand the dynamics of a growing church organism. At times that meant stopping to get retooled to understand that different leadership abilities are necessary at a 400-person church than at a 250-person church or a 75-person church. There are different leadership issues I need to be aware of to mentor a team of three versus a team of thirteen or thirty-three.

These are the things we need to calendar in as appointments or multiple appointments. The alternative is that our learning ends up being moves in crisis management to fix areas that have degenerated into problems. If we intentionally have a learning plan, we won't lose momentum and run into a headache.

Pull or Push

A principle of change related to the future is that we'll always have to change sometime tomorrow. We'll either change due to the pull of a more brightly visioned tomorrow, or we'll be pushed out of the present due to the pain of obsolescence and exhausted skills. The pull of the future is more fun than the push of pain, but it does take some preparedness.

The basic LifeWare is now in place, and you are starting to find your way around it. You can easily monitor what areas get "worked on" naturally and what ones seem to get neglected most often. There are still a couple other things necessary to complete our LifeWare package. We need to have a built-in review process. We not only need to review our actual LifeWare; we also need to review the being and doing goals in our LifeWare. A good deal of why this is so helpful has to do with reviewing the things we have written down. We need to establish a good rhythm for moving ahead in our growth.

Creating Rhythm

Rhythm captures the need we have for a periodic check on our three lenses and the color filters we view them through. In addition to weekly glancing at our journal as we "appointment" our week, we also need periodic time to reassess our journal entries and dig into some of the lifelong learning goals we have set from the last chapter. A couple of things are valuable to work into your annual calendar.

Take half a day on a quarterly basis and simply read for a few hours to evaluate your journaled goals and lens labels. In a space of four hours, you can easily get a handle on the updating you need to do and goals that are accomplished and can be replaced with other things, as well as do some reflecting on next steps. Couple that with a bit of reading and prayer, and you have a mini-retreat. No phones, beepers, pagers, or media input allowed.

Twice a year take a day or even an overnight to recalibrate. You are doing a similar thing as when you did your quarterly review; this is just more in-depth. A good deal of the time should be spent sourcing the next big steps ahead or a major growth area needing attention. If I do an overnight, and I try to at least one of them a year, I always try to read one leadership or spiritual formation volume and one other book, depending on my current needs at the time. Some of the time should be spent reflecting on thorny issues that have arisen in the last six months.

The discipline of scheduling quarterly and semiannual downtime is critical. There are always a dozen good reasons we can't afford the time to do it. The real question is can you really afford missing it? You will come to see such great ideas and creativity emerge from these downtimes that you will quickly see their benefit and uncompromisingly schedule them.

The method and model presented here are simply one way of doing it. There's nothing sacred about it, and it isn't necessarily the best way. The massaging process, fiddling with lens labels, and really wrestling with your being and doing goals is a tough and, at times, a long process. The payout, however, is hard to calculate. Don't wait around to get to it; you never will. Morphing is made of this stuff. Your working some model and giving permission to others to do the same will dramatically leak into the ethos of the church and will create an environment in which missional accomplishment and the learning necessary to make it happen are high priorities.

InnerAction

1. What is the state of your current LifeWare? What specific things do you build into your schedule to keep all the balls in the air? Periodically, software designers submit upgrades to consumers to keep the software up to speed and to

debug any problems in earlier versions. Are there any needs for an upgrade or to fix some bugs in the current version of your LifeWare?

2. Walk through the exercises of identifying your lenses and creating your categories and labels.

3. What would you say is your dominant disposition toward change? Are you pushed from the present due to pain or pulled into the future due to possibility?

4. If you don't have an annual, semiannual, and quarterly rhythm, chart one. Figure out what's the best way to stay fresh and tooled, and then get the necessary permissions to make it happen. Don't wait. Waiting is the game of procrastinators. They watch things happen; they don't make things happen.

Endnotes

1. A large pad of paper and colored markers should be standard material in the office of any leader. Mind-mapping will be discussed later on in the chapter on creativity, but pads and markers are the backbone of creativity sessions.

IDEAGRAPHER: DISCOVERING A CREATIVE WELLSPRING

Creativity is immensely important to 21C ministry. In fact, I don't feel it's hyperbole at all to say without creativity, ministry to the natives of this postmodern world will be next to impossible. Be careful to hear what I'm not saying. I'm not saying we have to be cute or coy in our presentation of our message because people won't hear it without bells and whistles. Don't confuse creativity with cuteness or slickness or Hollywood. We're not trying to be cute or Hollywood when we're being creative.

The intersection of the biblical message with our culture is mediated through the organism of the local church. The meeting of those three factors is impossible without some measure of creativity. I open with that qualifier because I think many people view creativity with disdain as a trendy, fashionable intrusion into the church that hopefully will pass unnoticed. That's simply a profound misunderstanding of creativity—its theological basis and its absolute necessity (yes, the word there is *necessity*) for being effective in this new world. Creativity has to be one of the generative components in the life of every leader. We need "ideagraphers": generators, synthesizers, and catalysts of great ideas.

Missions 101

Let's frame the critical context demanding our creative energy. Missiologists tell us that effective communication in any cross-cultural context requires a few clearly defined steps. First, understand the message you're trying to communicate. Make sure you are crystal clear with what you're trying to say. Second, study and understand the target culture, the culture in which you're trying to communicate your message. In missions this means understanding language, metaphors, stories, and anything else that assists a faithful translation of the original message. The third step is obvious: Translate the message into the idiom of the new culture you're trying to reach. While creativity is usually not talked about in the context of missiology, it should be. Good missiology is a creative endeavor.

Look at the creativity in just a couple areas of culture. We live in a highly niched, customizable culture. From the rage of bod mod (short for body modification) to customizing your computer's desktop environment with icons and colors, we like making individualized statements. Piercings, tattoos, eyelid tucks, liposuction—these are simply moving our interest with individuality to the realm of our bodies, the one true domain in our control. Entire companies and Web sites are devoted to the ability to have customizable icon sets for your computer. Almost everything in your computer is "skinable"; that is, it can take on the design and coloration of a covering made by an artist. All of this is creativity, our most primal core-seeking expression. Of course, the quality of the expression is sometimes debatable.

We need to jump on the creativity bandwagon and better wrap our message. In reality we live in a cross-cultural context. The message of Jesus, though ever relevant, continues to be communicated in forms primarily conceived in and targeted at our modern world. Outmoded music, architecture, delivery style of linear talking head, nonparticipatory format, and dense and obscure language all contribute to the **We may be clear on the message, but we haven't understood our target culture well enough to translate the message faithfully.** message being rather obtuse to those in this new native world of postmodernity. In missiological terms, we may be clear on the message, but we haven't understood our target culture well enough to translate the message faithfully.

Faithful translation surely means more than a simple statement of the gospel. Many will balk here and say results are God's business, and our role is simple proclamation. But just how do we define simple proclamation? Those who are negative about using creative means as a way to do good missiology have, at the very least, agreed that language translation is a prerequisite to understanding the gospel. Nobody I know is going around proclaiming the death, burial, and resurrection of Jesus in Greek or Aramaic. So if language is an "assumed" and legitimate necessity for "faithful" proclamation, why not the necessity of metaphor and image, as well as other cultural issues to take into consideration?

Faithfully translating the biblical message into the language of our culture is our primary job. The message remains the same by impacting the understanding of

the target audience the same as it impacted the original hearers. This requires creative translation; not a retranslation of the biblical text, but a translation of the way we communicate it in a culture that is constantly changing. In other words, we must be both exegetes of Scripture and exegetes of culture. If we read Scripture carefully without reading culture, we have an important message that's not understood. If we read culture carefully but fail to communicate the biblical message, we've been relevant but for no reason. Both biblical and cultural exegeses are necessary for effective postmodern ministry.

Beyond Newfangled

When we say creativity, immediately what comes to mind is contemporary church efforts to try newfangled things. Many don't like the departure from the old and familiar trappings they've grown accustomed to. We would be well served, however, to be reminded that every piece of classical music, every old stained glass window or stately cathedral was at one time fresh, creative, new, and, in some cases, riding the very edge of innovation. So let's make sure this simply isn't a discussion of the old sacred ways versus the new and unproven ways. The issue is more about effectiveness than chronological age.

The soul ergonomics chapter gave what could be looked at as an apologetic for why creativity on the spiritual morphing front is simply mandatory equipment if we want to experience dynamic morphing ourselves and then catalyze it for others. But there are plenty of biblical bases for a theology of creativity. "In the beginning God created." This is the most fundamental and primary thing God did. He created out of nothing what appears to the naked eye to be infinite variety.

God Is All About Variety

God could have gotten the point across with a few hundred colors. But we have millions of colors, and unless we have computers and monitors capable of that kind of display, we feel like we have an old beater. God could have had a few different beetles, couldn't he have? But he opted for thousands and thousands of varieties. Have you ever watched a tarantula up close? I had one that I let crawl around my office for a few years. Herman lived in a cage, but when I was studying, I'd let him crawl around on me and the desk. Have you ever watched one closely? You talk about God's creative ability! I'm in the desert of Arizona right now writing part of this book. I run the mountains every day (well almost every day). How many different cacti are there? How many shapes? colors? sizes? Now we could go on in this vein endlessly. How can we possibly escape the conclusion that God is into variety, creativity, and making sure we don't get bored?

Why not simply black and white everything? Why not create a world with one bug, one kind of flower (black and white, of course), one kind of tree, one shape of person (oh, that could be an ugly sight). Why not? God wanted to say something through variety. God is big-time into creativity, variation, and uniqueness. Not only that, but he has passed it on to his creatures.

When God created the world, he created man and woman—each unique, by the way. He isn't just into creativity; he's into uniqueness. Every human has unique fingerprints and DNA. God not only passed that form on to his creatures, but he has also passed on to us a measure of his creative ability. When God breathed into Adam and Eve, part of what he gave from himself was the craving for uniqueness, as well as the ability to create.

What's the significance of Adam's first activity in the garden? Immediately after creating Adam, God brought all the animals, birds, and fish to Adam to see what he would name them. He invited Adam's creativity and validated it by memorializing the action and keeping the names Adam used. Notably absent from the text is any reference to Adam's creative training, brainstorming sessions, free association, or lateral thinking exercises.

Now I'm far from saying those aren't important. In fact, this chapter is about becoming more creative and what we can engage in to assist that end. I look at Adam to point out that his very created nature was creative. God passed on to him, as one of his communicable attributes, creativity. While you won't find it listed in a systematic theology text in the doctrine of God section, it's easily defensible.

The implications of this kind of observation are actually quite staggering. God expected Adam to be creative. The Genesis text says quite certainly that God brought the animals to Adam to "see what he would name them" (Genesis 2:19). God fully expected Adam to create, to draw out of his interior a wide and lengthy host of names. I think there's a further implication: Creativity is the antidote to boredom.

We never answered the earlier questions we posed: Why so many colors, beetles, trees? Why variety? God wanted a creation void of boredom; a creation of vast, even incalculable visual interest.

I would contend the end point of all that creative genius is impact on the human heart. Creativity has impact deeper than simple window dressing. Creativity creases our emotions, imprints our hearts, and piques our minds. Great music, art, and drama all have the ability to move us. It's simply undeniable—we love creativity and the variety it births. The female penchant for shoe-collecting would be further confirmation of this. My wife is no exception. She is initiating my nine-year-old daughter into this addiction—I mean art form.

Why variety? God wanted a creation void of boredom; a creation of vast, even incalculable visual interest.

Personal Discoveries

I want to say that whenever the issue of creativity came up during my first eight years of ministry, I was quick to point out that I wasn't creative. My gifts were leadership and teaching, not the whole squishy, artsy thing of creativity. The mad artist who hadn't slept for days, was covered in paint, had canvases all over the floor, and had matted hair all over his face was everything I was not. I simply didn't *see* my creativity or how I was already expressing it.

Then I underwent a significant shift in my thinking. One of my main hobbies was cooking. In reading an article in one of my gourmet magazines, cooking was referred to as art. I nearly had a religious experience. Cooking for me was not only therapeutic, it was also artistic. I created meals and embellished on the styles of other chefs, and when a meal was completed, I felt something of a work of art had been created. None of that took persuading. What was harder to see was how this isolated, or what I thought was isolated, area was a much more dominant stream flowing through my life than I realized.

Here I'd been in an entrepreneurial church plant for nearly a decade. The church was certainly creative, and my leadership had something to do with it, even if it was minor. But then I began to reflect on preparing messages and the artistry involved; oh, not often very pretty art, but art nonetheless. My high school debate coach used to wax on and on that artistic word selection, when combined with good evidence, would almost always win the day. He had lots of state championship bids as a coach to back up his point.

Slowly it began to dawn on me. I *was* creative. And if I was creative, then it could be developed. This was a huge dawning for me. It was one thing to say I'm not creative. That's a done deal, end-of-story statement. You look no further and have no further expectations. It was another thing to see that I already was creative. I didn't need to obtain something I didn't have, and, therefore, I could develop it.

My hope is that you will own from here on out that creativity is part of being human. It's the breath of God in you. If we can agree on that, then we can begin to make progress. You may say, "But I am pretty left-brained" or "I am not into art" or "I like things plain" or "I don't like painting of any sort"...or...or...or...The point is, if we can agree that part of **My hope is that you will own from here on out that creativity is part of being human.** the divine imprint of God's image in you has a creative dimension, then we can move forward from there. To where, you ask?

I already said I couldn't see ministry in this postmodern world going very far without immense expenditures of creativity. That means you and I as leaders must morph in the creativity areas. You and I must build into our lives and schedules ways to be creative and to specifically get creative for ministry initiatives. The burden of almost everything we've looked at so far in preceding chapters is the need to have things happen in our lives if we're going to authentically catalyze them in others—morph of the leader, morph of the team.

The collision of our culture, our local ministry, and the biblical message of relationship with God in Christ has an infinite number of potential variations. God is obviously OK with variety. But I think *haphazard* intersection of those three is one of the most obvious reasons for ministry ineffectiveness in the local church. A good deal of the time, ministry ineffectiveness is because we're unwilling to do a little creative thinking about things.

Cloned Predictability

The United States is full of cloned churches. Every denomination has as an unstated goal: the "McDonald's-ization" of the church. From orders of service and liturgy to song selection and building design, the hope is that if you enter into the denomination's local church in Detroit or in Sarasota, you'll have a very similar experience. I like to count on that kind of consistency for a Big Mac, but for my worship experience? We act like God is in a rut. And this isn't just a gripe with the traditional church.

The nontraditional church often hasn't done much better. There isn't a traditional liturgy with prayers of confession and creeds, but there's the standard drama or video clip with a couple of song sets thrown in. The nondenominational church has liturgy. It's just a bit more flexible but almost as predictable.

This issue lies with creative design teams.[1] But it also lies one step further back. If our point leaders aren't fostering creative environments and training their teams on creativity, then it's no wonder our teams are stuck in a rut. For some, just the idea of having a team of volunteers get together and talk creatively about the design of the service is an immensely helpful thought.

Kindergarten Creativity

Something happens to us between the time we're very young and the time we become junior high students. Put a small irregular chalk mark on a blackboard, and ask some junior high or high school students about it. They'll look around at each other, stare in disbelief at you, and someone will finally blurt out to the relief of everyone else present, "A chalk mark on a blackboard." Do the same thing with a group of kindergartners. The diversity of response is refreshing: a smashed bug, a paint blob, some cotton candy, my daddy's cigarette butt, a stone, a snowball, a mound of salt from our saltshaker. These kids can generate an endless list. The moral of the story? Have kids on your creative team. Well, no not exactly, but that isn't a bad idea.

What this illustrates is probably the first principle in learning to be more creative. There's never only one right answer. But our schooling system creates a "there's only one right answer" mentality. With that training comes a shutting down of options that are the grist for thinking out of the proverbial box.

Our education system primarily trains and then tests for two or three of the eight intelligences. Howard Gardner started doing work in this area several decades ago. He became skeptical that our tendency toward mathematical, logical, and verbal-linguistic dominant training may leave out some very important areas in which people may show great aptitude but never really have it discovered, affirmed, or developed.

How would Mozart have scored on the ACT or SAT tests? He began to question the standard way we understand intelligence. He came to conclude that the IQ test was good for testing two kinds of intelligence but largely ignored six others. He identified eight different intelligences, all equally important but not all equally affirmed or acknowledged within our standard educational contexts. He asked questions, such as "How would Mozart have scored on the ACT or SAT tests? Could he score high enough to get into an Ivy League school?" The fact is, musical intelligence is one of eight intelligences but not one we have an IQ test for.

What does this mean to leadership creativity? Quite a bit! More important, we've been funneled into certain kinds of thinking due to our educational paradigms. As a result, we may be somewhat dwarfed in other areas. This is hopeful for those of us who desire to learn more creativity. The typical intelligences highlighted in our K-12 schooling are logical/mathematical and verbal-linguistic. The scientific method built upon testing, measurement, and verifying further confirms our default settings. Lecture-drill-test is a relatively fair depiction of our educational model; a model that by design creates competition among peers with really very little proof of competence at the end of the day.

Choosing Your Grade

Conductor of the Boston Philharmonic Ben Zander decided he would eliminate that nonsense and instead affirm each student's worth and latent ability by awarding them an A grade at the beginning of the semester of his Art of Musical Performance class. He desired to see his students take the risks necessary to go out on a limb and play with interpretive passion and fire. The one prerequisite for the A grade was a letter written to Zander by each student that first week of the semester. They had to postdate the letter May of the following year and in the letter tell Zander why they deserved the A. They had to write in the past tense as if they really were writing it in May. The letters Zander has received are more than heartwarming; they are moving. When students get in touch with their deepest fears as they head into the semester, they purpose to deal with them in the upcoming weeks. Zander says the results are staggering.[2]

Our churches continue in the exact same vein as our public schools. We do the lecture-drill part and usually omit the test, although to become a member in some churches, it appears there is something approximating a test. We need to move off our linear talking-head approach and breathe some life into our ministry contexts. Creativity in the leader will help spawn creativity in the team. What are the things we can do individually to help this along?

Understanding how creativity works is the first step toward fostering it. Have you ever noticed how you have great insights, creative ideas, or solve a lot of intractable problems either in the morning foggy zone between sleeping and actually waking or in the evening between being awake and drifting off? If you haven't noticed this, you're unusual. Something very interesting is happening in that zone. Your conscious mind is slowing down and your unconscious mind is coming to a place of getting a bit more of a "hearing" from you. When this happens, all sorts of insights burst out.

I hate taking naps—you know the two- or three-hour jobbers my wife feels are what Sundays were made for. Because God said rest on the Sabbath, she's taking it literally. For me that just wrecks the rest of the day. I'm groggy until I go to bed. But I'm the master of the ten- to fifteen-minute power nap. I come out of one of those fresh *and* often very, very creative.

Wouldn't that be something if we could figure out a way to get those insights at will. We obviously can't do that, but we can begin to understand the process better and, in so doing, create the increased possibility of those insights happening. We're going to start with a quick primer on brain research, much of which has become so well known that it's commonplace.

Two Halves Make One Creative

In the '70s Herbert Benson began publishing popular books on the phenomenon known as the relaxation response.[3] Through a variety of experiments, often using meditation, Benson was able to watch the change in brain wave patterns between the two hemispheres of the brain.[4] In meditation, the logical left side of the brain and the rhythmic right brain worked in harmony. The physical results of this are what so intrigued Benson. They literally saw a change in the blood pressure of those who were meditating. Apparently, meditation induced a tremendously relaxed state that even affected the heart rate and blood pressure. Yet that state was different from a state of sleep.

For our purposes, that's the key insight. The two sides of the brain working together induce a creative state. And the state between sleep and wakefulness

is similar in brain pattern to that induced through meditation. This explains why my ten-minute power nap helps the creative process. I never fully sleep but reach the dreamy in-between stage where I experience right- and left-brain harmony.

Getting Them Together

What are some things we can do to bring about this kind of tandem harmony in the halves of the brain? The list goes on and on. Juggling is a great exercise. You may say, "Come on, Ron. Are you serious?" Quite literally! Juggling is an exercise requiring both kinds of activity from your brain. I discuss this in the team chapter where we did this as a staff exercise.[5] Can you think of any other juggling-type things your grandma used to engage in that used both sides of the brain? How about knitting and crocheting? Skipping rope is another (I haven't seen my Grams do that one though). I know this seems a bit out there, but don't knock it until you've tried it.

Have you read about runners who get into the "zone"? There are certain brain chemistry things going on with a good deal of that. But there's also a kind of meditative state that kicks in and brings about harmony between the sides of the brain. Anyone who has run even eight or ten miles has easily felt this kick in. Again, this raises the meditation issue.

Meditation is the dominant exercise that brings spiritual depth and quieting before God, promotes a harmony in our brains, and results in states of heightened creativity.

As Christians we're urged to meditate day and night.[6] Obviously none of us believe we should sit around 24/7 and chant a mantra. But I think the hyperbole of "day and night" in both texts is pointing out something we've paid little attention to. Meditation is the dominant exercise that brings spiritual depth and quieting before God, promotes a harmony in our brains, and results in states of heightened creativity. I had the blessing of getting tuned to this early in my Christian experience, and then years later I had a professor in seminary who was really big on it.

Earlier I mentioned reading outside your frame. Fewer exercises have been of more profound impact on me than this discipline. A mentor early in my life told me I should be reading far more than theology and ministry topics. His essential thesis was that breadth outside of my basic discipline would provide me with inane connections that may prove helpful. Of course this doesn't have to just be reading. It could be taking a class, joining a group, or engaging a hobby totally outside the normal scope of your learning interests.

Out-There Ideas

I had the luxury of having our church-design architect have an office in our church office cluster for a number of months. The short course I received in architecture has been one of the most enriching experiences I've had in a long time. My understanding of how space creates feel and flow has been immensely insightful and practical.

Any area outside of church ministry may have more of a connection into ministry than you realize...from biographies to color theory, the impact of scent (interesting for worship and seminar purposes), quantum and superstring theory, art appreciation, travel, surfing the Web in unfamiliar areas. The list could go on and on.

If you begin opening yourself up to that which appears to be merely a tangent, over time your mind will amazingly make connections. The more grist you provide, the more connections your brain will make. This isn't just so you are a more interesting person, although you'll be that. This isn't just so you can have broader illustrative material, though you'll have that too. The real reason is the new fusion of elements that emerge. I genuinely believe the most effective ways of seeing ministry happen, the most powerful ways of connecting people to God, are still to be found.

> I genuinely believe the most effective ways of seeing ministry happen, the most powerful ways of connecting people to God, are still to be found.

Learning About Creativity

Let's not allow the most obvious thing to elude us. Learn about how the creative process works and what "great creatives" did and still do for their creativity. A couple of years ago, a book titled *How to Think Like Leonardo da Vinci* came out.[7] A follow-up volume by Gelb just came out, focusing more broadly on the world's ten greatest thinkers.[8] This is one of those books on my kids' reading list. They read the first one when they were preteens. We discussed it and did some of the exercises.

Some consider da Vinci to be the greatest of all geniuses who ever lived. He actually did things to cultivate both right- and left-brain dexterity. He did backward handwriting, simultaneous right and left handwriting. He did mirror writing. He did mirror writing with both hands. Those are just some of the things he did on the writing front to train his brain to be more ambidextrous.

Geniuses often have a higher level of fluency in all the intelligences than the average person. Multiple intelligences? Remember Howard Gardner, the Harvard professor who introduced us to the theory of multiple intelligences? He has written about it from a leadership perspective as well.[9] Geniuses seem to have a higher incidence of fluency in multiple areas than we average folks.

If you read about someone like Einstein, you would think he was all logical left brain. Not at all true. Most mind experts have noted that a good deal of Einstein's discoveries were through visualizing and creating pictorial scenarios long before they were mathematically worked out. Gelb's book, which helps us think through the minds of ten of history's greatest thinkers, is a great book to start with. What a way to spawn creativity and get outside the realm of our own rutted thinking and creating processes![10]

Mind-mapping is another discipline that's responsible for many of the ideas I've had. Of course, the value of those ideas is what some would tell you is rather dubious. If you aren't familiar with mind-mapping, it's sort of an idea-generation method that gets you out of typical linear outlines. Mind-mapping, by its very design, is spirals of thoughts using colors and even art to stimulate further ideas. The great part is that it takes hardly any time to learn, and the benefits are almost instant. The industrial artist who designed my office built a standing desk for me because I like to journal and sometimes even write while standing. I almost always have a huge pad on that desk with all sorts of markers to mind-map an idea when something hits me.[11]

Knowing Your Primary Vein

Do you know the primary creative path or vein you typically plow? In other words, if someone were to ask you what your creativity method is or how it works inside you, would you know how to respond? If not, you should think through your "faces of genius," as they are called by Annette Moser-Wellman. Her recent volume *The Five Faces of Genius*, is a treasure-trove.[12]

When a leader begins to fiddle with the creative process, there's an interesting leak that happens. Part of it just overflows. The story and demeanor are altered. Expectation levels change. Ideas begin to flow, and a kind of contagion kicks in. Others enter the arena, and the creative synergy ignites. Here is the real value of the leak. When a morphic leader leaks a value, idea, pattern, or practice to a team, the whole team's synergism with that new pattern or practice increases exponentially. The kingdom will advance.

InnerAction

1. Where do you consider yourself on the creative scale? Look carefully in your life. You are creative, but where? Where do you see hints that maybe you are more creative than you first imagined?

2. Look around. Where do you customize your environment to suit your creative sensibilities?

3. Where are you when you are most creative? What's going on? How did you get into that creative vein?

4. What are you doing to design a creative work environment? What are you doing to get out of your familiar learning patterns and engage some things beyond your usual realms?

Endnotes

1. That is the term we use at Westwinds for the team who does worship design, what elements will be used each week, how they will be configured, and so on.

2. Rosamund Stone Zander and Ben Zander, *The Art of Possibility* (Boston, MA: Harvard Business School Press, 2000), 25-53.

3. Herbert Benson, M.D. with William Proctor, *Beyond the Relaxation Response: How to Harness the Healing Power of Your Personal Beliefs* (New York, NY: Times Books, 1984). Herbert Benson, M.D. with William Proctor, *Your Maximum Mind* (New York, NY: Times Books, 1987). Herbert Benson, M.D. with Marg Stark, *Timeless Healing: The Power and Biology of Belief* (New York, NY: Scribner, 1996). Herbert Benson, M.D. with Miriam Z. Klipper, *The Relaxation Response* (New York, NY: Avon Books, 1975).

4. While Benson allowed people to meditate and focus on a variety of things, sometimes it was just their breathing; other times they actually used Scripture.

5. Michael J. Gelb and Tony Buzan, *Lessons from the Art of Juggling: How to Achieve Your Full Potential in Business, Learning, and Life* (New York, NY: Crown Trade Paperbacks, 1994).

6. Both Psalm 1 and Joshua 1 say essentially the same thing.

7. Michael J. Gelb, *How to Think Like Leonardo da Vinci: Seven Steps to Genius Every Day* (New York, NY: Delacorte Press, 1998).

8. Michael J. Gelb, *Discover Your Genius: How to Think Like History's Ten Most Revolutionary Minds* (New York, NY: HarperCollins Publishers, Inc., 2002).

9. Howard Gardner, *Leading Minds: An Anatomy of Leadership* (New York, NY: BasicBooks, 1995). Howard Gardner, *Extraordinary Minds: Portraits of Exceptional Individuals and an Examination of Our Extraordinariness* (New York, NY: BasicBooks, 1997). Howard Gardner, *Frames of Mind: The Theory of Multiple Intelligences* (New York, NY: BasicBooks, 1983).

10. Gelb, *Discover Your Genius*.

11. Gelb, *Thinking for a Change*.

12. Annette Moser-Wellman, *The Five Faces of Genius: The Skills to Master Ideas at Work* (New York, NY: Penguin Books Ltd., 2001).

KALEIDOSCOPIC IMAGINATION: SEEING TOMORROW BEFORE IT ARRIVES

Endless curiosity, wild imagination, incessant wonderment—these are the building blocks of all great visions of tomorrow. Jesus said he would build his church, and the gates of hell would not prevail.

So what does this organism called the church actually look like? What are the shape, color, smell, dimensions, ethos, flavor, magnitude, and method? What it's supposed to look like as Jesus is building it may be a more germane question. Imagining the future is not our best effort to build on the past but a foresight for intersecting the future.

The fundamental assumption is that rightly aligned and spiritually tuned in leaders will be moving the church toward interception of the new emergent thing God is doing. "I am doing a new thing!" he says (Isaiah 43:19). As morphic leaders, we have the honor and scare-me-silly responsibility of morphing local churches—morphing them by pointing out the new thing springing up and letting it dent the activity of the present. Jesus left few details about how to do this. No doubt he said he would build the church. But like it or not, the agency of leadership is his preferred instrumentation for doing so. You would've thought he could have come up with a better plan, huh?

Right Place at the Right Time

We said earlier that cellular leadership is coming to grips with what you deeply believe about leadership, vision, and people. I said I believe leadership is about God releasing his outlandish hopes and dreams through a certain personality, through a certain people, in a certain place, at a certain time. We need to develop the definition a bit more here.

My cellular belief is that leadership and vision are mediated through a personality—through an individual—and God takes into consideration that individual's strengths, weaknesses, outlook, disposition, and context. In other words, my placement in Jackson, Michigan, for this time, to lead this church, in this direction, is what has led to the dynamic we're experiencing at Westwinds. I believe that in a different context, at another time, in another church, things may have turned out very, very different, and I may have been a miserable leader.[1] Who, where, and when determine leadership leverage. This is the divine and sovereign side of the leadership event. The convergence of all those factors is a unique and often potent elixir.

Some eyebrows may be raised at my statement that I believe vision is mediated through a personality. My point is that vision comes through a person or a tightly woven team in which issues of philosophy of ministry have already been clarified. Even with a tightly woven team, however, there's a leader who eventually emerges as the primary vision holder. And that's who the team depends on to cast the vision. I've heard it said over and over again by many great leaders before me that people will follow a person before they follow a vision. I have yet to find a person on a team who has cast, owned, or articulated the vision better than the visionary point leader.

Aaron just can't be expected to be as passionate, clear, compelling, and detailed as Moses. Aaron can articulate it, own it, enlist others to it, and be willing to die for it, but it won't be with the burning bush history or authority of a Moses. This isn't license for a personality cult, nor does this model have to lead to that, though it can. This is only observation. God gave vision to Moses, Jeremiah, Daniel, Nehemiah, Paul, and Peter...not to the committees they chaired.

> **God gave vision to Moses, Jeremiah, Daniel, Nehemiah, Paul, and Peter...not to the committees they chaired.**

Does this mean vision discernment or building a shared vision is impossible as a team or that Moses and Aaron couldn't have seen the burning bush together? Definitely not. In fact, outside the context of pioneering church plants, it's probably in the very arena of teams that vision is discerned. But I remain committed to the fact God uses point leaders to discern, hear, and cast the vision. A liberating turning point in ministry came when I finally moved this insight from mere information to something transformational. When you say vision is given through a

leader and you are the leader, that puts huge onus on you. A team or a committee feels so much safer. When it became clear that I was responsible before God and he really intended me to lead, something happened to the courage level in me. I was responsible, I had to hear clearly and communicate passionately. Those two skills are the seeds of building shared vision.

On the heels of these changes going on inside me, I had to begin a series of hard talks with people who simply wanted to be power brokers in the church. They wanted things done their way, on their terms, with their ideas. After understanding better the leadership dynamic I was authorized by God to flow in, I could sit down, not without a lot of prayer and mustering courage, to have talks with these people about their subversive agendas. I quickly rediscovered why I hated "confrontation" so much; it is just so messy. But those were the beginnings of me inviting people to hop on God's heading for Westwinds or to invite them off the train to find one heading the direction they wanted to go. Did we lose some people? We did. Were we stronger and more unified because of it? We were. In church planting contexts and new start-ups, this may seem easier. In established, or may we even say entrenched, contexts, this is a morphic art requiring lots of finesse, and without it the church won't move too far.

Future-Map

Allowing tomorrow to come knocking on the door of the church and to answer it surprised is simply abdication of our responsibility and entirely inadequate for the magnitude of the task at hand. Every leader I find in Scripture was sent into the future. Against their protests, second-guessing, bad attitudes, and abounding excuses, they were sent into the future with a future-map of just how things were supposed to play out. Some maps were detailed; others were quite vague.

But interception of a new thing God had in mind was almost always at the forefront of the reason one was sent. Moses was sent armed with a future-map. Abraham was, David was, Jonah was, and Nehemiah was. All of them were sent into the future. There's no denying the plans were at times audacious, mind-blowing, difficult, chaotic, and complex. But there were future-maps given to leaders for that time, in that context, for that purpose.

Another way of saying it is leadership is historically occasioned. At this instant in history, given all the variables, God is going to do something unique in and through us. Morphic leadership is exactly that: God deeply changing us and then using the catalytic nature of that change to

> Morphic leadership is...God deeply changing us and then using the catalytic nature of that change to provoke, produce, and prod the same change in a group of people to move them forward.

provoke, produce, and prod the same change in a group of people to move them forward.

Our location in history makes a shared understanding of where we're heading tomorrow more important than ever. Witness the chaos of culture and how people are groping for direction. Psychics and tarot card readings are only a phone call away. I'm absolutely fascinated by how much science is increasingly talking of spiritual things. The proliferation and increased interest in religions of the East seems to continue unabated. Couple those developments with the perceived rigidity and irrelevance of the church, and if we're not careful, our already-marginalized location could worsen.

Intercepting the Emergent

The urgent imagining work of intercepting tomorrow's opportunities and intersecting them with God's "new thing" has to be a high priority. And yet the trudging on of most ministry entails little, if any, forward thinking. Hear this staggering statistic from the marketplace. The average executive responsible for understanding tomorrow spends 2.3 percent of his or her time on it. I'd love to say things in God's ark are different, and the pastoral tribe is more on top of it. Informal surveying, however, shows we're no more prepared.

To be the permission-giving systems we need to be for effective ministry, we must have clarity at the core and flexibility at the fringe.[2] Postmodern churches don't need and may not want clear boundaries on a host of things if they want to respond well to the host of turbulent conditions of our postmodern environment. The mission of why we exist, the vision of how to accomplish it, and our core values are clear and constant. Our doctrinal statement, though beyond a shadow of a doubt Christian, engages no doctrinal detailing. Of course, the only people who care are those with any Christian background, which is always a sinking percentage at Westwinds. We're black and white on the black and white and remain gray on the gray. We have "left-behinders" who are adamant and amillennials. We have infant baptizers though we baptize adults. For communion we have "real presence" mainliners and "no presence" Baptists. We have predestinarians and freewill theists. We have teetotalers and wine collectors, Democrats and Republicans. But none of that is necessary or even asked about to be a part of Westwinds.

There's tremendous permeability at the edge into the life of Westwinds. To attend, to find your way into a group, or to join any number of serving areas is easy, no-brainer stuff. But from the first moment on the campus, in a gathering, on a team, or in a group (sorry, we never had a committee), the core of what we are about is being clarified, restated, storied, and modeled. The responsibility of morphic leaders is to make sure the core is clear, the image of the future clarified, the opportunities being invited by God known, and the self-understanding and ethos in the body healthy.

The Kaleidoscopic Dance

Having grown up in the '80s (oops that should read '60s), I have a pretty good idea that the grade school–age birthday party favor of choice was cardboard tube kaleidoscopes. Call it a dearth of creativity, too much campus unrest, or too many burnt orange VW vans, someone in the birthday party favors arena in the '60s was obsessed with kaleidoscopes. Maybe that person was also obsessed with the psychedelic...ummmm...that was a '60s phenomenon.

Kaleidoscopes from my single digit birthdays were cardboard tubes with three mirrors arranged in a triangle the length of the tube. The real guts of the kaleidoscope wasn't the mirrors but the pieces of colored plastic shapes in the end. A glance through the tube and a turning of the end piece holding all the pieces created quite a dance of colors and shapes. The interaction of color, light, and three mirrors is what made these party favors so interesting.

Morphic leadership knows that the careful alignment and convergence of three mirrors of the kaleidoscope provide a dance of elements making up the future we're trying to see before it arrives.[3] The three mirrors are the "new thing" God is doing (the prophetic mirror); the unique gift mix, resources, and local vision that mediate God's message (the poetic mirror); and the current and emergent contextual setting of the ministry (the apostolic mirror). When a local church can glance at the understandings reflected in those three mirrors, she'll be prepared and ready as the new opportunities emerge. Welcome to 21C missiology.

The apostolic mirror reflects the landscape. The church as "sent" performs the apostolic role of seeing the context into which she has been sent. The poetic mirror is the creative translation of the biblical story using our gifts, abilities, and resources. It is what assists the local church in her self-understanding. The prophetic mirror reflects, in the context of the other two, what new thing God wants to do.

We may croon about the good old days, which really, upon closer examination, weren't all that good.

Kaleidoscopic imagination takes seriously the "sent-ness" of going into the world and understanding into what instant the church has been invited. We may lament the challenge of our world. We may croon about the good old days, which really, upon closer examination, weren't all that good. We may wish we had been called to another time or another place. But it remains that this is the moment into which we've been called. This is the context into which we've been sent. This mirror of the apostle is going out into the culture to see how the church can be the church and also to better prepare the people in the church for those who will come. This takes cultural tooling, sensitivity, and a desire to understand the currents of culture. We've already mentioned the often-quoted text about the men of Issachar. They understood the times *and* knew what Israel should do. This is apostolic.

The "going out" to understand culture better so we can better design understandable ministry within the church is part of the apostolic function of this mirror. Understanding people's stated needs, their perception of the world, their fears, struggles, hurts, issues—this is an apostolic "going out" to understand future ministry design. These kinds of findings should impact program selection and design, the language we use, and the topics we choose. Of course, all of these have to be aligned with the mission, vision, and values. But that goes without being stated. The litmus test of anything is mission/vision/values alignment. Without alignment, no program, plan, or idea can ever get past discussion stage. In our context, after we finally understood what we were about, it took several years to really get good alignment of our staff, people, and programs. Call us slow learners; it simply took us awhile.

Putting Out Ears

Every local context is different. So doing your own fieldwork here is very important. Reading the typical trend books and newsletters is always helpful but never a substitute for your own ears in your own context. There are simple ways to start. Ask your people to start listening to their unchurched friends. Nothing could be simpler, more accurate, or less expensive (last I checked, listening was free).

Brian had come for several weeks. He had hit a tough spot in his life and wanted to reach out to God but felt like his upbringing prevented him from really exploring faith very much. His close friends and neighbors were Westwinds attendees and gently but persistently invited him. Brian's story could be multiplied scores of times. "Every time I walk out of a service, I feel like God was talking directly to me. And yet that is what I hear from so many of the people walking around here. They all feel like it was designed for them. It is just hard to believe." Brian's story was recounted to me in the lobby after one of our Fusion services, unsolicited and honest. By the way, Brian is following Jesus now and is slowly but surely making progress as he is learning to live the life of Jesus. We need to do all we can to help those stories flow.

Two things happen when you encourage this. You create ethos, and you get information. What kind of ethos is created when listening for where unchurched family and friends are "living" slowly becomes a value? Morphic leaders are immensely concerned about ethos because that's what sets the temperature for the whole feel and flavor of the church. Make no mistake about it; this will take time and persistence. Creating ethos, casting vision, and aligning the team always take time, and usually more than we anticipated. Ethos is so worth it, though. By constantly asking the question "What are your friends saying?" you're passing on

a value and making a statement.

Creating ethos is only part of the benefit of having a listening force. You genuinely end up with useful, applicable, and specific information for your context. Of course, there are other ways to do this, too, but they require more sophistication, money, and effort. The informal information you get here can lead to all sorts of initiatives.

As we've listened in our situation, we've found huge brokenness in the people in our webs of friendships. How we speak to people, the kinds of groups we provide, and the kinds of training we offer our leaders had to be adjusted. Think about that. When you get information about divorce, abuse, lack of relational social skills, poor communication patterns, and the kinds of things that often come from contexts of brokenness, it impacts every dimension of ministry.

As we've listened, we've heard people asking lots of spiritual questions: world religions questions, "Is Jesus the only way?" questions, "What is God doing in the world?" questions. When we start to hear our people and leaders say, "I'm hearing that too," we feel it's something to pray through and discuss as a team to determine how we should respond. Do we need to do a message series or an evening class, launch a program initiative, or let a small group dig in? All of these are options.

What isn't an option is to have everyone in the church give the staff all the good ideas of what they would like us to do. Permission-giving churches allow people immense freedom in launching initiatives if they are mission/vision/values aligned. Whenever someone comes with a "great idea," and there are a lot of them, the staff attentively listens and then asks, "And you are leading the team for this?" You quickly find out who has an idea and who has a passion.

One of the big shifts in ministry already underway is the concept that more ministry will happen "out there" than "in here."

This apostolic sent-out-into-the-culture-to-understand-it mirror is also responsible for reflecting to the local church the question "Just how sent are you?" We've done some hard thinking and praying here. In recent days we've had to say that a good deal of what we're about is getting people "out there" to come to our gig "in here." While that hasn't been the case across the board, too much of what we do is invite in instead of be apostolic. One of the big shifts in ministry already underway is the concept that more ministry will happen "out there" than "in here."

So from a new full-time staff position for outreach into our community to the formation of new kinds of small groups whose function is apostolic "going out," we're trying to really understand what this mirror is reflecting back to us. Our sending has mostly been for the purpose of inviting back in. No complaint as far as that goes. It's a huge value and the dominant way people come to Christ. But we also felt prompted by God to become more involved in the lives of those who are marginalized and have needs for the gospel, as well as other physical, emotional, and social skill needs. The apostolic mirror is what keeps us on mission. It's the outward mirror.

The New Thing

The ability to discern and then proclaim the new thing God wants to do is the prophetic mirror. The prophet in the Old and New Testaments, though functioning on an entirely different authority base, was to discern God's next steps, God's next new thing, and God's heart now poured out. Isaiah is the one putting in the language we're using here. "See, I am doing a new thing! Now it springs up; do you not perceive it? I am making a way in the desert and streams in the wasteland" (Isaiah 43:19). The assumption by the prophet is that perception of God's new thing could be missed if we're not careful. As you think about, consider, discuss, and pray before God about the reflections in the apostolic mirror, what are the new things you sense God wanting to do? You can see where the apostolic and prophetic reflections share images and fuel imagination. Kaleidoscopic imagination is a tri-unity; one grand dance of imaginative opportunities as each mirror contributes its part to the dance.

Two things seem to be reflected in the prophetic mirror. One is the freshness in which ministry is done. Are our methods in keeping with the language of culture and faithful to the biblical material? This is always a hot topic but shouldn't be. Jesus and Paul were ultimate pragmatists—to win some we will use whatever methods necessary. Do we want to communicate in language people understand or not?

When we say language, we mean more than choice of words. We mean musical styles, interior design and architecture, topics of talks, service design, interactional elements—these all qualify under the heading "language." We are constantly trying to make sure we're doing things that are fresh and allow people to hear and experience God in new ways. Changes are good for that reason alone. I'm afraid we haven't glanced in the prophetic mirror often enough. If the feedback we get from the general population of unchurched is any indication, we aren't catching on to much of the "new thing" God wants to do.

The second thing the prophetic mirror reflects is the "new thing." What is God inviting you into for this next eight- to twelve-month run? What new initiatives is he asking you to trumpet? What new ministry opportunities are on the docket?

This last year our youth guy decided to have just a hangout time with high school guys in our parking lot. He invited them to bring their small skateboard ramps. Until just recently, there was nothing in our town for this. We started having sixty, seventy, or more youth appear. Many of them don't come to our youth group, but it's a great bridge.

That was one of those last year mirror issues. This year we're contemplating what paving a couple of acres on our property with an outbuilding for ramps would look like. We need more parking, and if we thought ahead on how to do the lighting so we didn't have poles all over the middle of the pavement, we may be able to do a ministry initiative and deal with some parking constraints, too. Is this a "new thing" God wants to do?

What about our fourth-service flavor? Is God announcing a new thing there? We don't know, but prayerfully and in the context of our teams, we're trying to hear God's fresh word and see what he's showing us in the mirror.

What new thing is God announcing to us on how to broker help to other churches in our region? We're trying to hear what new thing God may be proclaiming. The list always seems endless and diverse. Whether it's extreme sports or three hundred and sixty degree projection, whether it's staffing new initiatives or helping other churches, what is God showing you in the prophetic mirror?

Ethos comes to mind again as we consider the prophetic mirror. How can you not begin to create expectations and heighten anticipation in the feel of the church and community when the questions being asked are "What new things does God want to do in us and through us?" The connection we're trying to make is that interior change going on in a leader and team of leaders, if properly shared, creates excitement, anticipation, and a sense that God is at work. When this type of leadership leak happens, over time the marinating effect is nothing short of a feel and flavor change in the church.

Waxing Poetic

Every local church mediates its ministry through its local unique gift mix and leadership base. Churches have gift mixes. Look at places like Willow Creek, Saddleback, and Ginghamsburg. They're all great churches, but each one has made a significant contribution in an area or two. No one is great in every area, nor is that even a goal. Local churches mediate their messages through the local flavor and feel of their unique blends of elements, people, properties, and resources. The church body's self-understanding, then, is critical. Metaphors, images, songs, history, gifts, victories, fresh births, baptisms of scores of adults who six months earlier didn't know God from a hatrack—all of these are the tools of the poet.

The poetic mirror helps artistically reflect the self-understanding of a local church so it can be ever clear on God's deposit in it. The poetic mirror reflects to the body "This is who you are, this is what I've done through you, these are the things with which I have gifted you to give away, and this is your identity in Christ." The poetic mirror keeps the song playing, the highlights in focus, the story clear, and the metaphors fresh.

Local churches mediate their messages through the local flavor and feel of their unique blends of elements, people, properties, and resources.

God has made very clear to us that for the next couple of years, we are to have a two-prong focus: spiritual conversations and replication. Now, of course, it is easy to note that these are not revolutionary foci or out of the ordinary. Spiritual conversation is another way of focusing on evangelism, and replication is another framework for discipleship. These metaphors, however, are powerful for communicating well-worn concepts in new and powerful ways.

Our understanding of the process of conversion is much more accurately reflected in the metaphor of spiritual conversations. So we are spending the next run of ministry helping our people learn to engage in conversation about Jesus things. In conversation, things like listening, asking well-placed questions, and seeking first to understand others are all just as important in the spiritual conversation arena as anything we say. The recent series we did on this topic was one of the most liberating for our community. People may not feel like evangelists, but they can converse on Jesus things. Spiritual conversation is poetic language, and it helps redefine self-understanding both individually and churchwide.

Replication is a term more associated with DNA and cell division than with discipleship. But we have taken the term and used it to represent the whole of the Christian life, not just spiritual things. We have used six icons, designed digitally in-house, to represent six different arenas that comprise full replication. We then did a three-week mini-series on each icon, unfolding how the life of Jesus was to be replicated in us and how we were to be replicators in the life of others. Icons on T-shirts, replication, fresh language, old ideas—this is the poetic mirror reflection.

The poetic mirror accomplishes two things as we're tapping the kaleidoscopic imagination. Poets tell stories, and stories connect and align people. Connection and alignment are the two necessary things this mirror reflects. When we hold up the poetic mirror, we're asking if the story is clear. Is our personal story, our church story of God's grace to us and his divine story, clear and clearly shared? Few things could be more important.

Again the interaction of the poetic and apostolic mirror is apparent. The story must be clear so it can be told "out there." Any church wanting to imagine the future has to have people clear on the story—individual, collective, and God's. Yet, as already illustrated, many even in leadership posts don't seem too clear on this very central thing. If we're trying to discern God's heart for the future and want to intercept opportunities, how can we do anything of value unless the story is clear?

Earthy Stories

Concerning story, this is something that requires our full learning potential to do well. Story is *the* communication mode in this postmodern world. Story has never been out of vogue, but it is highly fashionable these days as we move away from the sterility of an Aristotelian rationalism that's into points, principles, and expounded propositions.

Jesus didn't say anything to the disciples without using a parable, an earthy story (Mark 4:34). We may have reversed Jesus' method, yet one more area in which we've sanctified our methods and claimed for them special divine status. Jesus always spoke to the disciples in parables, and then when they were together he explained. We expound, explain, propound, complain, and throw in a poem for good measure. The old homiletics line from seminary days comes home here; our preaching is three points and a poem. Should I say, "Point made"?

The reason story is so important is its connective and aligning power. Stories bond us to each other. They create shared community and enable us to create history together. The collective stories of a group become the shared bond only they have. The stories that emerged from our small group leader training are lifetime memories. Using the *Survivor* theme, our small group leaders, coaches, and apprentices went to camp for a Serve-Ivor weekend. From tribal names and gear to immunity challenges and pitch dark, middle of the night wake-up physical challenges, those tribes have stories. The group leaders from AMENers (Ageless Mature Empty Nesters) wanted me to know that, in their opinion, they'd kicked royal behind in the forty-eight-foot zip line experiences. I was deluged with stories as soon as they all returned. I think they were trained in the process, at least that's what my small group teammate Amy told me. The year previous they did a "Mission: Impossible" training weekend. The stories and excitement were similar.

In Jackson, Michigan, we are in the heart of NASCAR mania. Our Team Westwinds Racing team just finished a weekend of showing its cars at a local mall. This outreach team not only races stock cars at local tracks, but also provides chaplain services at the track each week. Racing is a huge sport around here. Why not go out to where the people are and meet them? The stories being generated already are exciting.

Stories also are the primary means for aligning the team behind mission, vision, and values. Mission and vision take on life in and through a life. The poetic mirror reflects back to us whether or not our stated values are actually our values in practice. Through video clip faith stories, illustrations, baptism services, and a host of other delivery systems, stories fill the heart, stir emotions, and cause us to ask questions about ourselves. When a high school teenager with numerous piercings and pink hair got up and went to the live video terminal that projected onto a screen what was being typed on the terminal, we were about to hear a life story. As a line at a time posted live on the far left of the auditorium, the rest of the congregation was singing lyrics off a huge center screen. As her story began, she recounted her entrance to Westwinds as an addict to drugs, sex, and alcohol. Her story was a celebration of all that God had begun but had not yet completed. As that poetic story was weaving through the lyrics of our worship, God's presence was unmistakable. Our very reason for existing as a church was being written by a teenage girl who found God.

The poetic mirror is the inward mirror that keeps us on the path of clarity and celebration for what God has done. When it's coupled with the other two, we can see how the story will be retold in fresh ways and new contexts.

Dance in the Mirrors

Kaleidoscopic imagination taps the very best of the creativity breathed by God into us. The colorful dance of elements in a kaleidoscope is the result of three mirrors. The same will be true for us in intercepting and intersecting the future. Talk of interception and intersection may not be the best way of saying it, but I haven't come up with an alternative. We say we're trying to discern the future so we can prepare to meet God there. That makes it sound as if the future is the end for which the present is the means. Do "all these things" so we can arrive at the future. Might it not actually be the other way around?[4] The future is the means to shape our present? When we look out over the horizon and say, "A year from now the evangelistic value needs to have soared into the stratosphere," we are beginning with that statement to shape our present. The team serious about this statement is going to craft discussions with leaders, weekend talks for the congregation, and training events for the leaders that all lead to the outcome of a year from now seeing the evangelistic value soaring. Seeing into the desired future enables us to do things differently today which usually ends us much, much closer to the hoped for and stated outcome a year later. Seeing tomorrow shape our today. The future is the means to our present behavior, and in so shaping our present, we create the future that God invites us into. Kaleidoscopic imagination is trying to get a sense of the reflections in the three mirrors because those three will alter our behavior and activities here and now. "One doesn't creep up on a big future. Rather, the future is boldly declared and serves as the catalyst for all that follows."[5]

Our definition of leadership now has an interesting connection to articulating the future. Leadership is paraklesis for releasing God's "what ifs." Paraklesis comes in two moments: the moment of understanding and the moment of action. The moment of understanding helps establish the framework of understanding that we act upon for bringing about change—that is the moment of action. Kaleidoscopic imagination is the source material for framing the moment of understanding.

The dance of elements and possibilities in the three mirrors of the apostolic, prophetic, and poetic are simply concrete ways of uncovering "what ifs" and God's divine destiny for any local body. This makes the sharing of kaleidoscopic imagination a central role of leadership and the mastering of encouragement a critical skill set in helping a church come to the moment of action of choosing God's new

Leadership is paraklesis for releasing God's "what ifs."

thing. Kaleidoscopic imagination is far from a sacred method or even necessarily the best method. But it is one relatively comprehensive way of getting the main elements to work together.

The exciting thing in all this is the profound clarity in which God is present in the process and delivery of the imaginative possibilities. I think we often construe imagination as humanly concocted hopes and wishes, a kind of dreamy, wistful maybe in the by-and-by. Given our understanding of the divine origin of creativity, it's simply impossible to view imagination as anything but a tool God has given for realizing potential ministry initiatives not yet even dreamt of. One of Adam's first actions in the garden was engagement with imagination. Imagination as we've used it here, being sourced by the triplicate mirrors, is part of leadership paraklesis and the source of the "what ifs" for the local ministry context.

The Best Is Around the Corner

We constantly say the best, most effective ways of doing ministry have yet to be imagined. The most creative ways to reach people haven't been seen in the mirrors yet. What if the most outlandish and yet successful outreach initiatives have yet to be considered? What if the most potent service design that connects people with God to allow them to interact and cut a new path that will be the next standard in your context has yet to be dreamt? What happens if the day of major "models" of worship services is over? What if every church willing to glance at the three mirrors creates models truly indigenous and not susceptible to comparative description? What if holographic projection is a dominant instrumentality in the next wave of what God wants to do? What if the next wave of meetings are in the main auditorium around a computer terminal after a ten-minute talking head drops a nugget for study, discussion, or prayer?

These are "what ifs" focusing on the service of worship, but there are a hundred other areas with hundreds of other "what ifs" begging for expression. The most helpful "what ifs" will come dancing off your apostolic, prophetic, and poetic mirrors. And yet these are far from just human inventions. They may be discovered on an off-site day with a staff team or at a Starbucks brainstorming session, but kaleidoscopic imagination is a divine enterprise.

InnerAction

1. How curious are you? Is it a dominant stream in your life?
2. Do you and your team react, respond, or create tomorrow?
3. How is the visioning process for your tomorrows accomplished?
4. In looking at the three mirrors, which one do you need to pay more attention to, and what will you do to ensure that happens?

5. What will you do to convince your team that the best ideas have yet to be thought up, the best ministry model yet designed, the best way of reaching and growing people yet uncovered? Can this be inserted into a church's DNA?

Endnotes

1. Three authors I know of mention this. Leith Anderson mentions it in passing. Leith Anderson, *Leadership That Works: Hope and Direction for Church and Parachurch Leaders in Today's Complex World* (Minneapolis, MN: Bethany House Publishers, 1999). Gary Wills develops this idea through excellent biographical examples of leading national and global leaders. Gary Wills, *Certain Trumpets: The Call of Leaders* (New York, NY: Simon & Schuster, 1994). William Berquist, *The Postmodern Organization: Mastering the Art of Irreversible Change* (San Francisco, CA: Jossey-Bass, 1993), 99.

2. Permission-giving is the term Bill Easum uses for churches willing to let almost anything happen as long as it is aligned with the electromagnetic field of mission, vision, and values. *Leadership on the Other Side* (Nashville, TN: Abingdon Press, 2000).

3. My cover article in Rev. magazine was entitled "Kaleidoscopic Leadership" but developed entirely different ideas related to ethos, not vision, hence my chapter title "Kaleidoscopic Imaging."

4. Richard T. Pascale, Mark Millemann and Linda Gioja, *Surfing the Edge of Chaos: The Laws of Nature and the New Laws of Business* (New York, NY: Crown Business Books, 2000), 72.

5. Pascale, Millemann and Gioja, *Surfing the Edge of Chaos*, 72.

CHAPTER
TEN

EXPERIENCE
ENCOUNTER

God is always doing something fresh. The question is are we content with yesterday's moldy bread? Morphic leaders aren't just constantly experiencing a personal undercurrent of change themselves; they are also sensitive to the gale force winds bringing change on the larger landscape. Part of the role of morphic leaders is to keep things stirred up and to ask uncomfortable questions frequently enough that God's voice can be heard speaking in fresh ways through fresh voices charting fresh directions.

One of those questions we've been asking recently is where are the fresh, new ways of connecting God and people? The question emerges from bread on the verge of molding. The "contemporary church" for the last two decades has been largely locked into a model of worship that has nearly calcified. How can "contemporary" and "last two decades" occur in the same sentence?

What's fresh in our worship format for the last twelve or fifteen years? We've seen new worship songs emerge during that time. More churches use video and drama and even continue to mix up those elements with music and message week to week. But that has become rather expected and has emerged as a whole liturgy in its own right. We used to pride ourselves on the moniker "contemporary"; that, too, is looking a little green.

I think I first heard Erwin McManus say he didn't like the term postmodern because it's simply a description of what we aren't, and it keeps us tied to the previous movement. As usual, it's a great insight from Erwin and one we should take a cue from. What is this new age then? I suggest we're entering the Aesthetic Age.

People like Bill Easum and others have chronicled the vast similarities between the 1C and 21C. Bill says we're entering a pre-Christian era. Len Sweet says his goal is to "demodernize the Christian consciousness."[1] We hear statements that we're post-literate, post-Christian, and postmodern. I think Easum is right. We seemingly have lots of overlap with the first century, the birthplace of aesthetics. I like the Aesthetic Age for a lot of reasons.

Our world is moving past Gutenberg. In the good old tradition of "posts," we could say post-Gutenberg. The observation isn't mine but can be found in almost every volume written about church ministry in our emerging Aesthetic Age. The implication this has for how people come to know and experience truth has simultaneously ancient tonalities and technological ones.

We're moving to a world in which the printed page is being replaced by the Web page and the linearity of text is being replaced by the hypertextuality of image streams and word bytes collated from various corners of the world. Technology has always shaped our spirituality. When the printing press hit the primarily aural culture that relied on the four S's of storytelling, sculpture, scent, and stained glass, it invited a heads-down approach to God, making much of finding God in the words. With our heads down, we've actually missed much and have shaped expectations that are linear, spectator, and informational.

Technology has always shaped our spirituality.

Going Mental

The advent of text brought several developments that may be seeing adjustments in our time. The enlightenment, with all its cognitive and rational focus, raised communication to highly deductive and propositional models of learning. The church was no different. Read the sermons of the Puritans, the Wesleys, or Jonathon Edwards, and we've entered into the acute mental world of propositions and doctrinal astuteness.

The same essential model holds sway today. The main event in almost any worship service is a talking head segment that usually takes about half the gathered service time. The rest of the space is filled with a variety of elements depending on the flavor of church. We're quite safe to state that the model is designed to explain to people how to get to God, what to believe about God, and all the principles about a relationship with God. If people perchance experience God in a gathering like this, it's a bonus.

Some say to suggest anything other than this is to diminish the primacy of preaching and the role of God's Word in the church. Such a statement only confirms modernist enlightenment moorings, not biblical ones. We've again run up against one of those areas in which the church has made sacred her methods but with little or no biblical warrant for doing so. To say these methods help us achieve biblical ends may be true enough, but to sanctify those methods as if they are biblical runs close to idolatry.

Reflect with me on how people "come to Christ" in our churches. We claim that Christianity is about relationships, not rules. But we introduce people to Christ through a set of rules or at least propositions. Then we wonder why people don't understand the relational basis of their walk with God. Think about this. The average person coming to Christ in the typical evangelical church is asked through an act of his or her will to mentally subscribe to four or five truths: "You're a sinner. You should pay for your sin. Jesus came and lived a perfect life. He died the death you should have died." Those are the types of propositions where we seek mental affirmation. Believe those propositions, raise your hand, ask for forgiveness, pray this prayer, and, *voilà*, you're in. You may claim that's a bit cavalier and shallow for how the process really happens. I disagree. I speak as an insider on this. I'm in no way taking potshots at a tradition outside of my own. The personal decision model of evangelism is the one I've dominantly subscribed to as a church planter and lead pastor for over fifteen years.[2] The process described is a rather fair depiction of how things really work in hundreds and hundreds of churches.

Now I'm in total agreement on the truthfulness of each of those statements, but the whole model of the "appeal" is no doubt extra-biblical. And while I say that, I say it softly. I hear with frequency the question "Do you present the gospel here at Westwinds?" Subtext? "Do you go through the 'gospel presentation' as we understand it so people can get saved?" In some circles, this has become a litmus test of orthodoxy. Yet it's clearly not found in Scripture.

Much of Evangelicalism felt Romans was too long, so we created the Cliff's Notes version called the Romans Road—something a bit easier, briefer, and more usable for our "gospel presentation" purposes. I want to suggest that's more a collision of our modernist rationalism and evangelical boundary setting than it is careful extraction of biblical models of evangelism.

Process or Point?

The model proposed by Jesus was much more "process"-oriented. No doubt the process had to eventually issue forth in a surrendered life, but Jesus invited the disciples into an experience first. I began to be troubled by this a few years ago when I asked what Jesus would think of our "getting people saved." Even more troubling to me was Jesus' own method—a sure sign I needed to make some adjustments on the topic. He simply invited the disciples to hang out. Way too relational for most modernists. Where was the doctrinal and expositional message from the Old Testament? Where was the clarification on the God they were really following?

Jesus knew that if he hung out with these guys, over time their lives would change. Jesus would slowly raise the stakes, and they would either continue deeper in relationship with him or abandon the enterprise. Experience preceded explanation; relationship preceded doctrinal training; encounter with the transcendent preceded exposition about the transcendent.

In our experience as a church, this has been true over and over again. Experience is what finally led to surrender. Take a current work in process. Tad came because his wife attended. He checked things out and got intrigued—intrigued by the fact that he was moved...intrigued by the fact that there were credible people there he knew and respected and there seemed to be something going on in them...intrigued because week after week he had heard someone's story through a media clip or in the lobby and the whole "church is unbelievable" began to evaporate into "this may be credible." Tad decided to try a small group. This was a big step. He wasn't a Christian and didn't want to be buttonholed, but nine months into the experience, things seemed rather safe. Now Tad has heard tons of FaithStories from his small group friends.

Jesus knew that if he hung out with these guys, over time their lives would change.

What's happening in all this? Tad is having bits and pieces of God's story mediated through the personal stories of dozens of people, and the realness and authenticity of it all makes a dent in his life. We're now two years into this with Tad. He's in process and closer to Jesus than ever. Where exactly is he? Again, who knows but God.

I used to take lots of stock in raised hands or walked aisles. But my suspicions were confirmed when, after fifteen years in the same place and lots of careful questioning, nearly all people raising their hands in one of our services (we don't have people come forward) were not actually coming to Christ at that time. They were on either end of the experience. Some were acknowledging with a raised hand that something was going on in their hearts, and they wanted to affirm it by saying, "I'm experiencing the presence of God. I understand what I'm hearing, so I want to affirm it."

Some were on the other side. They were saying, "I've been here nine months. At first I didn't believe any of this mumbo jumbo. But you know what? Something happened in the last several months. I don't know when or where it happened, but I do believe all this about Jesus and what he did for me. So I guess I'll raise my hand."

Directional Heading

For some people the thought of not knowing "who's in and who's out" is exceedingly unsettling. But Jesus seemed less concerned about that than about making sure people were heading the right direction. The rest was up to God. Only God knows a human heart. Raising a hand doesn't make it more certain. God doesn't need that from us. I'm relatively certain that if we needed the Romans Road in Romans Road form then we would been given that form. Experiencing God is where it begins, and it's our job to mediate those experiences.

IMAX on Mount Sinai

Explore Israel's experience when they came out of Egypt, or their IMAX, Dolby Surround Sound event at Mount Sinai. Instead of Israel having propositional truth about God and then hopefully an experience, it had exactly the opposite. The Israelites had full aesthetic and ambiance art as they were encountering God on the mountain. It was something so powerful it would make George Lucas and his crew at Industrial Light and Magic weep.[3] Apparently, God's stage props team pulled off such convincing thunder and earthquake effects that people were fearful—fearful enough to say, "Mo (they preferred one-syllable nicknames in 1600 BC, I think), you go. We'll wait right down here." After their divine IMAX theater experiences, whether you look at the Red Sea event or the Mount Sinai encounter, then and only then do you see explanation and propositions forthcoming.

Many other examples could be cited. How about Moses' personal DVD viewing of a fire-engulfed talking bush or being put in the cleft of the rock with full sound effects? God was concerned about the Israelites experiencing him at least as much as he was about what they knew about him. All of this is aesthetics and ambience, big and bold.

Experience preceding propositions has already met with resistance in many quadrants. We're told that experience may be counterfeited; it could lead to excess and could cause people to become emotional. My response? "And your point is?"

Of course, all of those are possible and, therefore, risky. But let's not live under the illusion that a propositional, talking-head Christianity, highly rational and full of perfunctory recitation is somehow a utopian alternative. The risk is just as severe, simply different. If we think insulating people from experience is a solution to excess and, therefore, a good safeguard, maybe we ought to rethink our control-freak tendencies.

If the alternative to experiencing God is a good head-filling of ideas and propositions—even biblical ones—then I think I will opt for the former. I know I'll be accused of overstatement here. But let me be clear. I'm not saying we don't need propositions or biblical truth as a standard against which to evaluate experience. But in many contexts, heads are filled but there's no experience. For that I'm deeply saddened.

We need to lead people into an experience with God and then help them understand what they're experiencing.

I had one old-time Westwinds attendee nearly come unglued when I introduced this basic idea from the Old Testament. He said, "But, Ron, people have to have right doctrine. They have to know what to believe about God or they'll end up heretics." I pointed out that while we're enamored with dispensing right doctrine in experientially sterile conditions, spiritual questioners are out dabbling in a hundred and one opportunities to experience God. Leonard Sweet says, "If postmodern worship can't make people furiously *feel* and *think* (in the modern world the church made people only 'think'), it can't show them how God's Word transforms the way we 'feel.' "[4] I couldn't say it better myself.

We need to lead people into an experience with God and then help them understand what they're experiencing. People desire to experience something of the transcendent. Only then will they care to know more about it. Balance in all things is a good adage here, but let's be clear. If we're going to err on either side, let's err on the side of the biblical material. It seems quite clear that was the side of experience. One of Paul's concerns was that people might be more engaged and persuaded by eloquence than with demonstrations of God's power.[5] Stated simply, experience, then explanation; power, then proposition.

Deeply Moving Experiences

A few years ago, Donald Miller wrote a very important book for churches of every stripe. In it he was looking for the common elements in a host of fast-growing church movements. What did this University of Southern California sociologist conclude? Churches on the move, those that were growing and seeing people come to Christ, had this in common: They all mediated deeply moving experiences with God.[6] Our culture is craving connection with God. Only in connecting with God will people care about cognitive elements.

Our culture is clearly crying out. The rock concert is a modern worship experience that the church has often failed to provide. Only now is that being corrected.[7] Turn on TV any given night, and surf the channels until you find a concert of people weeping, swaying, putting their hands in the air, lighting candles, and singing. Looks like worship to me, just the wrong God. They're experiencing something deeply visceral that's moving them to tears. It's interactive, communal, yet still individual. There's a mystery to the whole thing. They're aurally stimulated and visually stimulated with layers of video loops (sometimes with multiple screens), the stage presence, lasers, and so on. This sounds like a good description of the Mount Sinai event or the Red Sea crossing.

For many, this analogy will be found sacrilegious. The intent, however, is to show what our culture craves and how we fail to provide it. Again, you may say the church is not to just give the screaming public whatever it claims to want. And I couldn't agree more. However, the craving to experience the transcendent is God-designed.[8] When the church fails to provide an engaging experience of God, then the seeking individual has no choice but to seek filling that God-shaped void in other ways. Far from us buckling to "consumer demands," we're raising the need to return to biblical models of experiential encounter so those looking will find.

I am sitting looking at a check stub from an Applebee's restaurant. I was recently there for lunch with another pastor from out of town. I saw Sherry, a waitress

When the church fails to provide an engaging experience of God, then the seeking individual has no choice but to seek filling that God-shaped void in other ways. there, at a distance and just waved. She had been to Westwinds three or four times over the last several months. She was absolutely unchurched in every way. She walked over and said, "Ron, I just have to tell you that Westwinds is the coolest." Mark, the other pastor I was with, looked at her and said, "Well, Sherry, give me one reason why you think Westwinds is the coolest." I am thinking, "Oh, no, what is she going to unload to this out-of-town friend?" She quickly replied, "I could give you ten! Let me deal with this table over here, and I will be back in a minute." Sherry returned later with "10 Reasons Westwinds is the Coolest" written on a check stub. Simply put, Sherry had experienced people who knew God, and she had been to services where the incidence of her bumping into the presence of God was so probable it had become inescapable. She is still in her searching mode.

A good deal of this movement back to the experience of worshipping God artistically is our drive to return to the most basic murmurings in our Spirit. In the chapter on "ideagraphy," we talked about people automatically and naturally differentiating themselves, expressing their creativity, and being interested in art. From varieties of music, art, clothing styles, eyeglasses, architecture, interior design, haircuts, piercings, tattoos, and car selections, the list is nearly endless of all the things from which we can choose to create a differentiated self.

While we're already unique, we assume it as a divine right to shape and express that uniqueness through all sorts of exterior props that make life the rich and variegated experience it is. This is a powerful observation. Some people I know who are most outspoken against creativity in the church deeply affirm other areas of creativity such as symphony, opera, or Renoir.

So the issue isn't so much creativity, but it's creativity I like. Creativity is a neutral medium. It simply is. You can't say *that* is good creativity and *that* is bad. All you can say is I don't prefer this or that expression of creativity. Some people prefer the powerful brass of Shostakovich; others the delicate piano of Jim Brickman. But no one would say one is good creativity and the other bad.

Cloning Mecca

Our culture is looking for experience across the board. This is no reason to simply jump on the experience bandwagon, but there are sufficient hints in Scripture to cause us to rethink and recast our head-heavy models. I've no desire to set forth a paradigm of worship. Every time someone articulates what they do in a particular area, the cloning rush begins. Whether we speak of contemporary modernist church Meccas like Willow Creek or Saddleback or the emerging church models like Solomon's Porch, Graceland, or Warehouse 242, our goal is not to suggest cloning or copying. And I think that bears repeating. I know leadership in every one of the churches just listed. None think you should clone them, even though some churches have clearly tried.

We must come back to the place where Christianity is a missionary movement. There we study the culture; understand the metaphors, stories, and language of the culture; and then faithfully translate the biblical message and experience into something that's understood and relationally entered into. The need for this missions emphasis has never been more important.

If you care about effectiveness, the tremendous diversity from community to community makes the issue of indigenousness simply nonnegotiable. We can't talk about what works in the Midwest or rural settings or metro areas. Such designations that appear to be helpful assume that there is some agreed-upon collection of shared assumptions and **One-size-fits-all has become one-size-fits-no-one because it was meant to fit everyone.** contextual similarities. Those kinds of monolithic labels and assumptions are dying with the world of modernity. One-size-fits-all has become one-size-fits-no-one because it was meant to fit everyone.

Our God is a God of experience. Knowing that, what are some of the next steps to take in this Aesthetic Age? We're constantly trying to figure out a better way to help people experience God and, at the same time, allow the first-time visitor the safety to bail out or not participate.

A Desert Encounter

We're currently doing some experimental worship that is stretching our previous conceptions about a worship gathering. Picture our most recent Encounter.[9] Four of us responsible for core-idea generation began incubating an idea. I was working through the Gospel of Mark and really felt God prompting us to use the desert theme of Mark as a potential point of departure. The team talked about the interesting usage of the word *eremos* in Mark's Gospel. Several different English words are used to translate the Greek word *eremos*. In the first chapter of Mark, John the Baptist is in the desert. Jesus is tempted in the desert, but the text also notes that the angels minister to him in the desert. Several other times in the gospel, Mark records Jesus going to "solitary places" or "quiet places" after he experienced intense ministry. Each time, the word used is *eremos*. For Mark, the *eremos* isn't simply a desolate, arid, forsaken place. It's also a place of provision to which Jesus intentionally returned. The team began to dialogue about how this might take shape for a worship Encounter.

Our design goal for each Encounter has several components. We believe all worship experiences are moment collections. We feel our job is to mediate through that moment collection a set of activities that will hopefully increase the incidence of participants bumping into the presence of God.

There are several things to note about this philosophy of worship. We've definitely been influenced by the work of Donald Miller. His "mediating deeply moving experiences with God" had one of those haunting qualities the first time I heard it. I simply haven't been able to escape it. As mediators of experience, we don't pretend to control, bring about, or predict how God will be experienced. We don't need to invite God to a worship gathering as is so commonly done. God is always present with us.

The question is are we aware of his presence? Awareness is crucial. Each element needs to "heighten the odds" of creating space for God to touch, heal, move, speak, blast, or do whatever he wishes. Quite humbly, we come to the task of recognizing that our role is to simply create environment, to be space designers, to be moment architects.

Space Designers

I think the theology of space is foundational to our experience of God. I intend the ambiguity with which the word *space* is used. There is space in music, space in buildings, space in worship, and space in our lives. In creation, God not only created something out of nothing; he also created space out of nothing. The shroud of darkness over the face of the deep was punctured with light. It was then punctuated with space against which the rest of creation could be seen and identified. Without light and space, there's nothing else, and there's no way to see. Space and light bring structure to creation. They bring the same to our lives and to our worship with God. We need as much "space" in our worship of God as we do activity. We *are* space designers.[10]

Our Encounters are community designed and built. While we have a small administrative and idea team, those ideas are embellished upon, and the execution of prop-building is done by a rather large group of volunteers. In terms of our monthly goals, we're trying to decidedly alter the feel month to month. Essentially, that means varying everything from auditorium configuration and seating to coloration and staging, scent, poetry, digital art, tactile props, and "lobby as prelude to the experience." These are all up for discussion and design. We almost always have a one- or two-word phrase for each Encounter. Hands, Pendulums and Fire, Water, Hungry, Bask, Online, Restore, Vibrant, Infuse—these are all themes we've recently done. You can see that we try to land on themes that are not "spiritual" (but actually are). We want people to instantly connect when they walk in and see the auditorium. They need to instantly know what the evening is about—something real and authentic they face, deal with, need, or struggle with.[11]

The idea team landed on the word *eremos* for this particular Encounter. It gave it more of a mystical feel and made the experience more memorable. I created a digital art title cell with a single set of footprints in sand and placed the word *eremos* so it looked like someone had actually drawn it in the sand. The team decided we would try to have one simple but massive prop this time: an actual desert! Sometimes we do exactly the opposite and attempt sensory overload where we design multiple props and have a tremendous number of visual layers divergently going on. We had the prop leader figure out a way to build an "authentic desert" inside the auditorium. We wanted it to be as massive as was practically possible. This would be more convergent; one prop supported by media.

Forty people with wheelbarrows and shovels converted our empty auditorium into an authentic desert (we have movable seating). They had a section about eighteen feet wide right down the center from the doors all the way to the stage. The desert mounded two to four feet in places. Cacti were brought in and planted throughout the desert. (They were borrowed from a local florist.)

Layer Upon Layer

Interactive elements in addition to communion are always a priority. For this we decided to have people remove their shoes in the lobby. (This was optional, but 99 percent did it.) Each person was given a smooth stone. No explanation was given as to what they were to do with the stone. As they walked in, ambient music was going and an oil named "Earth" was burning to give it an earthy scent. On our large center screen was a slow-motion, close-up video loop of bare feet walking through desert sand. On our side screen was the *eremos* title slide. As the participants entered, they also saw eight separate communion stations embedded in the edge of the desert sand. Eight separate sisal mats created kneeling communion altars. Each space had a large earthenware bowl sunk in the sand for communion juice, along with large woven rugged baskets for bread chunks.

Capture the elements people experienced just as they entered. Shoes off, stone given, one motion video loop with the theme quite obvious, side screen with title, scent, desert, cactus, communion stations, sisal mats, no auditorium chairs, ambient music—they were in sensory overload before we said a thing. After everyone entered and was seated, music gave way to desert wind blowing in the sound system and art slides began scrolling of all sorts of desert scenes. I climbed barefoot into the desert facing the screen and sat down in the sand so all the attention shifted back to the screen. Then I read a piece of poetry that functioned as the first three-minute message segment. The heart of it was to express how we all want to avoid desert experiences, and yet there can be some powerful things learned in this type of desolation. We made no clear scriptural allusion or application of any sort that early in the experience. We were trying to connect the environment with a personal life-issue. We were focusing on the question, not the answer.

The rest of the service moved between music, talking-head segments with Scripture, and *eremos* explanations. In this particular service, I had three three-minute talking segments. The first one was a piece of journaled reflection I wrote about how I love to avoid deserts—how arid, lifeless, and undesirable they are. After some reflective music, we unloaded the biblical nugget for a time of pondering. We looked at Jesus' desert experience. Jesus was tempted there but also ministered to by angels. Rhythmically throughout Mark's Gospel, Jesus returns to the desert for times of refreshment. I was able to biblically paint the picture of how rugged deserts feel in our lives but how important they can be to our formation. Since we are to follow Jesus' footsteps, then we really ought to see the two prongs of desert experiences. The last talking unit was an action step directed toward the interactive options they had, related to their desert experience for the evening, as well as communion instructions. We took some time to explain how we were going to do communion and what they were going to do with the smooth stones they received when they came into the auditorium. The stones represented their lives and the solitary aloneness we often feel in life. Desert experiences almost always have that effect. The stones were individual touch points for them to personalize the experience. Communion had a horizontal and vertical dimension. As they knelt on a sisal mat in the sand (we also had a rock altar built up out of the sand with communion elements that were wheelchair accessible), they brought their rocks and tossed them into the middle of the desert.

Placing your rock in the middle of the desert and watching the accumulation of hundreds of others rocks during communion was a reminder that not only did Jesus have an angel minister to him in the desert, but we also have a community we can "do life with" when things are going tough. No matter how much we feel like a solitary stone when in a desert time, we're always in the midst of a community—a community we need. The horizontal dimension made more communal what is typically very individual and private.

For the vertical, they took communion at their station. The service concluded with a bit more music. This hour and twenty-minute experience literally flew by because there was so much going on and so little talking head (only three different three-minute segments).

Worship Experience or Entertainment?

A college class from Spring Arbor University was in attendance that night for an "alternative worship experience" a class of theirs had to have. A question emerged that's worth unpacking here. One of the professors said, "Are you concerned about this just being entertainment?" I think the spirit of the question is "Do you think people will simply come to check out what the next attraction is?"

I think that's certainly possible and actually a good thing. The *Oxford English Dictionary* defines *entertainment* as "the action of occupying a person's attention agreeably; amusement." Under this definition, we want to entertain. We want to hold peoples' attention agreeably. I think this professor was concerned that entertainment implied superficial or glitzy. I think that's simply a confusion of definition. One student shared a story about growing up in her home church her whole life but never worshipping until the *eremos* experience. "I was so immersed in the presence of God that I simply couldn't help but respond; I never knew what that was like before."

Rachel and Paula are another good example of how experiential worship can really put a dent in your spirit. They were roommates who were both inquirers. They had very little religious background

We want to hold peoples' attention agreeably.

but had made a commitment to "check out some churches." The two of them had only attended our weekend Fusion service a couple of times when our Encounter was announced for that Sunday evening. They came to our Pendulums and Fire service and were blown away. Rachel said to me, "Ron, I have never experienced anything I would call spiritual, but this was so powerful that I was moved to cry." I asked what was so moving. She said, "I really do need forgiveness, and for me to see God as one willing to forgive me and to actually write the wrong things in my life down on a slip of flash paper and watch it disappear in a flame was overwhelming. I really feel like I need to look into God. I guess I need to look into Jesus a little more seriously."

Rachel experienced something transcendent. All of the details were not clear to her, but a good deal of her experience she understood and could articulate. Our willingness to help people debrief their experience through dialogue is a helpful step in the inquirers faith formation. In fact, to assist this process, we are launching cybergroups that will meet online starting one hour after the Encounter experience so people can interact about their feelings, discoveries, and learnings. We are doing the same thing for our weekend Fusion services.

Something very interesting has happened with these Encounters. We originally thought these would be for our believers a kind of in-house communion time where we didn't need to explain everything we did. But we have as many guests and spiritual questioners as we do Christ-followers. Why? The experience is something our culture and our people crave.

Our weekend Fusion services are more geared toward outreach. Don't read "outreach" as antiseptic or beat people with "the gospel." When I say outreach, I mean introductory Christianity and more basic design. These are also quite experiential with incredibly powerful music, digital art, message, and even limited interactives.

We made a digital prayer altar last Thanksgiving to accomplish the same type of horizontal and vertical experience as we did in *eremos*. In the middle of the auditorium, we placed a computer surrounded by candles. At the end of the thanksgiving message, people filled out a postcard of thanks (it was already stamped so no one had any excuses). If they chose, they could lay it in a basket at the digital altar where they could type in a thanksgiving to God that was on an e-mail screen. That thanksgiving went right up on the big center screen so the thanks to God became part of the community expression.

Leading the Creative Charge

The issue of leadership creativity, I think, becomes quite clear. If we don't have leaders thinking out of the box and cultivating teams that think out of the box, how will we engage people in multisensory and interactive ways? We've done everything from large water pools to floating tea light candles, anointing oil stations to fire pits and large hanging pendulums. The sky's the limit. I can think of no better employment for God's breath of creativity than to use it to mediate deeply moving experiences with him. We must cultivate this in our own lives so we can train our teams to do it well.

> I can think of no better employment for God's breath of creativity than to use it to mediate deeply moving experiences with him.

As for the ethos question, think about this. What kind of expectancy is generated in a church, even among new attendees, when Encounter-type experiences are happening? The experience itself is phenomenal, but the overflow and residual from those monthly surprises has all sorts of benefits. Actually, these are not just big deposits in the saints who attend; there's a big credibility deposit with them as well. They know they can count on the church to do something excellent and powerful. As a result, they'll invite friends.

Remember Chad and Christina? Chad and Christina are still in process but heading closer into the kingdom. They're now regular Encounter attendees. Even though we thought this would be an experience to service the Christ-followers, it only took one time of seeing the two of them kneeling at the water pool, lighting several candles with tears in their eyes, to move me to tears. Then and there it became clear to me that this is the direction God will move worship in the next decade.

We're currently trying to make our Fusion service more Encounteresque...a bit more interactive, less talking head, more layered. The options are vast, but so is the harvest field. Morphic leaders create ethos where people want to grow and share their lives.

InnerAction

1. How would you characterize a worship service? Get your team together and try to think up as many adjectives as possible.

2. How do you feel about the "experience precedes explanation" model of worship? What kind of support biblically would you cull for your position?

3. What are the little things you could start doing right now to move worship to a more experiential and interactive experience? What will you do to ensure that the space and experience remain safe for visitors?

4. What could you do to tap a wider creative base in your church?

Endnotes

1. Leonard I. Sweet, *Post-modern Pilgrims: First Century Passion for the 21st Century World* (Nashville, TN: Broadman & Holman Publishers, 2000), xvii.

2. Personal decision is really one of three dominant expressions of conversion in our church culture and history. Scot McKnight's new book *Turning to Jesus* is one of the welcome additions to a broader and more biblical understanding of conversion using the tools of sociology. Scot McKnight, *Turning to Jesus: The Sociology of Conversion in the Gospels* (Louisville, KY: Westminster John Knox Press, 2002).

3. Arguably the greatest "effects" company in Hollywood: www.ilm.com.

4. Sweet, *Post-modern Pilgrims*, 43.

5. 1 Corinthians 2:4

6. Donald Miller, *Reinventing American Protestantism: Christianity in the New Millennium* (Berkeley and Los Angeles, CA: University of California Press, 1997).

7. The kinds of places really getting this are Warehouse 242, an intersection of arts community in a coffee house atmosphere where a rock concert is going on, poetry readings, and so on. Kurt Olheim at Pinnacle in Texas has also figured it out along similar lines.

8. Ecclesiastes 3:10

9. Encounter is our monthly meeting geared to believers (or at least we thought so). It's also where we do communion.

10. As an aside, but not too far to the side, how we design physical space is also very important. How do we design space to communicate the language of our ministry to the world of onlookers? How do we design worship space that depicts God's outrageous creativity and genius and at the same time points to transcendence instead of trendiness? How do we create space for community life to transpire in the context of worship?

11. The idea of actually designing a worship experience with the worshippers in mind shouldn't seem so novel. For the single best volume on this notion, see *Interactive Excellence*. Edwin Schlossberg, *Interactive Excellence: Defining and Developing New Standards for the Twenty-first Century* (New York, NY: The Ballantine Publishing Group, a division of Random House, Inc., 1998). Leonard Sweet says every preacher today should read this one book to improve his or her preaching. Wow!

CHAPTER ELEVEN

TEAM ARCHITEXTURE

The verbal statement by the staff of a large church where I was consulting was "We really want to see this church move forward." However, the reality of their team dynamics was one of competition, irritation, lack of leadership, and simply lack of any real direction. Their team texture was rough and prickly; not surprisingly, so was the church's.

I was recently in another church for a twentieth year in ministry celebration. The staff was getting ready to celebrate their lead pastor's years of service. I know this team, too. Their expectancy, vibrancy, and genuine affection for kingdom things made their texture plush, inviting, and very, very comfortable. Two church teams, two textures, two totally different church cultures.

Morphic leaders know that the texture of the team around them is the single most influential factor in the texture of church ethos. What is texture? Texture is the appearance, feel, or distinctive and identifying quality of something. Silk has a different texture from cotton or brick, velvet different from wax or asphalt. Teams and churches also have textures. The way and with whom we build our teams creates a certain feel within our team and within the church at large. The "building" of teams and leading them to "feel" come together in the word "*archi-texture*." The feel, the flow, the expectancy, the level of excitement about God, the intensity of prayer, the creative initiatives attempted—all these hinge on the right team in the right slots. In Jim Collins' latest volume *Good to Great*, one of the few characteristics separating the merely good from the great leaders is the ability to get the "right people on the bus" and then to get them in the right seats on the bus.[1]

The Right People on the Team

How do you create the right team? How does staff focus on the big stuff? How do you source the team and keep things fresh? What about spreading the leadership culture? How do you do that? These are common questions. I had them early in ministry and still get asked them all the time.

Answers to nuts and bolts questions like these are tough to find in the resources we can run out and consult. I think a good reason for the dearth is simply that there are no obvious guidelines, cut and dried rules, or accepted standards on how all this works. Much of it is context specific, has denominational guidelines, or is assumed to be intuitive. All senior leaders learn to pick their way through this minefield in the hopes that with some spotty mentoring here or there, they'll avoid any explosions. My experience was exactly that: hopes of survival with some mentoring encouragement along the way.

Enviable Environment

Being in a church plant brings with it some obvious start-up challenges and headaches. But the tremendous latitude and opportunities in a nondenominational plant far outweigh the downsides. One of my written goals early on was to create an enviable staff environment. I wanted to create such a great learning environment, such a fun feel, such a place where God was so obviously at work that the average person would say, "Man, I'd love to be on that team." To be honest, I don't know what my motives were in writing that goal years ago, but it has remained a priority for me. Church ministry ought to be a great ride.

If we really love what we do, if we're called to it and aligned with the mission, vision, and values of where we serve, why shouldn't that be a blast? If those three things—loving what you do, being called, and being locally aligned—aren't your context, do yourself and everyone else a favor: quit! Without those three in place, longevity in any context is impossible. Even one of those out of synch will, at the very least, lead to dissatisfaction and will probably have you constantly looking for the next job. Neither of those dispositions is optimal for serving the kingdom and leading God's people.

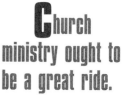

Church ministry ought to be a great ride.

While we'll start with the first obvious team in a larger church, the staff, many of these things can easily apply to the board and unpaid servant team of leaders. With no exaggeration, it can be said these three teams will make or break the whole church. This is the fountainhead of the leak. A major misalignment in any one of these, and you will have headaches.

From the very outset, we can say the issue of values alignment is a make-or-break enterprise with anyone on the team. From staff to board, from unpaid servant leaders to partners of the church (our term for members), if you have a lack of buy-in and alignment with the mission, vision, and values of the church, you're eventually going to have issues surface. Of course, this assumes you're crystal clear about your mission, vision, and values and align your programs, hiring, and initiatives around them. While this seems obvious on the surface, it's not in practice. I can recount a half a dozen stories of church fiascoes due to staff not aligned with the mission of the church.

Since our mission is just a rephrased and shortened Great Commission, most people give buy-in fairly easy. "Leading people to full life development in Christ" is our one breath effort at crystalline clarity. There's an elegant simplicity about that phrase, and it motivates all of us to want to be the best in the world at it. Every word is pregnant with meaning and freighted with mandate. New hires have to love this and own it. The same thing is true with our vision statement and four core values. These have to be deeply owned and modeled, or alignment will always be a problem.

While the mission statement is something that anyone in Christian ministry should be able to affirm as a kind of universal mission because it's based on the Great Commission, the vision statement is very different. The vision is the distinctive "how" of our mission. The Bible is quite clear. Vision emerges in the context of a personal encounter with God. As a result, all visions have a personal dimension. As such, visions are highly specialized and flavored. We seek to accomplish our mission through creative means, contextual understanding of culture, and a rigorous pursuit of intellectual credibility to answer the hard question, and to do it all in a caring environment.

In a multiple-staff church, the staff team is clearly the most important organism in communicating the mission, vision, and values, as well as the imaginative "what ifs." Injecting a steady stream of talent here sets the whole tenor and trajectory of the church. Care needs to be exercised in the team-formation process. While I don't want to spend a lot of time on the staff acquisition process, when it comes to team discussions at conferences, it's one of the top questions. "How do you hire? What do you look for?" There are few easy answers, but there are some broad handles we can discuss.

Remember the C's

Four C's help frame the basic contours of staffing interviews. *Character* stands at the head of the list. It's the first foundational piece. Things like honesty, integrity, and sound reputation are what we have in mind. You could fill in a host of things here, but little probably needs to be said.

There are a couple of items I do want to highlight, however. Teachability and coachability are biggies. Openness to receiving constructive criticism, correction, and feedback is critical to the ethos of any staff. In the interview process, I ask, "What are some examples of being able to receive criticism and be coached?" "When are some times you've needed to be corrected that you are willing to share?" These are helpful indicators. Without this in place, further interviewing is totally unnecessary.

In this character section, a prospective team member's walk with God fits in. What is his or her walk with God like? How is a typical time with God shaped? What are the typical patterns and practices he or she engages in? What are the other patterns in his or her arsenal of experience? I like to know what constitutes growth and health in team members' minds. I want to know if they really understand grace or if they are on the performance plan.

Chemistry

Provided the character piece is in place, we can move on to what, for some, may be a surprising second component: *chemistry*. While character is first on the list, chemistry is second and even ahead of competence. What is chemistry? It's the subjective feel of "they click with our team." We like them; they like us. They seem to fit, and the reciprocity of feel is mutual. Many will say this is highly subjective and a bit nonempirical. This is true on both counts but exceedingly important. Everything about hiring is nonempirical, other than some potential inventories that can be used. But they're only empirical for what is measured.

Hiring staff with experience is a bit like those mutual fund disclaimers: "Past performance in no way guarantees future performance." Chemistry is the intuitive side of hiring. We have a blast as a staff. We want someone who wants to join the party. Of course, this doesn't mean everything in ministry is fun or that we don't have difficult times. But this does mean our basic disposition and staff ethos is fun-loving, crazy, and basically the envy of anyone who doesn't get to have fun on the journey.

A recent volume on leadership by Daniel Goleman says one of the dominant roles of a leader is to create resonance. He defines resonance as a reservoir of positivity that frees the best in people.[2] While this may sound a bit fluffy, Goleman is hitting on what we usually label "chemistry."

My attitude on this one is quite simple. Several years ago I heard a noted author on human resource issues say, "Never hire anyone you wouldn't enjoy a whole day of golf with or wouldn't invite on your family vacation." While I don't think he literally expects us to invite staff on our family vacations, his point is transparent. If you can't enjoy them, don't hire them. This is tough to identify in simple interviewing, but it's one of the reasons we have almost exclusively hired from within or from a network of people we already knew. This obviously reduces the unknown variables significantly.

Our pastor of leadership development was not within Westwinds when he was hired, but he and I had traveled in fifteen countries of the world together over the course of seven years, so I knew him quite well. Competence was the biggest issue with him, but the other things were fully in place. To date, he remains one of the most coachable and teachable guys I know and is one of my closest friends.

Getting It Done

Competence is the next agenda item. If someone has great competence but we absolutely share no chemistry, they won't be hired. The reason? Chemistry precedes competence. Slightly below par competence you can make up for in training. Not true with chemistry. Either you have it or you don't. I learned this lesson the hard way. I hired competence ahead of chemistry early on in my ministry experience; the result was a train wreck that hurt everyone involved.

Chemistry precedes competence. Slightly below par competence you can make up for in training. Not true with chemistry.

On the other hand, when we needed more administrative support in the office, we hired chemistry well ahead of competence. We only had three full-time employees at the time and needed another for small group administrative support. When we interviewed Amy, she was all chemistry and teachability but a little weak in certain skill sets. In fact, she had never used a computer. We hired her because the basic things she needed to do were easily trainable. She did have one thing we desperately wanted, though—great people skills and chemistry. She now does all of our in-house publishing, writing, and brochures and is our director of guest services and small groups. She is coming up on her tenth year, and she's a gem.

The last major area we look for is *creativity*. We need people who love to do things different and fresh. People who don't get juiced by creativity won't enjoy Westwinds. We talked about this in the "ideagrapher" section. Personal creativity is important, so you might as well try to find it in those you hire.

There are other things you'll need to add to your hiring profile specific to your context. These will be things that bring tighter alignment with your context and culture. Simply asking yourself some blue-sky questions can get a list of traits going. What are the most desirable traits I'd look for if I could customize a person for our staff?

Personalize the Profile

Several specific things are indicators for me of good fit with Westwinds' culture and staff. Are they learners? What are the most important books they've read in the last six months? in their lives? That tells me a lot. What are their senses of humor like? Do they take themselves too seriously? Our staff has an illegal amount of fun, and we want others to join in. Notice that I said illegal *amount* of fun; that's different than illegal fun (thought we better clarify that). Are they global or local thinkers? I'm not thinking world missions here; I'm thinking if they see the big picture organizationally.

This has been a struggle for us sometimes. We want everyone to own his or her area with passion. At the same time, we need people to see the systemic implications of little movements in one area. Are they self-starters? How do they handle complexity? Do they have a good work ethic? Do they move quickly, or are they plodders? Are they allergic to mediocrity? Are they incurably curious? These are the types of things that help us check on basic fit.

Doers and Developers

The single biggest shift a church can make is to have leaders move from being doers to developers. This should be taken into consideration in the hiring process and clearly discussed. We pay people to develop others, not to do ministry alone. In a small church, it means the pastor must move from being a doer of ministry to a developer of others. This is simply a direct application of Ephesians 4. It's a very hard and painful transition, but one that must be made if the church is going to move numerically. A lot has been written about this shift in churches of 250 or fewer.

In the medium-sized church, staff has to make the same change. Again, this is another hard transition. Ideally, all staff should be hired to be people and leader developers, not doers of any significance. Of course, certain areas of ministry require this ability a bit more than others. How this applies to a staffer leading the small groups area may look quite different from how it looks to the music staffer who may have been hired for certain performance and stage abilities. The fact still remains that the shift in seeing staff become developers of others is critical.

The real home run comes when staff can convince unpaid servant leaders that their main job isn't doing but developing others. This, too, is a major shift, but if it can be placed into the very DNA of the church, it's a recipe for a constantly expanding infrastructure. This needs to develop ahead of the church's growth in attendance.

Develop, Develop, Develop

Once you have the team in place and its basic objective contoured, you have one major responsibility as a leader: develop them. I spend about 25 percent of my ministry time on developing my leaders. Help team members succeed in their areas. Encourage them toward the fulfillment of the wild "what ifs" in their ministries. Create a permission-giving environment in which off-the-wall ideas are encouraged and can come from anywhere on the team.

Two years ago in a staff team meeting, Taryn, our full time music director, had an off-the-wall idea. "What if we turned the auditorium into a jazz club for Valentine's night?" Now there is a crazy "what if." "We could use it as an outreach to provide our people a place to simply introduce their friends to the Westwinds community." The first year it was such a success that we had to have two separate sittings the following year. The key was a permission-giving environment that says if it's aligned with our mission, vision, and values, then it is fair game to consider.

What's the Point?

Whether staff leaders, board leaders, or unpaid servants, we must resource, develop, and support our teams. Our weekly two-hour staff meeting is essentially about personal development. I'm surprised how often I find staff from other places who dread staff meetings because they're simply boring information-sharing. Staff meetings need to be a time to look forward to hanging out, not a dreaded obligation.

Ministry is a challenge on a good day. We don't need to add a dreaded meeting to the mix. We start our meetings by connecting with each other. It's almost always light and often just plain funny. Someone usually has a story of some goofy thing that happened over the weekend. Our youth guy, Ed, may walk in wearing a huge wig (check our Web site for a picture of that one). In that case, discussion could go a hundred different directions. Or someone fesses up to some boneheaded move he or she recently made, and we laugh at that person's expense. Don't worry; we spread it around pretty well. Ministry is a challenge on a good day. We don't need to add a dreaded meeting to the mix.

Calendar items and major initiatives are also discussed during staff meetings, but the bulk of our time is spent in personal, biblical/theological, or leadership development discussions. Then we share where we are personally and take prayer requests. One year I wrote a weekly little nugget called a Leadership Health Habit. These were two or three paragraphs long. Each one was to be digested and discussed the next week. We talked about everything from creativity processes to systems thinking, from credibility building to spiritual temperature-taking. The variety was vast and the results remarkable. The brevity of each Health Habit, coupled with the diversity of topics practical to our current situation, made staff discussion quite lively. Everyone could find time to read and think about a few paragraphs.

We've read all sorts of books together. From leadership volumes to theology or the latest in evangelism, culture, or creativity, we'll read them for staff discussion. We read Christian and secular stuff. I want the team to be aware of the best material out there, and I want them to ingest writing that affirms our mission, vision, and values.

Our most recent commitment is to always be reading and ready to discuss one of three areas: life and time management, leadership development, and spiritual formation. This is a slightly different approach to the "let's read the same book and discuss" format. Every staff person, unannounced, has to be ready to give the rest of the staff any current learning they're working on in one of those three areas. A model like this, though a bit more intimidating, provides built-in accountability and diversity of current learning.

Those are the items usually comprising our staff times. Sometimes it's good to end the meeting by an impromptu lunch or just tell everyone to knock off at 1 o'clock for a matinee of a new flick. Staff team ethos leaks.

Team Competency Targets

The system most helpful to keep me on track with helping the staff along is what I call my staff competency targets. In my computer I have a listing of target areas I feel the staff needs to be working on and growing in. I have eight areas listed as categories. Since the automatic next question is probably "What are the eight?" let me reel them off real quick. Spiritual formation is an obvious first. Leadership/team development, mission/vision sourcing, creativity/innovation, community-building and people skills, organizational architecture/ministry models, change initiatives, and lifelong learning provide the other seven.

I use those headings as a file keeper. I constantly watch for what I think might be important resources for the staff. I have said that part of what morphic leaders do is provide resources that help the staff morph themselves. Think of this as an intentional resource system. I log articles I find, book chapters I think are helpful, Internet discussions or sites, or entire books I think are future "staff reads." I then leak those resources as necessary.

The biggest thing this has done is to give me a growing proactive list of staples for us individually and as a team. Again, your areas may be different, but I would encourage you to think about keeping a list somewhere.

Support Structures

There are a couple support structures that help staff stay focused. At the end of each calendar year, each person gets a review/planning sheet. Each year it's intentionally different with varying questions and format. The review/planning sheet is an exercise that gives staff an opportunity to reflect on the year, celebrate accomplishments, learn from the performance plan of the previous year, see their personal growth process, and draft a new plan for the upcoming year. Their performance plan is something they draft based on the questions I give them. It includes everything from big picture objectives to how they'd like to be coached in the coming year to personal growth goals such as fitness and hobbies. They also tell me what I do that demotivates them.

After they've drafted their plans, we review them together. We tweak them, adjust them, and settle on them. During the year they're encouraged to consult their plans at least quarterly. This is simply a tool to keep the big picture in front of them. It's amazing how quickly we forget something we've planned, only to glance at the sheet two months later and say, "Oops, I need to get on that one."

How do we keep the main thing the main thing?

One other little sheet is brand-new this year—staff health checks. I needed a coaching session recently with a gal who is in human resources in a very large church context. She helped me on this one. Staff pressures are constant. In addition to the product of weekly services, there are the pastoral care issues, emergencies, and all the other surprises that come in a week. Staff mission drift is easy. How do we keep the main thing the main thing? How do we stay focused on the important constellations and not the periphery? These sheets, in either electronic or paper form, ask five questions to keep us focused. They are submitted prior to each staff meeting.

Adventures in Learning

Every leader has to decide how they will develop their teams, how to broker resources to them, and how to provide learning adventures. What can you do to create team camaraderie? What can you do to raise the fun quotient? At one staff meeting, everyone walked into our conference room where there was a set of three tennis balls for each person. This was unannounced, and they had no idea what we were going to do. For the next four weeks, the entire staff learned to juggle. Now apart from this being an absolute scream, what leadership lesson could be learned from this? We had a learning experience over the next four weeks that was unforgettable. The little volume *Lessons From the Art of Juggling* provides great observations about how learning a new skill is intimidating.[3] It talks about how our conscious left-brain often works too hard when learning a new skill, but once learned, there's an interesting balance between intuitive and rational minds at work. Juggling is a great metaphor to get the two sides of our brain to function together.

Essentially, I was trying to create empathy on our team for the new people they were all training in leadership. By being put in the juggling exercise, they had to get in touch with what it felt like to do a totally new skill. They learned how over-analysis harmed their efforts at juggling and how the intuitive "go with the flow rhythm" made juggling easier. Lessons were learned, laughter was raucous, and a reproducible learning adventure was experienced.

The sky's the limit of what can be done with our leaders. We need to think out of the box. A few years ago, our staff drove a couple of hours to one of those large outlet malls that have sprung up across the land. They knew we were going, but they didn't know why until we got in our vehicle. I handed them instruction sheets which simply asked them to observe certain things in the mall—things like how they separated space, flooring and ceiling changes, color scheme shifts, music changes (did different music in different locations go with any of the other changes?). They were asked to carefully investigate how public congregating space was designed. What about the mall's computerized information kiosks? How and what did the mall do with its main staffed information center? What was its purpose, and how was it designed? How did it feel? They were asked to carefully note the food court design and layout—differences in seating, lighting, kids' space, decorating. How were those similar or different compared to the rest of the building? How did stores make physical outcroppings architecturally into the corridors, and what was their purpose?

Our little observation trip was five hours of observation, a stop at the Ben and Jerry's counter, a free lunch for all, and a parting shot at a coffee bar. The point? How does space make us feel? How does space define experience? How do the layers and textures of audio and visual cues define our experience unconsciously? We were moving into our new building and wanted to think about our space and how we could learn from the experts about feel.

The "Necessity" of Team Time

Now was this necessary? That depends on how you define the word. It was a tremendous learning tool. The team was invited to look at the world in a way most of them had never even considered. Their lives are forever enriched by it simply because they were asked questions they'd never asked before—questions they'll ask in other contexts again and again.

The byproduct was great team time. As usual we laughed our heads off about inane observations and crazy things we did to each other. We shared a meal and created bonds that couldn't have been fostered at the office. Trips like these are worth every minute and dime. And by the way, it seems that Jesus did the same. How often did he jump off the road to another town and soak a line with the disciples and have a fish fry? Were they simply engaged in deep Hebrew exegesis of the Torah? Or discussing the finer points of Stoic or Epicurean philosophy? I rather doubt it. They were having team time, bonding time, get-to-know-you time, and let's-laugh-our-heads-off time.

Trips like these are worth every minute and dime. And by the way, it seems that Jesus did the same.

Off-site days are full, one-day times away from our office when we go to plan, dream, or work on some brainstorming time. This is different from a learning adventure. We usually do reading ahead of time and have some definite issues we're trying to solve, get on the table, or learn about. We do one of these every four months or so.

I remain amazed at the number of pastors and nonprofit executives who claim that such adventures and off-site days are simply too expensive in time lost from the office and in money to pull them off. These pastors and leaders are profoundly wrong on both scores. There are plenty of low-cost ways to do this. Our off-site days are in the lobby of some big hotel or on someone's donated pontoon boat. The mall trip cost gas and lunch.

In terms of time lost from the office, it's actually time well invested. The refreshment and bonds created contribute to teamwork and a culture of excitement for weeks. The moral of the story is don't be stingy; you'll reap what you sow.

Volunteer Sourcing

The most important thing we do to source and vision our volunteers is our monthly leadership training event called Frontline. Over 120 unpaid servants attend—those who lead or apprentice to lead a group or a ministry area. These are the leaders on the front lines of ministry, and this is the way we try to keep them fresh. Only Frontline leaders can attend. One of the ways we've created a leadership culture is by keeping Frontline closed to anyone except leaders who pour it out week in and week out.

Another way we affirm their leadership each month is by giving any insider information that hasn't been given to the congregation yet. New building initiatives, mission possibilities, new ministry launches, staff situations—these are all given to them first. It's a quiet reminder that they are leaders. We allow them to be part of any staff discussions or initiative deliberation we may be involved in.

We give awards monthly (usually wacky ones), just simple acknowledgements of a job well done. Sometimes they're designed to simply help us laugh at a staff blunder or some church idiosyncrasy.

The main thing we do is train and equip the leaders. From personal spiritual formation and freshness to learning to delegate, train an apprentice, or become more personally creative, we try to cover a host of things.

In addition to a skill as the focus of our training, I always do a little road charting—a charting of our current course, the next mile markers to watch for, and reminders of our destination. We try to be as motivating as possible. For me, it's the highlight of the month. We've also had meaningful times of pause from training to simply share impromptu war stories or times of foot-washing and prayer.

The board at Westwinds is an incredible team. They are so behind training and sourcing it that they put up half the fee for a major leadership training conference for anyone who will be a first-time attendee at the conference and is a Frontline leader. This is just one more perk of leadership.

Conflicting Reports

Few things are more universally experienced in ministry than conflict, and with it often comes poor conflict resolution. The leak of leaders is critical to the ethos and texture of the church. Another way of saying it is that people are attracted to a healthy upbeat morale. Nothing can squelch good morale more quickly than poor conflict resolution patterns.

I literally sat in a consultation with a church that said to me, "When someone comes gossiping to me about 'him,' what am I supposed to do? Just tell them to stop and be quiet...to quit talking?" As it came out of their mouths, it became clear that they were having an aha experience. The entire staff felt helpless at what they all knew was an "out of control" gossip problem. They simply didn't know how to deal with it. Gossip is a sure sign that poor conflict resolution patterns prevail.

Regularly, we pause and walk through the conflict resolution policy, which is essentially a statement of Matthew 18. The staff must follow it and constantly teach it to others on their teams. We will ruffle each other's feathers, we will hurt each other's feelings, and we will sin against each other—things that happen in a fallen world. To not have healthy ways to deal with such things is to shoot ourselves in the foot.

Nothing can squelch good morale more quickly than poor conflict resolution patterns.

We require people to go to the source of the offense, lovingly tell the other of the offense, and deal with it there. Anytime someone comes under the guise of "wanting to share" with us something that's clearly an offense with someone else, we cut that person off and send him or her to the source. Matthew 18 doesn't give us the permission to build coalitions with others en route to sharing our offense with the offender.

Hopefully this gives a big picture of some of the ways we create a sense of team texture. The flavor and feel of Westwinds is largely the result of the things talked about in this chapter. Team ethos is the critical factor in church ethos. A failure to build compelling community in the team or to be able to laugh at our fumbles and foibles or enjoy the accomplishment of mission in relationship will translate to a church with the same lack. We will always teach what we know, but we'll reproduce who we are.

InnerAction

1. Do you have the right people on the bus? Are they in the right seats? If you know that someone shouldn't be on this bus, how proactive are you being about making the hard call, and how much are you procrastinating?

2. What is the dominant "feel" on your team? How does your read on the feel compare to what the rest of the team thinks? Give them the opportunity to give

feedback anonymously about their sense of the feel of the team. How does the rest of the team describe their sense of the feel?

3. What is the primary function of your staff meeting? Is the meeting a highlight or a dread of the week? What could you change or adjust to make it a huge time of development for the team?

4. What things did you read in this chapter that you need to put into the calendar to try? Don't wait. Record them in your calendar and then make them happen!

Endnotes

1. Jim Collins, *Good to Great: Why Some Companies Make the Leap...and Others Don't* (New York, NY: HarperCollins Publishers, Inc., 2001), 42.

2. Daniel Goleman, Richard Boyatzis, and Annie McKee, *Primal Leadership: Realizing the Power of the Emotional Intelligence* (Boston, MA: Harvard Business School Press, 2002), 5.

3. Michael J. Gelb and Tony Buzan, *Lessons From the Art of Juggling: How to Achieve Your Full Potential in Business, Learning, and Life* (New York, NY: Crown Trade Paperbacks, 1994).

ECOTONIC EDGES

Ecosystems are complex, self-sustaining systems. The aquatic world of the ocean is an ecosystem, as are the rain forest of the Amazon and the Everglades of Florida. Very interesting things happen at the edges of ecosystems. Where one system comes up to and intersects another, we have collision. In those overlapping edges of the ecosystem, we have the death of some organisms and the spawning and reordering of creative life in others. When the jaguar of Mexico is forced out of its habitat, its main food source—the rabbit—multiplies. When the rabbit multiplies, literally millions of acres of grasslands get eaten up and turn into desert.[1] Two ecosystems of grassland ecology and the animal kingdom have overlapped. Change in one impacts the other.

The edges of the ecosystem are called ecotones. Where the aquatic ecosystem of the ocean overlaps with the ecosystem of the geothermal vents in the ocean's floor, we have ecotonic edges. Ecotonic edges are places of risk. Death is there. New forms of life-giving opportunity also reside there. The ecotonic edges are the zones of tremendous challenges potentially leading to extinction and tremendous opportunities potentially leading to new and creative life. Think about the organisms living in this "overlap" area called an ecotone. The water temperature undergoes radical change at the nexus of those warm geothermal vents and typically ice cold depths of the ocean. What does the temperature change do to the organisms that live in either of those environments? Those used to warmth are hit with a bone-chilling blast of cold, a cold that for many will cause death. The thriving organisms of the ice-cold climate of the ocean depths are faced with potentially dying due to a fiery furnace blast. There is an alternative however. Instead of dying, what if those organisms are able to make do and innovate survival in their new environment? What if they reshape certain things in their life patterns that cause them to not only survive the ecotonic overlap but to in fact thrive in it?

We're living in a cultural ecotone. The overlap of two ages has given us the tremendous opportunity to reconfigure the medium of the life-giving message of Jesus in new and interesting ways. Or we can simply be relegated to the marginalized edge of culture, becoming one of the many options on the spiritual buffet. The overlap of modernity with postmodernity is an ecotone presenting us with the grueling options of extinction or hard thinking about how to reconfigure and redesign in a new environment. History will probably record that we are the transitional church, the church surfing the potentially innovative overlap of the two ages of modernity and whatever the next age—now usually referred to as postmodernity—ends up being called. We are the transitional church, and our goal is not survival, subsistence, or getting by. To quote the title of Seth Godin's latest book *Survival Is Not Enough*, God expects the church to play her chosen role of incarnationally intersecting this world. Survival is too unambitious.

Every generation must freshly imagine, image, re-metaphor, and rework the never-changing message of God's grace and love. This chapter will affirm our earlier developed theology of creativity and help us practically think about ministry challenges in new ways. From worship design to discipleship, the best, healthiest, and most effective ways of doing ministry have yet to be discovered. Every generation must freshly imagine, image, re-metaphor, and rework the never-changing message of God's grace and love.

Our tendency is to find someone else's video series or implement someone else's program. What would happen if we learned how to innovate, create, and design contextually unique answers to our ministry challenges? The ecotonic edges of chaos spawn new opportunities.

What are some of those new opportunities? Where can we allow our current chaos to reconfigure fresh ways of doing this thing called 21C ministry? We must come to love constant change and the hard questions that provoke it.

Menu Expansion

All organisms survive by adaptation to the environment around them. The church is no different. For decades it has thrived in a culture where it was the dominant spiritual selection on the menu and where generations had unquestioningly attended, even out of obligation. Such ease lulls one to sleep. For when attendance happens automatically and you're the primary show in town, the methods and avenues by which you get things accomplished are absolutely irrelevant to the final outcome.

The denominational church I grew up in illustrates the challenge on this front. In the late '60s and early '70s, it was a church among over 250 in the community; it had stable attendance and a balance of age groups, and it seemed to have a promising future. Many of the people there went to church because that is what you did on Sunday. In the ensuing decades, the landscape had radically changed. Denominational loyalty ranks right down there with watching grass grow as a top priority. People choose churches not based on the influence of their upbringing but based on the pragmatic question "What can I get out of this?" In addition to those two factors, the pluralistic spiritual climate has made the Christian church one of several options. Self-help books, community college meditation classes, and spiritual recommendations from Oprah all now vie for attention every bit as much or more than the typical church. The church used to have a nearly captive audience. Due to irrelevance and mission drift, the church is well off the charted course of fulfilling the Great Commission through cultural penetration. In fact, in many quadrants of the Christian church, contextual intonation might as well be four-letter words.

The linear, post-enlightenment, didactic, deductive, and mechanical is colliding with the nonlinear, narrative, inclusive, and organic. The new is simply the old with "post" in front of it because we're still uncertain what to call it. But the new postmodern world in which we're ministering is having devastating and marginalizing effects in the Christian church. With thousands of Protestant churches closing every year, according to Lyle Schaller the only other alternative is to get creative and determine how God's life and invitation must be expressed in fresh and practical ways. According to Schaller, there's a very good reason why in just one year 9,000 churches closed their doors. His opinion? Churches would rather close their doors than think and compete.[2] Thinking was too hard; closing the doors was easier.

If the church isn't living on the edge, it's taking up way too much space. What are we to do in this context? We have the option to become risk-resilient and change-ready or to die a slow and ugly death. Here's where all the creativity of a team comes into play.

The world into which we have been invited is a world impatient with tired and withered expressions of Jesus. Morphic leaders must be ecotonic experts. We must rise to the challenge to understand what new, creative ways the church can offer the message of Jesus that will survive the collision of two worlds— the old of modernity and the new of postmodernity. Morphic leaders believe this current context is an opportunity. Morphic leadership teams are convinced that the best ways of doing ministry have yet to be discovered, and major mental map rewriting will probably take place before everything is said and done.

If the church isn't living on the edge, it's taking up way too much space.

Honestly Now...

One of the characteristics of truly great organizations is the ability to be brutally honest about the facts. We can never get to our destination unless we're brutally honest about our current location.[3] Leaders of the morphic sort have a built-in GPS for where the church is really sitting at any given time. The reality is that the church for far too long has misapplied Scripture and ignored Jesus' clear words.

We must look at the facts. Faithful proclamation has often been held up as the goal and mandate of the church. Far too many times, this has been construed to mean just preach the message and the results are up to God. Passages like 1 Corinthians 4:2 are then quoted in support. Faithfulness under this reckoning has absolutely no indicator to identify faithfulness. How can you have no Great Commission results and claim "faithfulness" for what you're doing? Jesus said the fields are ripe and ready (Matthew 9:35-38). The problem is not one of harvest readiness but of the harvest tools we are using. To simply sit in an unripe field and attempt harvest month in and month out under the guise of faithfulness is maybe better characterized as foolishness. The image of farming that Jesus uses is apt. No farmer would ever spend one second trying to harvest in a field that isn't ready for harvest. He would do one of two things: He would prepare for an eventual harvest—for us, engaging in spiritual conversations and relational interchange, observing signs that preparation was progressing—or he would move to other, more ready fields

Honesty means really doing what Jesus said: Make disciples, and teach them to obey. There is no faithfulness where those two things aren't going on. Bill Easum says in *Unfreezing Moves* that faithfulness must be defined by whether the church is in mission...mission as defined by the Great Commission.[4] No fulfillment of the two prongs of the Great Commission, no faithfulness. To say preaching the gospel is "faithful" is to simply misread Matthew 28:18-20. Jesus didn't invite us to preach our heads off. In fact, the word *preach* isn't used in the text.

Jesus gave us an outcome-based indicator that could demonstrate our effectiveness very easily: make disciples. More disciples and better disciples are the goal...not proclamation. I think this misunderstanding is largely responsible for our informational transmission love affair. We often feel that we have accomplished our God-given mandate if we just make sure what we say is "biblical." Unfortunately we've defined "biblical" as good textual exegesis. But most of the time, we've left cultural exegesis behind.

I have been in my share of conservative Bible-believing churches where careful biblical exegesis was reflected in the message communicated from the pulpit. Few seminary

Without careful biblical *and* cultural work, we'll never faithfully translate the message into the target culture we are attempting to reach.

homiletics professors would find a gripe with the message and how it was unfolded from a biblical perspective. But when it comes to communicating that message in the context of our current culture, many of these messages entirely miss the mark. The problem is that they continue "to preach the Word of God" so they say, but the Word of God is miscommunicated and not faithfully rendered when the culture to which it is spoken doesn't understand the categories, Christian-ese language, and in-house slang we use in most of our churches. A person in our culture today, without any background in Bible stories or Christian language, has no better chance of understanding the typical pastor than the audiences I speak to in Asia or Eastern Europe have of understanding my English. Without careful biblical *and* cultural work, we'll never faithfully translate the message into the target culture we are attempting to reach.

The most helpful advice I ever received on this front was a pastoral friend saying to me, "Ron, go sit in a bar or in the middle of the mall, or go to the bus station, and write your messages there. Ask if that single mom with three kids tagging along would have any idea what you were talking about if she showed up this Sunday with no church background." When we begin to put ourselves physically in the locations of the people we claim we are trying to reach and begin evaluating our message topics, language used, and action steps given from the point of view of their eyes and ears, our weekend talks will undergo a radical change. I am so thankful for that instruction. It changed the entire trajectory of my speaking.

What Is Really Sacred?

What is sacred in our ministry? When you ask questions like that, you have to know what is genuinely up for grabs and what can't be touched. Here's your first step in wrestling with this new era we have entered. What can you modify, change, dismiss, or destroy? Where are there sacred cows that need tipping?

Risk resilience is the ability to look at risk and, without aversion to the pain of change, be able to say, "If this furthers the mission of the kingdom, then whatever it takes, we will do it." A pastor from northern Michigan was recently visiting us because his daughter who was attending a local university attended Westwinds. He walked out of our weekend Fusion service and said, "This is exactly what I would like to do. This is what I have dreamed of doing, but the biggest risk the church I serve has taken in the last five years was changing the color scheme of the church sanctuary, and that took months of meetings to get passed through." He was saying we have no risk resilience; the cost in terms of the pain of change is just too much to venture out into the unknown waters of risk.

I have a large, clear, glass cylinder filled to the top with water and a rock sitting in the bottom. It sat on my office coffee table for over a year. It is the image I used in one of our monthly leadership training events that was titled "Deep Water Churches." Using Luke 5 as a launching pad, we looked at the risk involved in the disciples leaving the shallow, familiar, no-risk, fishless waters of the shoreline to strike out into deep waters. At Jesus' bidding, they went into the higher risk, drowning-potential, capsizing-possible deep waters. The real key is that only in those riskier deep waters are there fish, and yet in those deep waters, there is always a solid rock upon which we can stand. Jesus has invited us to be deep-water churches, risk-resilient churches, churches where we are out in the deep risky waters with him.

Knowing what can be questioned and changed can become watershed events in the life of a church. Is it the service times? the traditional service? the altar call? the frequency of communion? Just what are the strongholds that can't be touched? We've tried very hard to create an environment in which anything can be questioned. The truth is that methods are always up for modification.

We've tried very hard to create an environment in which anything can be questioned.

The following areas have all been experiments. I'm not suggesting that you clone our efforts. But I am suggesting by giving these extended examples that you consider everything in your ministry portfolio as something that possibly needs redesign or deconstruction. The goal is not cloning but indigenous ministry, ministry that's so culturally snug that people can't help but be compelled. The whole reason for reconfiguration is to better fulfill the mission. No other reason is worth it.

Some of these are simply practical ministry issues. In the chaos of this new world, a change was warranted and is bearing fruit in one way or another. Some of these issues, though practical, have much deeper philosophical or theological implications. You may find these a bit unsettling. That's good.

Any reading you do or seminar you attend that merely affirms what you already believe should give you your money back. Real learning causes you to think about new things and old things in new ways. This is the essence of the ecotonic chaos. What feels like a threat is simultaneously an opportunity.

Membership Has Its Privileges

When people "join a church," it is almost an axiom that they now have the "benefits" of membership, like American Express' "Membership has its privileges (MHIP)." While this appears innocuous enough, it's one of the most dysfunctional notions in church circles and is reinforcing all the wrong values that we're constantly fighting against.

Take, for instance, the special relationship people think they have with the pastor once they join the church. How about hospital visitation or appointments on demand? These and a host of other things are assumed now that they are members. Pastors who have moved through the two hundred attendance barrier will remember the agony of trying to convince people that others are equally able to pray at a hospital bedside. Without the head dude present, some feel slighted. I speak from the difficult and painful transition Westwinds went through when we gave the care-giving to small groups. The question was instantly "What is Ron going to do?"

Appointments on demand are another MHIP item. We have people who think they should be able to have an appointment with me whenever they call. Any explanation as to why that won't happen and the alternatives to it are one big, hairy deal.

Now why are these problems in the local church? We've created an ethos of entitlement and codependency. We call them members, after all. But since we don't define the term á la 1 Corinthians 12, we end up with American Express expectations. Here's an example of an item in need of reshaping.

We blew up the whole membership category. We no longer have members. They don't exist. We now invite people to "partner" with us to accomplish God's mission in the world through Westwinds. If you're excited about that and want to relinquish your time, money, energy, and best creative juice, then you just come on! You're what we are looking for.

Partners at Westwinds have no special relationship with the senior pastor or staff. They have no privileges in the traditional sense of that word. They're simply saying to the other partners, "Count on me; I'm counting on you. Let's accomplish the mission in community together."

Actually, under the partnership reckoning, you lose privileges. Your time is not your own. Neither is your money or your best energy and effort. They're employed in the interest of God's mission. You want privileges? Stay an attendee and avoid partnership.

You want privileges? Stay an attendee and avoid partnership.

One Option?

Morphic leaders realize that part of their role is to question conventional wisdom to see if it yields something better...such as unconventional wisdom. For years our church had basically one goal, one option for people: get them into a small group. Groups are where intimacy happens, growth occurs, and spiritual growth takes place with a small collection of other adults. What were we thinking?! Intimacy? Growth? In a church this means we may call on you to pray! Spiritual? In a church this means Bible!

One day we woke from our stupor. Essentially, we had been giving people one option beyond our weekend meetings where well over one thousand attend. Plug into a nine-month group of intimacy where we want you to share your heart of hearts, know the kings of Israel in chronological order, and potentially drink goat's blood in an animal sacrifice. Not really, but this is how new, unchurched people think. They have no idea what happens in these things called small groups, but their imagination tells them it could be classified as *Survivor* material.

We realized that we needed to think hard about alternatives. So we began to analyze why people stay away from groups. We were living in a new postmodern world where people really crave relationships and even rawness. But would they commit to months and months? Would they be vulnerable enough to share?

We came to conclude that there were two issues at stake. One was that they wanted to belong before believing. They wanted to tire-kick before committing. We needed something less than a nine-month option. We needed to shorten the commitment continuum.

The other issue was the vulnerability/disclosure continuum. Was there a way for people to be in a setting in which there wouldn't be the expectations on them to disclose anything if they didn't want to? Again, we needed some alternatives where *they* felt they would be safe. We had been asking people to commit to nine months—a level nine or ten commitment. We were also asking them to go to a group of ten to twelve people who were mostly strangers and interact—another level nine or ten commitment. Were there any ways to get a variety of options on both scales?

So we set out to create options that took into consideration both scales. We don't do potlucks, but in the past those were a "fellowship spot" for people. So what about lobby minglers—a 21C version of the potluck? Now at the beginning of every major series of new weekend talks, our hospitality team does some very nice hors d'ouevres, and we invite people to hang out after a service. Here's an event low on both continuums. No need for disclosure unless you want to. The commitment is a one-time shot for as long as you choose. The added bonus is great free food. The response was amazing. Lots of new people were willing to hang out for an extra thirty minutes and are now known by a whole raft of people who they would have never interacted with otherwise.

You get the idea. How can we create all sort of options that allow people to slowly (if they choose) enter into various stages of the process so they can tire-kick and test-drive the whole Christian community thing. We've since launched four-week, eight-week, and twelve-week small groups. These are obviously high on the disclosure scale but low on the commitment scale. Almost across the board, people go deeper once they've tasted. We have also created more big, fun events to which people can come one time but still have some measure of interaction.

Redrawn Evangelism

The ecotonic era we're in has moved us in highly relational directions. Discussions about relational evangelism have gone on for a long time. But the way things shape up now is a rather radical departure from the sharing of yesterday. I've tried to tell plenty of stories throughout this book that show how we see the process orientation of evangelism playing out. The old method of propositional presentation is probably not going to work. Attempts at that breed more suspicion than interest.

The gospels present a radical difference in the way "conversion" is viewed. Jesus said, "Come follow me," or "Hang out with me." For the peripatetic teachers of Jesus' day, followers simply chose who they wanted to hang out with, fell into the crowd of followers, and walked around (*peripeteo* is the Greek verb for *walk*). Jesus called out to his followers to walk with him. Strangely absent is a doctrinal exposé—membership requirements or some propositions they had to buy into. Jesus knew that his presence would, over time, up the ante, and the newly enlisted learners would either slowly morph his way or would fall out of the group hanging around him and dismiss themselves.

Jesus knew presence and process would bring about personal questioning and eventually surrender. We really aren't sure when the disciples became Christians in the evangelical 20C sense of the word. When were they converted and born again? When did they cross the line of faith? Was it the moment they left their nets and followed? Was it when Jesus in John 20 breathed on them and said, "Receive the Holy Spirit"? Was it on Pentecost?

Jesus said, "Come follow me," or "Hang out with me."

Here may be a better question: Why are we even asking? Are we captive to our modernist mantra to measure, quantify, and record? Is it important that *we know* exactly when? I've earlier listed the experience we've had at Westwinds of hand-raising only telling us that people are in the process. But nine out of ten times, the ones raising their hands don't know where they are in the process. We need to be biblically careful here. While I think it's obvious that God always knows when someone passes from death to life, and we as individuals know if we have inner witness of the Spirit of God (Romans 8:16), nowhere are we told *we* will know when *someone else* crosses the line of faith.

Spiritual conversations and relationships might be better things to count than conversions, if we are going to count at all. Jesus seemed more concerned with trajectory than clear lines crossed. Every time someone seemed to think they were "in," Jesus reversed it. When someone identified someone else as "out," Jesus redrew the circle. Jesus really wasn't nearly as much into boundaries as we are. Spiritual conversations lead to trajectory alteration and further movement into the kingdom of God. "Aisle-walking" tells us nothing for certain. These are some of the new challenges on the cusp of this ecotonic era.

Holiness Boundaries

The church, like many other organisms of the 21C, needs to develop more permeable membranes at the edges and more stability and clarity at the core. I'm afraid a good deal of the time we've reversed the two. We aren't sure about the central tenets, but we have the minutiae listed.

The hoops people have to jump through to attend many churches are a joke. This is often due to a profound misunderstanding of biblical holiness and what our mission in the world should look like. The postmodern church is moving more toward a centered set of definitions instead of a bounded set. The lifestyle issues, for so long the definer and boundary marker of who is in and who is out, will fall by the wayside. Instead, the center of Jesus being Lord and Savior and the life his lordship produces as a byproduct of that relationship will be the litmus test. This is clearly a return to the ancient biblical Jesus model.

Jesus constantly challenged the external bounded set categories of the Pharisees. He told them it wasn't what you ate or drank but what came out of you that mattered (Matthew 15:11). Jesus was constantly in the company of the wrong people and was in suspicious party contexts way too much, according to the religious leaders. He was accused of being a glutton and a drunkard, and apparently the label stuck for he never denied being in the context or that his behavior may have *appeared* to religious leaders inappropriate. Jesus simply acknowledged his mission was for the sick, not the righteous.

For the religious leaders of Jesus' day, holiness was defined by a series of rules and regulations entirely independent of heart disposition (Mark 7:1-11). Those are unnecessary boundaries, says Jesus. Real holiness works from the inside out, not the other way around. You could have someone who doesn't smoke, drink, or attend R-rated movies; who reads the Bible faithfully; who attends church every Sunday morning, evening, and Wednesday night; and you wouldn't know one thing about his or her holiness. In fact, you wouldn't know if that person were even a Christ-follower.

Our postmodern context has gotten us down to the nitty-gritty. Most people outside the church are sick and tired of the plastic, fake, and artificial in the church. We need to return to definitions that really come from the Scriptures instead of the reading offered by the Pharisees. Jesus invited guys to hang out with him. I don't see any discussion of their habits in his invitation. Does that mean we don't deal with bad habits or can let sin continue? Absolutely not! But let's be sure the habits we ride and the sin we call out are really *bad* habits and really *sin*.

Our postmodern context has gotten us down to the nitty-gritty. This is simply one example where we've attempted to make the gray black and white and let the black and white go to gray. We've identified our own selected slate of boundary markers that define who is "in" and who is "out," and those outside the church see right through it all.

How does a biblical take on holiness and a more conversational invitation to follow Jesus impact apologetics? Significantly is my guess. My experience with people searching for God is one not of skepticism about his existence or whether Jesus is real. The issues are far more complex. I encounter two extremes. One asks questions: What gods are the right ones to follow? What spiritual experiences in my life are valid? How can I tell which of the voices I hear is God? The other pole is one where the approach to God is more of passive disinterest—no hostility or heat but no real investigation either.

Apologetics Redesigned

The implications these two poles have for our traditionalist rational apologetics are far-reaching. Debates about cosmology, God's existence, or the historical veracity of the Resurrection will always take place, especially in our university contexts where a kind of skepticism toward things spiritual runs wild. At the grass roots, however, those aren't the questions we see being asked in our Midwest context. We have to deal with the raw yearnings of the human spirit. Solomon said there's a God-designed, God-shaped hole at the core of humanity's very existence. The apparent intention of God's divine design was to provoke investigation of what might fill that hole. Discussion of the most fundamental yearnings of the human spirit is rich grist for the spiritual conversation bin.

More than ever, our apologetics must take seriously the Holy Spirit's work in the life of every unbeliever. In all the evangelism training we do, rarely, if ever, do I hear us unpack a through-going theology of the Holy Spirit's pre-conversion work (John 16:8-11). God is at work in the life of every person who isn't following Christ. We need to observe where God is at work and learn to engage in spiritual conversation accordingly.

The need to couple our rational apologetics with a relational focus that explores the core yearnings of a person's heart in no way diminishes the role of our traditional apologetics. Our experience is that once people are connected relationally and address some of the more pressing existential yearnings, then, and usually only then, the issues surface that we've typically dealt with.

From Sequence to Parallel

I see a whole arena that will undergo radical reconfiguration in the ecotone of the 21C. It's in the area of leadership development. Our primary model of raising up unpaid servants has been to see them come to Christ, disciple them, get them into a small group themselves, make sure they have adequate biblical knowledge (an M.Div. is desirable), give them the opportunity to apprentice, put them through some reading and training seminar material, and then determine five or six years later if they could lead an interior cleaning team. OK, it's not quite that bad, but almost.

Have you ever noted the enlistment to deployment time frame of Jesus? Now I know you could say, "But that was Jesus." Let's take a look anyway. Be reminded that Jesus only had a ministry window of three years. How much training could the disciples have had? And to say, "That was Jesus," shows a pretty low view of how we can interact with him today.

A careful reading of any of the gospels shows an exceedingly small window of preparation, one I am frankly quite uncomfortable with. Again, maybe I need adjustment on the training schedule. It appears that the disciples had a number of months of training before they were sent out, if they were lucky. Incidentally, most of the training was not in the "give me the right answers" doctrinal arena. It seems to be more in the "hands-on, practical ministry" area. He did some training and sent them out. Then they came back with stories and debriefed their experience. He then sent them back out.

What does this bop on the side of the head tell us? Our method of training is serial sequencing—one step completed, followed by another and yet another. After all, it's what we do in education, isn't it? Here is a linear timeline approach that compliments our linear modern world. Again you may cry foul as did one of my Westwinds leaders: "But you have to have some baseline minimums they must know." Yes, that is true. I readily acknowledge that much.

Here's the question, though: What are they? I suggest that in place of our serial sequencing, we need to move to a more parallel simultaneity where the leader is simultaneously learner too—always learning, getting insights previously unknown, and answers to previously unasked questions—all the while leading others.

The downside we may say is "This is messier, has more potential for problems, and is riskier." But we talk as if the sequencing **We need to** model we usually use is really healthy and functional. I don't know **ruthlessly try to** of a church that doesn't need more leaders, and yet I know in most of these contexts there are people who've been Christ-followers **model the life and** years and years and still don't feel equipped to lead. We've created our own monster on this one. We're experiencing a little **pattern of Jesus.** Hebrews 5:12ff. We have far more questions here than answers. But, wow, what a fruitful field to probe!

We need to ruthlessly try to model the life and pattern of Jesus and, in so doing, recognize that only eleven of the original twelve stuck it out. All this stuff is risky, but this is what ministry is made of. I give these as samples of our attempt to rethink the results we are getting. The processes we go through to arrive at reworked models are spirited and, at times, come with some heat.

I'm not suggesting that you must or should plow in the same furrows we are. I'm only suggesting that we must always ask the hard questions, and in a time of cultural transition, it's sometimes easier to ask those hard ones. The best ways of doing effective, life-giving ministry have yet to be designed. Morphic leaders are at the forefront of asking the hard questions at the ecotonic edges. Creative life is a possibility there. Let's not miss the opportunity.

InnerAction

1. What is the real picture of where your church sits? How can you be sure this is accurate and not simply wishful thinking? Do you have clarity on where the church is and where it needs to go? The difference in distance between those two is called creative tension. The role of the leadership team is to make the current position clear to everyone. The next job is to create tension by dramatically painting the picture of where God is inviting you to go. What's your strategy for this?

2. What systems do you need to rethink or spend some brainstorming time on?

3. What are the sacred cows that need tipping? How will you generate discussion on this without blowing up the place?

4. What are the most controversial things you read in this chapter, and what kind of feelings did it stir up in you and your team?

Endnotes

1. Seth Godin, *Survival Is Not Enough* (New York, NY: The Free Press, 2002), 18. From Greenpeace ad in the New York Times.

2. "Pastoring with Integrity in a Market-Driven Age *(Part 2)*," Leadership, by the author of Christianity Today International/Leadership Journal, 2002.

3. Jim Collins, *Good to Great: Why Some Companies Make the Leap...and Others Don't* (New York, NY: HarperCollins Publishers, Inc., 2001), 71.

4. Bill Easum, *Unfreezing Moves: Following Jesus Into the Mission Field* (Nashville, TN: Abingdon Press, 2001), 9.

PENDULUMS AND PYROTECHNIC

A million great ideas, kaleidoscopic vision, and careful team texturing are all very important, but without the ability to implement the ideas, things will go nowhere. When we talk of identifying sacred cows, that's helpful only if we know how to cow-tip without destroying the whole farm. How often can you find a pastor or leadership team that has the ideas, desire, and persistence necessary but doesn't know how to bring its board or a big faction of the congregation around?

A big tool in the toolbox of morphic leaders is the ability to morph the organism through well-orchestrated change. Such language sounds like you can follow a carefully laid game plan with guaranteed results. Obviously, that's not true. In fact, while there are some things we must do, the change game is more art than technique.[1]

Early on in my leadership development, I had a major change initiative—a total overhaul of our philosophy of ministry. We had been stymied by absolutely no evangelism during the first five or six years as a church; only nine people that we knew of had chosen to follow Jesus. Call me spiritually deep or an undiscovered genius, but something told me that nine new followers in six years didn't sound too missional. And I was totally clueless how to reverse that trend.

While a redraw of our philosophy of ministry was clearly in hand and the board was in full support, I proceeded to make a carefully orchestrated montage of bad choice after bad call after bad timing in the change process. I have learned the hard way that the proper release of information so there is a sort of incubation time allowed is critical for the buy-in of the congregation. Instead of slowly leaking to key leaders and influencers that a major philosophy of ministry change was in the offing, and maybe even sketching the contours of that, I did exactly the opposite. I kept everything hush-hush. When we came to the congregational meeting (which, by the way, we finally abolished; we haven't had a congregational meeting in over a decade) to talk about the change, it was the first pass for everyone but our board. Ouch! Huge mistake. Nobody in this scenario can help champion the cause, answer questions, or assist in building consensus. A painful lesson with indelible impact, this was one of those early learning fiascoes that was erected as a monument to ignorance in our pasts. While it isn't the only such monument that elicits chuckles today, I'm quite certain it towers the highest.

Diets or Fire?

Knowing how to implement change is just about as important as knowing what kind of change to go after. Churches suffer much like people do from attempts to make changes. At first things look like they are moving, but once the dust settles, no real change has happened. The dieting industry makes hundreds of millions a year on the idea that the vast majority of people never really experience a significant change in their lives from dieting. As a result, they will try yet another diet.

In the therapeutic world of counseling, this is referred to as first-order change. Something new has been introduced into the system, but the net result is no change. William Bergquist has written what remains one of the most insightful and thorough pieces about the impact of postmodernity on leading organizations, in spite of its decade-old age. He uses the image of a pendulum to describe first-order change. The diet starts the pendulum moving, but it always returns to the same resting spot. The movement is real, but any change is an illusion.

The alternative to the pendulum is the irreversible change of fire.[2] Therapists call this second-order change. Instead of introducing into the system a "more of the same" solution, we actually introduce or change something systemic that catalyzes irreversible change. The goal of the counselor is to help the patient identify why the tried solutions never bring about change. The counselor then offers a second-order change solution, shifting the system to an entirely different plane. God is a God of fire—permanent, irreversible, powerful change. Morphic leaders need to be pyrotechnicians.

Let's look at these two images a bit more. The pendulum has an elegant simplicity, and no matter what path its hypnotic motion takes, it returns to the midpoint of homeostasis. Homeostasis is an important term for organizations, and maybe for churches especially. It describes the built-in tendency of every living organism to act like the pendulum and seek a re-balancing and restoration to its quiet resting point. Equilibrium and homeostasis are what organisms strive to maintain.

Morphic leaders need to be pyrotechnicians.

Ilya Prigogine, Nobel Prize–winning scientist, was the first to note that not all things in nature function with this pendulumlike return to homeostasis, much as science would like it to be so.[3] Some systems resemble fire more. Something ignites, and though matter is neither created nor destroyed, with fire it has been irreversibly changed. The burned down house can be rebuilt, but it won't be the same house.

Organism Unpredictability

It's God's desire to do a new thing. He sent new manna every morning; his mercies are new every morning. Freshness is God's trademark. Living a life of homeostasis may be playing it safe, but it may also be a precursor to death. The use of homeostasis takes us into the realm of organisms.

I rarely run into a point leader or team who doesn't know what it wants to implement, whether it's a small group ministry, church name change, introduction of some art form, or the launch of a contemporary service. Most people have the "what" well in hand.

The "how" seems far more elusive. The following will focus on the "how" of the change instead of the "what." A lack of knowledge about what needs changing can't be found in a book. That's the job of church consultants. With that in mind, what are the latest understandings that can help us with the "how"?

In the last several years, a number of authors have made important connections between the discoveries in science (like quantum mechanics) and chaos and complexity theory and what these mean for our view of organizations as organisms and our leadership approach.[4] One of the more recent entries into the melee is Richard Pascale. He gives four clues about the organization as organism.[5]

Clue #1: Equilibrium is a precursor to death.

Clue #2: When a compelling opportunity is presented, living organisms move toward the edge of chaos.

Clue #3: When these new opportunities present themselves, organisms self-organize and new repertoires emerge for the new possibility.

Clue #4: Organisms cannot be directed along a linear path, precisely because living organisms are living and creative.

What are the implications? How does this impact our leading of change, and what does this mean for the process of change?

Let's look at what we can learn from the church as organism based upon Pascale's observations. The first principle related to the living nature of organisms is their tendency to crave equilibrium. The problem is that equilibrium is a precursor of death. Churches, as a rule, tend toward equilibrium. Pascale's observations are as true for churches as for any organization, and maybe even more so.

Equilibrium is often sought in churches for two reasons, one cultural and the other historical. Massive amounts of change and turbulence in almost every area of life make stability and equilibrium in at least one sphere—the church—a welcomed haven. The historical reason is a perceived need to maintain the traditional ways of doing things. There seems to be some fog on where the methods and the mission start and stop. Stability for either or both reasons is deceptively dangerous.

Unstirred waters lead to stagnation, and stagnation can't support life. Churches looking for lack of change and preservation of "what has always been" are on course with slow, creeping death. Injection of new life, ideas, freshly surrendered lives, spiritual fervor, hunger to penetrate culture, and better ways to connect people in community all lead to disequilibrium. Disequilibrium is uncomfortable, unpredictable, and chaotic—the dominant reasons people don't like it. Pascale's point is that without fresh injections, organizations will be lulled into a false sense of complacency and end up "the frog in the kettle slowly brought to boil."

Leading for Stability?

The role of leadership is probably obvious. Stability and equilibrium can't be goals. Is it possible that stability and consistency are really overrated? Part of the role of any leader is to define reality. If the reality we are seeking is life-giving freshness, then stagnation can't be an option. The morphic leader is an irritant and agitator to the system. Leaders, at the very least, must act like fuel injectors, squirting the fluid of new life into the organism of church culture, even if it means uncomfortableness for the troops. Acting as status quo agitator takes internal fortitude, clarity of vision, and discernment. All of these are inside issues. Here's where the interior life of the leader has significant implications for the process of change.

We have just undergone the most significant staffing reorganization and jockeyed more ministry descriptions than has ever happened in our history. Our team designer (executive pastor) and I rolled out these changes in a recent off-site day with our staff. The agitating quality of this shake-up will bring new life to our team, heightened effectiveness, and most of all a new organic system of cross pollination that makes living in your own little ministry silo impossible. Three days of one-on-one meetings with the key players and an off-site day with the entire staff made that week one of those long weeks when my heart and attitude and my patience level and willingness to have chaos for a transitional time were critical.

The leader must help the church understand that without new life, new programs, and new ideas, stagnation and death are around the corner. You are trying to help the church avoid the pain of death while there's still life. You are trying to help people move because of the pull of the future instead of waiting for the inevitable pain that would eventually force movement. While some may buy in here, most will want to know what those new things are and what they are going to have to give up before they buy. Here the challenge begins.

Compelling Opportunity and the Curve

Pascale's second observation states that a compelling opportunity moves an organism to the edge of chaos. For a morphic leader this is both challenge and relief. "Compelling opportunity" means the vision of tomorrow needs to be gripping, as well as clear. No one can do this job for the leader. Either you have a powerful vision of the preferred tomorrow you want to intersect or you don't. The hard part is that what one finds "compelling," another may not. There are several things leaders can do to increase the incidence of buy-in.

First, realize that the bell curve on innovation acceptance kicks in at this time. About 2 percent of the population innovate ideas, and another 14 percent are early adopters. These two groups comprise the ones you can count on from almost the first breath about new initiatives. They're addicted to change, thrive on it, live for it, and will do what it takes to help it happen. You must know who these people are.

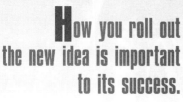

Another 34 percent are called middle adopters. They look to the early adopters, ask questions, and carefully weigh the idea before buying in. The middle adopters are a critical group because their 34 percent gets you to the critical halfway point. If you don't capture their willingness for your idea, forget it.

Second, how you roll out the new idea is important to its success. We leak vital information all the time in our Frontline meetings. What I'm doing is letting the innovators, early adopters, and some middle adopters get time to assimilate the news and talk about it among themselves before it goes public. By the time we go public with a major initiative, a critical 100+ leaders are already on board, and they help persuade and inform the rest.

In any change initiative, new idea, or change of program, people want to know two things: What do I lose if I buy in, and how does my life change if I buy in? The two are related but not the same. Clarity and careful patience here can make or break your idea. You have to be honest, clear, and ready to explain "why" ten ways from Sunday. You score no points by trying to convince people the change won't cause them to lose something.

Pascale says the compelling opportunity will move the organism toward chaos. Expect it. Plan for it. Help people understand it. The feelings of personal vertigo during change are real. Help them prepare to keep their balance by over-informing them.

Third Service and Systems

When we went to our third service, we opted for a Saturday night. The flavor would be identical to the two on Sunday morning but would give people an alternative day. Sounds like an easy one, right? Wrong! At least people could see everyone who attended church when everything was on Sunday. They might not be worshipping together, but they could connect with anyone in passing.

Saturday night changed all that. Volunteerism would also take a hit. We needed more volunteers to fill the slots of another day. Doing double duty on a Sunday was easy in a pinch, but not on another day. With more volunteers came the need for more leaders. And the domino effect continues. We need to be clear about what we lost as a church and then be compelling about what we would missionally gain.

In response to the "compelling opportunity," first we've seen the effect of the bell curve, and second, we've seen the need to inform the groups what is happening. Our third insight is that what happens on the macro group level works on the micro individual level. The information you used to help get groups unstuck and moving forward sometimes must be done with individuals. Usually, those are "must have" lunches. Don't send a representative. Any major initiative is worth your time to get buy-in from pivotal but resistant people.

New Abilities Appear

Pascale's third principle states that as new opportunities present themselves, organisms self-organize and new repertoires emerge for the new possibility. I've seen this over and over again at Westwinds and at other churches. A great idea or a new ministry launch emerges, but the "how" question comes up. "But how are we going to do it? Who has the gifts? How would it all work?"

Pascale's third observation is that because organisms are living entities, they have immense creative power. He shows tremendous faith in living matter. In the case of a church, though, we're talking about a talented, spiritually gifted collection of God-hungry, Spirit-infused Christ-followers. Surely it's not too much to expect that, as new opportunities appear, the organism of the body of Christ would "reorganize" itself in such a way that "new repertories emerge."

What a powerful insight! On one hand, it seems rather intuitive. But it's not how we think. Often it is said, "But we haven't done that before," or "But we don't do things that way." The subtext is "We don't have the abilities to do it." In the body of Christ, the starting point needs to be the God-sized dream. Then we figure out how the gifts will emerge to pull it off.

A couple of years ago, our children's department decided to do a huge summer outreach...huge for us, that is. Since we don't do the standard VBS (we don't do a "standard" anything), they needed to cook up something bigger than life. Over a period of months, they came up with "Super Cyber Summer Fest"—over two-story-tall "computer terminals" with eight-foot-wide "keyboards" that included video projection screens and large live stages, complete with live video feeds and live dramas.

Early in the planning, all the character development, complementary bigger-than-life props, and vision for hundreds of kids were simply audacious elements dancing in the kaleidoscope of what could be. How would we do it? Gifts emerged that no one was aware of. Ideas to embellish the original began to flow. Chaos struck with a vengeance (remember, Pascale warned about that), but teams came together and made it happen big.

We have Christ-followers today actively serving who decided to check out a church that would do such "out of the box" things.

At some point in time, morphic leaders must take the plunge and shift their team to the arena of possibilities. If what we *could do* isn't shackled by the past of what we *have done* or "what a church should do," then what we can do for the advance of the kingdom is overwhelming. If we thought about the "kinds of things churches do," we wouldn't have been the only church band at a Hot Air Balloon Jubilee with thousands of people or the only church with a car in a Mini-Grand Prix with tens of thousands present. But those two events literally brought people into the kingdom. We have Christ-followers today actively serving who decided to check out a church that would do such "out of the box" things.

When opportunities and needs bubble up, the body will reorganize itself and "new repertoires will emerge." We've seen appear all the gifts necessary to rebuild a struggling single mom's house that nearly burned to the ground or to obtain all the security clearances and badges necessary to have fifty-two people working Ground Zero six days after the tragedy of 9/11. The body of Christ can be amazingly adaptive and innovative.

Living Things Are Unpredictable

Organisms cannot be directed along a linear path precisely because living organisms are living and creative. Living organisms have elements of unpredictability. What's the moral of the story? Go with the flow. All organisms are going to have a measure of unpredictability. Here's a good reminder to keep our control issues in check. Our structures need to submit to the moving of God's Spirit. Form emerges from what is most functional in accomplishing the mission. We just need to relax.

When we finally enter into the truth of unpredictability instead of constantly fighting it, we enjoy the ride more, trust God more, expect the unexpected, and experience increased curiosity about what God might do. It's not a bad place to live.

Each one of these characteristics of living organisms applies to our churches and requires a tremendous amount of leadership savvy to navigate well. We must become great communicators and consensus-builders. Each one of the events I mentioned here (and many more could have been) were fire events. We've gone through a church name change, thirteen years in three different schools before our first building, a major philosophy of ministry change—all sorts of "out of the box" events. Most of them were fire for us—events that enabled the people to envision what could be.

Initially the steps were small, but those were confidence-builders. Those little steps showed people that change wasn't so painful; it was "doable." We had the gifts and sense of destiny from God to do it. When little steps are followed up with bigger steps, divine audacity starts to set in, and we experience a reckless trust in a God that wants to exceed our wildest dreams.

Learning Experiments

There have also been plenty of examples where we had learning experiments in our path that didn't turn out the way we anticipated. They could be called pendulum initiatives. We thought they'd work, but the system settled right back where we started. Some of those learning experiments had unanticipated outcomes and took us where we didn't want to go. Some were simply ill-conceived solutions or scenarios that were more complex than we realized.

One of those messy fiascoes was our banquet where we announced that we were abolishing membership at Westwinds as a permanent thing and we would have a banquet every year where people could recommit and affirm their membership again. Well, at the time the rationale of follow-up with inactive people, and an opportunity to vision-cast as to the importance of membership for this whole scenario, seemed smart. It was a disaster. Long-timers deeply committed to Westwinds were slighted; new people that had just become members felt like we did a bait and switch. In general, a bunch of people were really unhappy over the mess. Another monument to unexpected outcomes we had never thought of. We laugh now; we smarted then.

We've tried all sorts of birth methods and coaching structures in our small group ministry. I shared earlier our aha experience of realizing that people simply wouldn't go from the anonymous large group of a weekend service into a small group of intimacy with ten strangers they didn't know. Most of these solution-seeking experiments took multiple attempts and frustrating hours of brainstorming to finally land them. We've watched the pendulum settle at center point lots of times.

We've watched the pendulum settle at center point lots of times.

The reality is that all current "solutions" are provisional. Living organisms are in a constant state of flux. Environmental conditions, local geography, and other dynamics of church life all factor into what will make certain systems work well at one time and then exhaust their value for the next run ahead. A bit of understanding of systems thinking and creating a change-resilient culture can go a long way in helping us through changes.

Systems Thinking

All change initiatives have a ripple effect. In fact, this is true even of minor decisions. There's a whole field of research on this called systems thinking.[6] Systems thinking says the sum of the parts is actually greater than simple math would indicate. If you and I are in the equation, systems thinking says there are now three components, not two. There are you, me, *and* the relationship between you and me.

The third component listed is the most complex, is unpredictable, and is also full of the most possibility. In systems thinking, one plus one is three. Now muddy the issue a bit by adding two more people or six more. The sum of the parts plus all the relationships, not just one-on-one relationships but all the combinations present, has to be taken into consideration.

In systems thinking, this is the distinction made between dynamic and detail complexity. When you add another element into the mix, you add another detail. When another person enters the mix, the simple number of connections goes up. That's simple math. However, something else happens too. The dynamic complexity, which takes into account all the relationships between the people or elements in the system, also goes up.

Think about this as a church system. When we first decided to implement small group ministry years ago, we had no understanding of this ripple effect due to dynamic complexity. We had Sunday morning, Sunday night, and Wednesday night services. We decided to implement small groups for intimacy and growth. What happened? Wednesday night attendance, Sunday night attendance, and serving in ministry all went down within a couple months. Whoa! There was some very simple systems stuff going on. People had a set amount of time. So much would be spent on church functions. People were not going to add to their plates. They simply took some things off and put other things on. The feedback from the system was "Net time invested is the same. Do you want to multiply the options or focus your goals?"

You must understand systemic issues in the church. Every time even an element in the system changes, the whole system changes. Dynamic complexity says every relationship touched by that element is now altered. Sometimes those connections are not that clear to the naked eye. The larger the organism, the more complex and important this becomes.

Creating Resilience

I think it's safe to say the most valuable thing any leader can do is morph the outlook of the congregation toward the exhilaration of risk and outlandish possibilities of God. Spiritually speaking, there's more value in this than in learning any techniques. Risk and change resilience are essentially an issue of faith and trust. I think we come out further down the road if part of our leadership time is spent making sure the DNA of risk remains clearly in view. Remember, all children have built in "no fear" and built in "the sky is the limit." With age, there seems to be some loss of this muscle.

Talk about God's risk-taking endeavors. Preach about them, talk about them, and point out the Scripture about them. Sometimes our view of God is so clouded that we forget God is a risk-taker of the highest order. He expects nothing less from us.

Helping people make the connection between the magnitude of mission and the required risk is important. Our change in philosophy of ministry was necessary for only one reason: Lost people weren't being found. At some point in time, people have to decide if the mission is worth it. The change was hard for us and done with little knowledge of the process. I was in one of those places of grace, and we all survived.

> **Sometimes our view of God is so clouded that we forget God is a risk-taker of the highest order. He expects nothing less from us.**

Change should be going on in our spiritual lives. We expect it and assume it should be happening. Tying the change initiative on the table to that sort of expectancy is a helpful tool for assisting the troops to come to grips with what's to come. Everyone can instantly assent that our spiritual lives with God are to be dynamic. Old habits should be laid aside and new ones engaged. Relationship by definition is dynamic. How can the body of Christ be anything but changing and laying aside bad habits and adopting new ones when that's the pattern of individual growth and health? Status quo protectionism is actually an addiction and shows core dysfunction.[7]

Little Changes

Make little, seemingly inconsequential changes often. Here's a great way, especially for those in more traditional contexts, to start and create immunity to change. The vaccine approach says, "I'll change little things slowly but surely, and let people notice and talk about them." In working with a traditional church, the lead pastor begins making changes in the foyer, in the decorating, in the sign. All of these required no permission, no board approval, and no vote. All of them were visibly noticed and discussed. People were slowly being sensitized to change. Call it subversive, but I love it. How this works will, of course, be different in every context. Creating risk and change resilience in a traditional context is different than trying to bring it about in a contemporary, though no less calcified, context.

As time progresses, make dramatic changes not requiring permission. I mentioned earlier my friend not wearing his robe. Wow! He's got game! Dramatic? For his context...yes! A statement? Yes! And all well within his boundaries. He was creating teachable moments, instructional lessons. All of them provoke discussion and show where people's real concerns lie. These are great opportunities to teach about the biblical mission and vision of the church.

Lunch and befriend coalition-builders. Is this political? Call it what you want. Followers watch what people they respect buy into. You are smart enough to know which ones follow and which ones are looked at for their cues. When we went into our building-design program, I had lots of lunches. We were building a wild, artistic, unusual building for a church. There wasn't instant excitement from all quadrants on this. In fact, some people never got on board.

Help people understand the why's of any project: why it is missional, why the extra money spent is worth it, why this approach seems best. These are the long, tedious ways change resilience eventually gets worked deep down. I know that we have people in our congregation who were part of our building program who are more change-resilient and outlandish in their expectations than you can imagine. They now have the experience behind them. But part of that is due to hours spent wrestling with the issues—spiritually, practically, and functionally.

Broadband Zoom-width

While we need to learn how to implement change initiatives, we need a culture of change expectation. My goal as a certified, fire-starting pyro has been to create in Westwinds an entire ethos where routine is suspect and change and risk assumed. This is what Seth Godin calls "zooming."[8] We are looking for broadband zoom-width. Westwinds' people are incredibly resilient. We've come to conclude that if you like stability, consistency, and predictability, we are going to discourage your attendance at Westwinds. We want to help "disqualify" those who are looking for something more set in stone. Almost always, these are people already Christian who want something alive but not quite as alive as we have it. To disqualify them may seem crass. Experience indicates that they are happier in the long run, and we have less conflict to navigate.

We have come to understand that there is no way to please everyone. The vast variety of people and preferences mean there always will be people who are more comfortable elsewhere. There are hundreds of other churches in our county and the surrounding area where status quo stability and weekly predictability are huge values, and they are consistently delivered.

If there is anything that can thwart the leader from moving forward with vision, it's the lack of facility in implementing change. God is always a God of fire, never of pendulums. He's always interested in doing a new thing (Isaiah 43).

We have come to understand that there is no way to please everyone.

Israel experienced the bipolarity of fascination and, at the same time, the angst that comes from approaching fire. Mount Sinai was a pyrotechnic experience, not a pendulum experience. The dance of the flames and hypnotic color change is counterbalanced as we move closer with the overwhelming, all-consuming heat that will only allow us to get so close. And yet even with an event of this magnitude, there were days Israel complained and thought a return to Egypt might be best. Israel was flirting with the pendulum; a return to the status quo that had seemed so horrible but when looked at from the vantage point of currently difficult circumstances was seen in a more glorious light. The good old days are old all right, but not usually quite as good as they are remembered. God is looking for authorized fire-starters who will bring about the fresh, new thing he's introducing. Morphic leaders have a little pyrotechnician inside them and will use it to fan the flames of kingdom change.

Inner Action

1. What is your basic posture toward routine? Is your tendency toward falling into ruts, or are you automatically changing things to stay fresh? Your personal tendencies will automatically leak to your team and larger context.

2. Dieting as an illustration of first-order change is instantly intuitive. What areas can you look at in your own spiritual or leadership formation that have not been easy to change because you were actually introducing first-order change?

3. Look at your history of change initiatives. Where do you see a problem that didn't seem to yield to any solution tried? Are you able to see the differences between first- and second-order change?

4. What has been the typical plan for rolling out a new change initiative? Has it been successful or difficult?

5. Who are the early adopters in your church? How do you bring them along in a new idea? What about the critical mass group of the early majority?

6. What is the next change initiative in which you'll try out your new learning?

Endnotes

1. A raft of good books exists on change management. Some are even geared toward the church. My hope in this chapter is more on the organisms' behavior and how we navigate those dynamics as we try new programs and event initiatives.

2. William Bergquist, *The Postmodern Organization: Mastering the Art of Irreversible Change* (San Francisco, CA: Jossey-Bass, Inc., Publishers, 1993), 4-5.

3. Ilya Prigogine and Isabelle Stengers, *Order Out of Chaos: Man's New Dialogue With Nature* (New York, NY: Bantam Books, 1989).

4. Margaret J. Wheatley, *Leadership and the New Science: Learning about Organization from an Orderly Universe* (San Francisco, CA: Berrett-Koehler Publishers, Inc., 1992, 1994). Joseph Jaworski, *Synchronicity: The Inner Path of Leadership* (San Francisco, CA: Berrett-Koehler Publishers, Inc., 1996, 1998). Bill Easum, *Leadership on the OtherSide: No Rules, Just Clues* (Nashville, TN: Abingdon Press, 2000). Mark D. Youngblood, *Life at the Edge of Chaos: Creating the Quantum Organization* (Dallas, TX: Perceval Publishing, 1997).

5. Richard Tanner Pascale, "Laws of the Jungle and the New Laws of Business," Leader to Leader (Spring 2001), 21. The significance of his material may be found in the near simultaneous release of articles excerpting his thesis in both Fast Company and Leader to Leader; both publications arguably leaders in the field of business leadership, though differing in their genre and approach. For a quick glance at Pascale see http://www.fastcompany.com/online/45/pascale.html. His book is titled *Surfing the Edge of Chaos*. Richard T. Pascale, Mark Millemann, and Linda Gioja, *Surfing the Edge of Chaos: The Laws of Nature and the New Laws of Business* (New York, NY: Crown Business Books, 2000).

6. Peter Senge remains the classic here and still shows few signs of age. Peter M. Senge, Art Kleiner, Charlotte Roberts, Richard B. Ross, and Bryan J. Smith, *The Fifth Discipline Field Book: Strategies and Tools for Building a Learning Organization* (New York, NY: Doubleday, a division of Random House, Inc., 1994). Peter Senge, Art Kleiner, Charlotte Roberts, Richard Ross, George Roth, Bryan Smith, *The Dance of Change: The Challenges of Sustaining Momentum in Learning Organizations* (New York, NY: Doubleday, a division of Random House, Inc., 1999). Peter M. Senge, *The Fifth Discipline: The Art and Practice of the Learning Organization* (New York, NY: Doubleday, a division of Random House, Inc., 1990).

7. Thomas G. Bandy, *Kicking Habits: Welcome Relief for Addicted Churches* (Nashville, TN: Abingdon Press, 1997).

8. Seth Godin, *Survival Is Not Enough: Zooming, Evolution and the Future of Your Company* (New York, NY: Free Press, 2002), 60.

VIRAL EXCITEMENT

A few years ago, an old beloved brand of shoes just about sunk. Hush Puppies and their droopy-eared basset hound mascot were about to go the way of the dinosaur. The company had sold only 30,000 pairs the previous year. These were being sold in mom and pop stores, off the beaten path outlets, and second-hand stores. And then the unexplainable happened. Owen Baxter and Geoffrey Lewis, two Hush Puppies executives, ran into a New York fashion expert who told them the near-death Hush Puppies were becoming the hip rage in the clubs and bars of New York. Apparently resale shops in Soho had sold a number of pairs of shoes, and they were increasingly sought out. Pretty soon well-known fashion designer Isaac Mizrahi was wearing them and requesting them for his shows. The Manhattan designer Anna Sui wanted them for her show, as well. From New York to Los Angeles, a stir was created. The once-dying breed had been resurrected with surprising interest. But more than that, it had been resurrected in explainable ways. Did simple word of mouth generate the interest?

The following year Hush Puppies sold 430,000 pairs of shoes, and the year after that nearly four times that number. The prestigious Council of Fashion Designers awards held at the Lincoln Center every year noted the phenomenal success, and Hush Puppies were awarded the best fashion accessory of the year.[1] The success had almost nothing to do with the company; the success was due to the wearers of the shoes.

Yo-yos and Scooters

Hush Puppies is not the only story where we could identify this phenomenon. A couple of years ago, my sons all of a sudden showed interest in yo-yos.

Apparently a couple of kids at school had gotten some new Yomega yo-yos that were all the rage. Was there a big ad campaign, any billboard marketing, or slick TV commercials? No on all three counts! Word of mouth was the means by which the yo-yo craze spread. In local malls little yo-yo kiosks selling Yomega sprung up everywhere. Yo-yos must have something of a life cycle. I remember as a kid experiencing the same thing with yo-yos as my boys did. There was a six-month window in my grade school days when you just had to have Duncan Butterfly yo-yo.

Think about the wildly successful love affair with scooters all of a sudden. In the last couple of years, from Razor Scooters and the Xootr to Segway's motorized "thing" that had word-of-mouth hype surrounding it, buzz seems to be the way to generate public interest. So what does all this have to do with leadership and ministry? Lots!

When I observe cultural phenomena like those we've just mentioned, I automatically kick into my "parallel study" mode. I feel part of my leadership gift is "plundering the Egyptians"—learning what the leading edge of other disciplines are doing and then doing a parallel study to see if there is a church or ministry application. The principle is especially true when we discover that the principle operating in the other discipline is actually a biblical one.

Our goal is to discover what we need to reclaim, relearn, and then repackage for ministry consumption and kingdom purposes. Of course, my preference is that we, in the church, would be on the innovative edge and create our own contextual and biblical ministry initiatives. But we must always acknowledge that all truth is God's truth and be willing to sit at the feet of other disciplines and teachers to learn.

Isn't buzz simply a form of evangelism—people getting so excited about something or changing their behavior in such a way that it gets others' attention?

As I'm doing my parallel study, a couple of things emerge from these "buzz observations." Isn't buzz simply a form of evangelism—people getting so excited about something or changing their behavior in such a way that it gets others' attention? And isn't this kind of epidemic the thing the church would like to see happen concerning Jesus and his invitation to real life?[2] Isn't this actually what happened in the early church?

I think about the passages from the book of Acts that talk about God's Word spreading throughout the region and how it continued to increase and spread widely and that it grew in power. Obviously, in all those cases, word-of-mouth buzz is what happened (Acts 6:7, 12:24, 13:49, 19:20). Finally, if buzz is a component of evangelism or simply another word for it, isn't it the job of the morphic leader to help people buzz with life for God?

The Buzz About Buzz

The issue of buzz became quite the buzz a couple years ago in business literature. The cascade started with a very interesting guy named Seth Godin. As a writer for Fast Company, he already had something of a forum for his ideas. But he wrote a full-sized book called *Unleashing the Ideavirus* and gave it away...free![3] You can go to his Web site and get an e-book copy of it or a pocket PC or Palm Pilot version.

The interesting thing about Godin's approach was that he was trying to create an idea virus about his new book on creating idea viruses. And did he ever create one! Godin was modeling his manifesto. He did the counterintuitive thing in the marketing of his book. He gave it away like crazy and then, at a later date, came out with a hardback copy. Instantly it went to number five on the Amazon.com buying list. People found it hard to believe that you could give a book away in electronic form and then months later release the high-priced hardback and have it be near the top of the selling list.

Two other volumes hit around the same time dealing with similar issues, *The Tipping Point* and *The Anatomy of Buzz*.[4] All three of these volumes have much to offer to get us to think about how we can buzz the topic of morphic life in Christ. What could possibly be more valuable for us as leaders than understanding how we can get the troops on board and create a buzz that following Christ is THE thing to do and that surrendering to him is where real life is found.

A bit of reflection on the natural world surrounding us shows that buzz is actually built into the world at the most basic levels. Bees should probably get credit for inventing buzz. Their dancing within the hive is a signal that they have located a patch of flowers that shows promise. Black carpenter ants spray a secretion that acts as buzz. When the other ants get a whiff, they follow that leader to a newly discovered food source. Ravens have a servant model of buzz. When a raven finds a fresh food source, without taking a single bite, it will fly up to several days journey to return with a whole group of ravens. Then they'll eat together. The whole buzz thing seems to live at DNA levels of the created order.

What's the blueprint for buzz, and how does it work? Obviously, we have plenty of statements from Acts. In fact, that's what was happening. Buzz is nothing more than what we have called "sharing our story." But it isn't just any story-sharing. It is passionate, exciting story-sharing that's unavoidable because someone is experiencing real life change and the undeniable presence of God in his or her life. We have a story from Jesus' ministry that created buzz, and a large number of people became followers as a result. Think about the story of the woman at the well.

Well-Water Buzz

Jesus engages a Samaritan woman at a well (John 4). The woman instantly identifies this as irregular and even inappropriate. John provides us with a parenthetical statement to explain her surprise. The summary of the story might be told this way: Jesus meets this woman at exactly her point of need.

Her response to Jesus is what interests us. She left her water jar, presumably a valuable possession in those days, and went running back to her village. Why did

Why did she go running back to her village? She was buzzing.

John 4:28-29: "Then, leaving her water jar, the woman went back to the town and said to the people, 'Come, see a man who told me everything I ever did. Could this be the Christ?'" She was so moved at Jesus' entry into her life and by him possibly being the Christ that she ran back and started sharing her story.

Apparently, her personal story was passionate and compelling. The following verse records the people coming out of the town to hear and see what she was so excited about. John 4:39-41: "Many of the Samaritans from that town believed in him because of the woman's testimony, 'He told me everything I ever did.' So when the Samaritans came to him, they urged him to stay with them, and he stayed two days. And because of his words many more became believers."

The woman's excitement and story were found persuasive, and many believed. As the townspeople "sampled" Jesus for themselves, they urged him to hang out longer. They were able to taste and see for themselves whether her buzz was really all she had cracked it up to be. As a result, many more became followers. One person started to talk, created some buzz, and it went viral. A whole town was impacted.

Compelling Lives, Compelling Churches

How do we create an epidemic about following Jesus? How do we create momentum about being in community? How do we create cravings about a life directed by God's purposes?

Two related things seem to emerge as important for our understanding. First, we need to live compelling lives so people will see a credible example and reason to belong and believe. Second, we need authentic churches where people will long to explore their spiritual curiosity and find genuine community that is patient with their process. Saying we need both compelling lives and churches in no way mutes the fact that we're trying to point people to Christ and him alone, not to our churches. The problem, however, is all too well known. The church is perceived as boring, marginal, tired, and out of touch. Unfortunately, the charge is often true.

We are responsible to create what we've been calling ethos. More than ever we need an ethos of excitement about what God is doing in human lives and what he's up to in the local church. When people who go on vacation have mixed emotions about missing church because they aren't sure what they'll miss while they are gone, you're moving into the compelling realm. If Razor Scooters can go viral and yo-yos become epidemic and there is nothing at stake except a little pleasure, then why not every weekend service we do?

Jesus was committed to building his church against which the gates of hell could not prevail (Matthew 16:18). Those words sound serious. And let's not forget something: Scooters and yo-yos don't have the breath of the Holy Spirit motivating and moving the epidemic to ever-larger circles.

Personal Morphing Goes Viral

Let me give you my working thesis.

Quite simply, real life change of the morphic sort, coupled with excitement and storytelling, leads to momentum. Let's ask some questions. Would you characterize the people in your church or on your team or staff as being excited about what God is up to in their lives and their church? Or could you better characterize the dominant flavor as status quo, mundane, and predictable?

Momentum is excitement gone epidemic, and excitement is life change gone viral.

Think about this from the ethos and epidemic perspective. If the ethos is average or mediocre, it will produce little storytelling and excitement for people to share. If, on the other hand, there is an Ephesians 3:20-21 anticipation that God really wants to do things exceeding above and beyond our wildest dreams, then it's pretty hard to keep quiet stories of life change, addiction deliverance, restoration, relational healing, and a host of freedom from sin. So here is our next question: Where does excitement come from?

The Big Two Leading to Momentum

Two things seem to be at the very base of a generative spiritual excitement within a church—an excitement leading to momentum. First, my life is profoundly changing. Second, I get to see and catalyze life-change in others. These two things form the basis of genuine spiritual excitement, which is the juice fueling spiritual momentum.

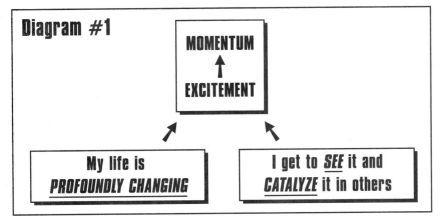

Diagram #1

MOMENTUM
↑
EXCITEMENT

My life is **PROFOUNDLY CHANGING**

I get to **SEE** it and **CATALYZE** it in others

If you eavesdropped on the people's stories in your congregation or on your team or in your small group, would they be talking about the life-change and how they are assisting that in the lives of others? If they aren't talking about those two

When people have deep transforma- tion going on in their lives, they simply can't keep quiet about it. things, it's fundamentally because it's not happening. Show me somebody experiencing dramatic life-change, and I'll show you someone sharing the good news.

Bill Easum poses a question that constantly rings in my ears, "What is it about our experience with Jesus that this community cannot live without?"[5] Few questions are more poignant for ethos and spiritual excitement. When people have deep transformation going on in their lives, they simply can't keep quiet about it. When we elevate and celebrate stories of lives morphed in our midst, it slowly becomes an expected part of the fabric of community life. We celebrate and parade stories, people buzz about them, others get motivated to experience change and growth with Jesus, and the buzz increases.

Let me give you an example of celebrating stories. We baptized over fifty people at our last baptism service. Thirty-eight of the people were adults who had become followers of Jesus in the last six to twelve months. For many of them, Westwinds is the first church they had attended in many years. Some had never attended. We allow the person or people instrumental in their coming to Jesus to be in the pool baptizing them. The baptizers may be small group leaders, close spiritual friends who invited them to Westwinds, or staff members or team leaders who assisted them in the process of coming to Jesus.

We start by having several people read their stories of how they found Jesus. Baptisms have become some of the most emotionally moving and deeply meaningful events in the life of our church. By the time those stories have been read, hundreds of Christ-followers have been reduced to tears at the wonder and awe of new birth in their midst. Those events and story times create spiritual excitement...excitement that fuels momentum forward.

How Can It Work Better?

If life-change in me and my helping to catalyze it in others are the bedrock elements of an ethos- and excitement-fueling momentum, then how can we see the life-change quotient raised in our churches? Morphic change—deep, lasting, life-change—is what we, as leaders, want as the dominant flavor and feel in our space. Seeing people anxious to look more like Jesus, talk more like him, think more like him, serve more like him, live and love more like him is our primary reason for being.

At Westwinds we've found two things that fuel life change in people's lives. The first thing is self-centered and self-serving. We help people answer the question "How can my life work better?" According to a recent study by the Alban Institute, that is the primary question unchurched people are asking. The church is consistently answering questions the unchurched aren't asking and is scuttling the real issue they do have: "How can I make my life work?"[6]

The reality of this self-centered approach to Jesus is seen throughout the

Gospels. Few, if any, examples can be cited of people from the crowds coming to Jesus to ask how to better glorify God or what doctrinal position is best. Those seeking out Jesus in the Gospels did so with tremendous human need driving their quest. Whether it was a thirteen-year hemorrhage, a death in the family, or an ailing servant, those seeking out Jesus had deep personal needs.

We are simply out of touch with the general population of unchurched if we think people come to our churches for any other reason. I have yet to meet a person from the ranks of the outside observer who decided to attend our church because they had some intractable theological question or wanted a deeper understanding of the biblical material.

Fifteen years into a church plant, and hundreds of people coming to Christ later, without fail I find people coming to Christ for only two reasons. Some come in crisis and think the church may have answers or help that they need. This is usually a tactic of last resort. The rest come out of curiosity because someone credible in their lives has experienced visible morphic change, and they want to see if maybe that is possible for them. In both cases, they come for personal, self-seeking reasons.

I know criticism will be leveled here. I heard it for years from my conservative brethren: "Are we to simply give people whatever it is they want to hear because we can create a crowd with it?" The answer to that is a flat out no! We're talking here about meeting the Samaritan woman where she is without pulling any punches. There's no need to whitewash the demands of the gospel and equally no reason to address questions no one is asking (a skill at which the church has been expert). Sin and the demand of surrender and allegiance to Jesus should be the core of what we talk about. But if we can't help people make the connection as to why following Jesus is the best decision they could possibly make, we're doing a poor job.

> **There's no need to whitewash the demands of the gospel and equally no reason to address questions no one is asking (a skill at which the church has been expert).**

Divine Conversations as Test Case

Westwinds just started a four-week series titled "Divine Conversations." The opening volley looked at the Lord's Prayer as an outline for conversation with God. Our unchurched people want desperately to communicate with the "transcendent," whatever they mean by that. We have people who are deeply spiritual coming to Westwinds; but they are just as apt to dial 1-900-888-CLEO for the latest psychic reading or to run out and buy the latest Oprah recommendation as they are to appear in church on the weekend.

For us to do a series on conversation with God is right up their alley. To open with a detail of the six-point discussion outline Jesus gives for talking to God the

Father, the creator of the universe, really meets a need in the people coming to investigate God. We used *The Message* translation of the Lord's Prayer to help people see the genuine outline nature of the prayer. We talked about the need to see the prayer as six topic guidelines instead of a rote incantation to be uttered in 24.8 seconds.

But note that this is still biblical, still feeds Christ-followers, still starts with the text of Scripture, and works outward from there. The need for clear, cultural, and biblical exegesis could never be greater. The first avenue fueling life-change is our ability to help people answer in God-honoring and biblical ways the question "How can my life work better?"

It should be obvious how getting at this question fuels spiritual excitement and momentum. When Solomon says God has placed eternity in the heart of every man and woman, and they finally find the Jesus who can fill the Jesus-shaped hole, excitement and stories automatically flow.

The Ed Story

Ed came to church because his wife was attending and volunteering on our hospitality team. She convinced him to come to our MSU vs. U of M football game party. We projected the game on our big central screen in our auditorium and had a big outreach event. College football in the Midwest is big stuff, local rivalries even bigger. Ed had never been a church attendee, but any church that would do a football event like this was worth checking out. He decided soon after that experience to join the hospitality team so he could be with his wife and serve also. Over a nine-month period, the hospitality crew modeled Jesus. They loved Ed, laughed with Ed, and simply let Ed's quest carry on.

One Sunday morning Jeff, Pam, and Leta could be seen in the kitchen praying with Ed. It was his day. The credible lives he had witnessed over several months and what he heard in weekend services finally convinced him.

Ed's story gets better, though. Just a couple months later, Ed approached his hospitality team with an idea. Ed was into muscle cars, car shows, tinkering under the hood of old cars, and restoring them to better than original condition. He had an inane idea. What if Westwinds had a car show with seventy-five to eighty show cars on the lot. This is the 21C version of a Matthew party.[7] The team got behind him. They saw this not only as a great outreach idea, but also as a huge permission-giving affirmation of Ed's newfound faith and desire to share it with the crowd with which he hangs out. As he sat on our stage, sharing his story for our fifteenth anniversary, there was hardly a dry eye. Helping Ed find out how his life could work better led to a reproducing disciple.

Deeply Moving

The second component is to help people have deeply moving experiences with God. We cannot for a moment minimize the tandem role experiencing God plays with the practical side of a life that really works better. For many (myself included) it's hard to adjust to this approach. Experiencing God is actually biblical. Wow!

As we noted before, Israel had powerful experiences before it had propositions and understanding. Our post-enlightenment, propositional obsession really works against us here. God invites people into relationship that is experiential by definition. Unfortunately, the very nature of most people's understanding of what it means to be a Christian centers on a set of propositions about Jesus, not a relationship with Jesus. God said the Word was made flesh and dwelt among us. The church has often taken the Word made flesh and attempted to turn it into propositions.

If talking-head services, low on experience and high on the rational, continue to be the primary approach of most churches, I'm concerned that we will produce primarily cerebral Christians. No one will buzz about a new doctrine understood or a biblical insight garnered. And for the few who may, nobody in the unchurched community will care.

But when experiencing God moves a heart, touches a soul, heals subterranean wounds, and pours tangible grace on dark sin confessed, stories will emerge automatically. The need for the church to spend significant amounts of time reflecting on how they can increase the incidences of people bumping into the presence of God has to become more central.

The reason for the church to really be on the ball should be quite clear. The average person ends up coming to church because of an invitation from a credible person in his or her life. If our invitee comes to church and experiences nothing or experiences a bunch of heady propositions without the immanent presence of the Almighty, then we simply will be ineffective at intersecting his or her private world. Incarnational intersection is the main event. We can't afford to blow it here.

The Conclusion to the Ed Story

When lives work better because of relationship with God and obedience to Jesus and people are moved by experiencing God, stories flow, spiritual excitement reaches a fevered pitch, and momentum organically grows from the soil of morphic change. Leaders, through paraklesis, release God's "what ifs." What if Ed had never been loved into the hospitality team? What if Ed had never seen credible lives walking the talk and talking about the walk? Leaders of the morphic sort are constantly trying to help catalyze an environment for the Eds of the world.

Only a couple months after Ed came to Christ, his son was diagnosed with a brain tumor. Ed's son has fought the fight and come out with victory. But Ed's story at the anniversary service was his confession that without Jesus and a community of Jesus around him and his wife, Lydia, they would have found surviving their hardship exceedingly difficult. Ed had been won to Christ through community and had been sustained through his challenges by his newfound community. No one has to ask Ed and Lydia to buzz about what has happened to them and their family or to tell the story of the incredible things God is doing in their lives. It's simply overflow of a life being filled by God.

The flow of how buzz creates spiritual excitement and, therefore, momentum should be clarifying. Momentum is excitement gone epidemic, and excitement is life-change gone viral. Here's what we have so far.

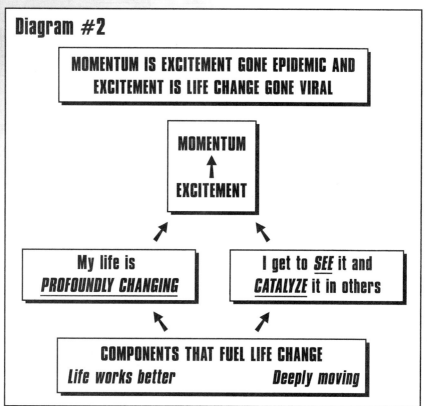

The last component that we've talked about but haven't fit into the picture yet is the role of storytelling. We have seen examples of this, but let's make explicit what underlies all buzz: the power of narrative.

The Narrative of God's Life in Ours

The power of story is the very foundation of buzz, no matter what the topic being buzzed is. Whether it is buzz among grade school boys about yo-yos or how cool old-fashioned Hush Puppies look, narrative is what moves the little trickle to viral proportions. The woman at the well in John 4 demonstrates the power of word-of-mouth story. When lives work better because people are coming to obey Jesus, and they begin to have deeply moving experiences with God, the natural overflow is storytelling. Without the storytelling, there is no buzz. The life-change virus never spreads. An epidemic never happens.

Personal storytelling will have to become one of the primary tools of the 21C church. The only thing eclipsing it will be the tool of listening ears. The church that doesn't listen carefully will be in no position to know how to respond to the people it claims a desire to reach.

Listening as a tool is simply the flip side of storytelling. By listening, we are inviting others to share their stories and their world. When *their* world opens, we almost always have the opportunity to story *our* world as well. The intersection of our story—which is really just a microcosm of God's larger story—and their stories is the essence of spiritual conversation.

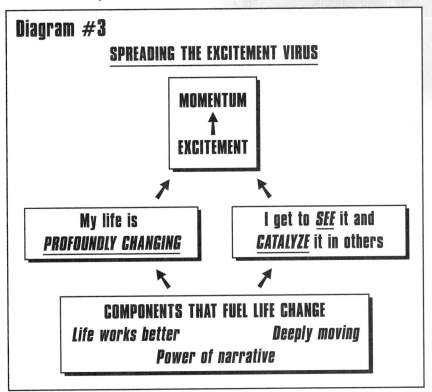

Our need to elevate peoples' stories of God's infusion of life demands creativity. Every medium possible needs to be used to parade God's work in people's lives. We use video stories, e-mail readings, and have even connected a computer to one of our video projectors. People type their stories on one of our two large screens.

We would be remiss not to acknowledge that our goal isn't to create a phenomenon, but it's to create, under the power of the Holy Spirit, storytelling that reflects the work of God.

The open computer terminal is the equivalent of the old testimony time many churches had in the past.

The momentum from spiritual excitement is obviously cyclical. The more people buzz about morphic life-change and talk about being inexplicably moved in a church service, the more people want to investigate. The more people investigate, the more teams in our churches recognize the stakes of the game we're in. The more diligence we see in prayer, the more diligence appears in creatively helping our people tell their stories, and the more diligence to be exegetes of culture and the Bible. As a team gets diligent and raises the bar, the experience level of those attending increases as well. When those levels increase, buzz increases. Before long, people want to know "What's going on over there?"

If yo-yos can get boys buzzing without the work of the Holy Spirit, what happens when God, by the power of the Holy Spirit, starts moving in people's lives and escalates the gumption to tell their stories? So far we haven't even talked about the role of God's Spirit. But we would be remiss not to acknowledge that our goal isn't to create a phenomenon, but it's to create, under the power of the Holy Spirit, storytelling that reflects the work of God.

The Great Commission seems to be smack-dab in the middle of the life-change charge. So I invite you into creating momentum in a very practical way. Hopefully, we can see that momentum is not mysterious, slippery, and unattainable as we may have thought it was. In fact, God has given us some pretty clear guidance and direction. When you head in that direction, you end up deeper in the kingdom of God and bring a bunch of others with you.

InnerAction

1. Think about some buzz examples with which you have had personal experience. What were the factors causing you to buzz? Do you think they were the same factors that created an epidemic for the product or thing you have in mind?

2. How would you rate the storytelling value in your context? What mediums do you use to cull and disseminate stories?

3. How much is life-change elevated as a goal of service design and the very structure of the church? What could be changed to raise the bar here?

4. What are you doing to help people see their lives work better? Is it a goal, desire, dream?

5. Is experiencing God the main focus of the weekly planning for weekend services, or is information transmission primary? What can you do to create experiential interaction with God for your people?

6. How will you train your people on the power of story?

Endnotes

1. Malcom Gladwell, *The Tipping Point: How Little Things Can Make a Big Difference* (Boston, MA: Little, Brown and Company, 2000), 3-4.

2. The way Eugene Peterson translates Jesus' promise of abundant life in John 10:10. Eugene H. Peterson, *The Message* (Colorado Springs, CO: NavPress Publishing Group, 1993, 1994, 1995).

3. Seth Godin, *Unleashing the Ideavirus* (Do You Zoom, Inc., 2000) www.ideavirus.com.

4. Gladwell, *The Tipping Point;* Emanuel Rosen, *The Anatomy of Buzz: How to Create Word-of-Mouth Marketing* (New York, NY: Doubleday, a division of Random House, Inc., 2000).

5. William M. Easum and Thomas G. Bandy, *Growing Spiritual Redwoods* (Nashville, TN: Abingdon Press, 1997), 50.

6. Alan C. Klaas, *In Search of the Unchurched* (New York, NY: The Alban Institute, 1996), 51.

7. Matthew came to Jesus and quickly threw a party for his friends so the others could rub elbows with Jesus. Creative and innovative Matthew parties will play a major role in 21C evangelism (Matthew 9).

APPENDIX

THE FIRST STRAND OF LEADERSHIP DNA

Leaders come in different sizes, shapes, genders, and temperaments. Leaders come with differing gift mixes, emphases, and areas of expertise. They come with different passions, intuitions, and sensitivities. To complicate matters a bit, leadership definitions are nearly as diverse as the packages leaders come in.

The leader's personal definition of leadership is the focus of this appendix. As we will see, the convergence of a personal leadership definition and the deeply held beliefs about leadership account for a unique leadership signature or fingerprint.

Every leader—biblical, political, and marketplace—has this unique leadership signature. The more we are aware of these factors comprising our DNA, the more clearly we'll understand our leadership and how every one of these factors shape our personal morphing and the teams and churches we lead. If we have a hard-nosed, dictatorial style, which obviously reflects a certain type of leadership definition, then we'll be creating a certain type of feel on our teams and in our churches. If we enjoy catalyzing self-directed teams, then the feel of the church will be entirely different.

Defining leadership is notoriously difficult. Consult a few hundred volumes on leadership, and you'll get a few hundred permutations, variations, modifications, and re-creations of how to define the concept. So why even try? I confess tremendous reluctance to enter this deep well and attempt to draw out fresh water, but I can't help myself. What we believe about leadership impacts everything else we do. So even though this appendix may be more detailed and academic than the rest of the book, the effort to digest it will be worthwhile!

What is distinctive about Christian leadership as opposed to leadership in general? The discussion here could take a variety of trajectories. Is it more than simply a leader who is a Christian? Is it their outcome and goals that set Christian leaders apart?

I want to suggest that Christian leaders, especially point leaders, have a unique encouragement or motivational ability that is more than simply good vision-casting. There's something spiritually powered when leadership is rightly conceived. Furthermore, I think this is a way to move the discussion forward and create some new possibilities to explore.

It Is Influence

Let's start with a common definition of leadership that circulates freely even in Christian circles. Early in my ministry days, I realized that I knew very little about the whole leadership enterprise. So I was off to the current leadership seminar guru, John Maxwell. While I'm sure it probably didn't originate with him, no doubt he has brought the "leadership is influence" definition into its prime. The stories surrounding that definition made it seem right on target to me in those early years. "Title means nothing," you were told. "He who is doing the influencing is the leader." This made total sense, and because I could see this scenario played out in so many different circumstances, I bought the definition. Of course, John Maxwell was always careful in his seminars to point out that we aren't talking about authoritarian or dictatorial influence; we're talking about compassionate but strong leadership that furthered the goals of God's kingdom.

Leadership, if it is anything, is at least influence. But is it more than that? Is there something making the "influence" of a Christian leader actually distinctive? The "leadership is influence" definition makes the Hitlers of the world incredible leaders. In the purest sense of that definition, Hitler was a great leader. He wasn't moral or good or right, but he was an influencer—a dark, demonic, massive influencer. So what I want to do is take a look at what kind of influence would comprise a Christian definition and toward what kind of outcome is the influence heading.

Leadership, if it is anything, is at least influence.

Let's cast our working example in less hostile light and use two relatively known leaders. Is there a difference between the leadership of Bill Hybels at Willow Creek and Jack Welch at General Electric? Certainly many of the components of their ability profiles would overlap. They both obviously excel in vision, communication, motivation, inspiration, and mission and values alignment. Some say the difference between the talented marketplace leader and the spiritually gifted leader is teleological; that is, it has to do with the end or goal of their leadership. Jack Welch has General Electric in mind; Bill Hybels has God's kingdom. You could also state the difference in terms of spiritual gift and talent. Bill Hybels has the spiritual gift of leadership, and Jack Welch has a talent. But that distinction only provides labels. We are curious about the operational differences and even the impact the distinction has on the follower.

Paradigms and Possible Proposals

In the absence of any clear biblical definitions or direction, we have a few approaches at our disposal: 1) Ignore the question and move on to more certain discussions. 2) Answer the question superficially. 3) Employ or design a construct in hopes of furthering the discussion, but always knowing a construct is a working model that's open to development and, yes, morphing. You guessed it; I opt for the third.

The development of any new paradigm or construct is done to answer questions previously unanswered in the current paradigm. The downside of such new constructs is well known; previously well-answered questions may not be answered as well under the newly proposed model. Only time, dialogue, testing, and lots of questions can determine whether a newly proposed paradigm will show any lasting promise. With those potential risks in mind, let's look at a possible framework for understanding a definition.

Jacob Firet, in his incredibly insightful book on pastoral theology, has a lengthy discussion on pastoral role fulfillment. To hear Firet takes patience, but I'm certain it will be rewarded.[1] In his discussion he speaks of modes of pastoral role fulfillment and identifies three. He seeks to answer a tough question: how does God's Word come to God's people through God's messenger?

The first mode is *kerygma*. Kerygma is the New Testament Greek word for "proclamation." In the New Testament, this is the good news of the gospel. This is the initial offer of salvation, the surprise of good news to those who have never heard it. It's the first moment of salvation. The response to kerygma brings people into the kingdom.

The second mode is *didache*. In the Greek New Testament this is the word for "teaching." Didache picks up where kerygma left off, painting the contours of what it would be like for the one who has responded to kerygma to now progress into the experience of living life in the kingdom. Kerygma announces that you can live in the kingdom; didache is how you live in the kingdom once you've accepted the invitation.[2] These two Greek words are relatively well known and necessitate little explanation. The third word and usage is a bit less familiar.

morph

Encouragement With Weight

Paraklesis is the New Testament Greek word for "encouragement, exhortation, consolation, and comfort." Its noun form is used of the Holy Spirit in John's gospel where at times we transliterate it as Paraclete (John 14:16, 26; 15:21; 16:7). Kerygma invites people into the kingdom; didache instructs the follower how to live life in the kingdom; and paraklesis stirs up, motivates, exhorts, and encourages people to so live. For Firet, these are the three dominant roles of the pastoral leader: You must preach (kerygma) to bring people into the kingdom; teach (didache) to instruct them how to live in the kingdom; and then motivate, encourage, and comfort (paraklesis) them to live and respond appropriately to situations they'll face in living out kingdom life on earth.

As the primary speaker in my context, I attempt to make the gospel clearly known. I also try to instruct people about the counter-cultural values, priorities, and ways we are to live as followers of Jesus in a land where we're really strangers. In weekend services, in one-on-one meetings, and in staff development contexts, I try to encourage and motivate people to live out the values of the kingdom. Paraklesis is the motivational "umph" that helps people close the knowing and doing gap in their lives. For most of us, lack of knowledge is not our primary problem. Few times do we run into a passage of Scripture that gives us something new to obey. Dominantly our problem is obeying what we already know. Closing the gap between knowing and doing is the function of paraklesis. So far this doesn't qualify for a leadership definition, but we're making progress.

> Closing the gap between knowing and doing is the function of paraklesis.

A Key Paraklesis Example

An example of paraklesis in the New Testament is important to catch the usage.[3] Hebrews 10:24-25 is a fairly typical example: "And let us consider how we may spur one another on toward love and good deeds. Let us not give up meeting together, as some are in the habit of doing, but let us encourage [parakalein] one another—and all the more as you see the Day approaching."

Several noteworthy items arise in this text. Paraklesis is a function of the gathered community. You can't have individual paraklesis. Encouragement, motivation, and exhortation always happen with at least one other person or with a group. Paraklesis is a mutual activity. We're all encouraged to be encouragers. Paraklesis flows back and forth among community members.

Paraklesis has a motivational dimension. Whether here in Hebrews or other passages where the "encouragement" family of words is the translational choice or in passages where Paul "appeals," "begs," "exhorts," or even "comforts," some way the word is motivational and comes with divine freight toward a given outcome. These observations may prove helpful to our discussion of leadership definition.

The Piercing Arrow of Paraklesis

Think about this from a personal perspective. Have you ever been in a small group setting, staff meeting, or team session and someone said something encouraging or challenging but the comment wasn't really central to the discussion? The import of what they said only came home to you days later when that phrase, line, or passing comment was still rolling around inside your spirit.

Or turn it the other direction. Have you ever had anyone come up to you days after a small group meeting or a weekend talk and tell you, "Do you remember saying this in your message last week? Wow, all week long I've been thinking about that"? You may or may not remember, but the point is that something landed in their spirit with divine penetration and continued speaking to them some time after the event. Paraklesis is at work: our encouragement receiving divine help in "sticking" to someone's spirit. The intersection of our paraklesis with the Paraclete finds tremendous weight and staying power.

Now some may question whether this is leadership. So far we aren't claiming that comments in a small group necessarily constitute leadership. But we are saying this may be one of the constituent components of how Christian leadership functions and, therefore, a piece of our leadership definition.

Is it coincidental that the Holy Spirit has Paraclete as one of his names? Is there a synergism in that as we engage in paraklesis there's a kind of breath of God's Spirit in it? How that happens and how frequently it happens is beyond the scope of this discussion. But when our experience is coupled with passages like we read in Hebrews, I think it's quite clear that paraklesis can come with extra force...a kind of "divine freight."

The Moment of Understanding

Paraklesis comes to us in two stages or moments; it has two separate functions. Firet refers to "the hermeneutic moment and the agogic moment."[4] We're going to call these "the moment of understanding" and "the moment of action." The word *moment* is used to distinguish two distinct features of paraklesis. It doesn't have to do with "time" as in a moment equaling a split second.

When we're encouraged toward a goal, two things have to happen in us for the paraklesis to "take root," to see us move toward change. First, we have to come to some understanding of the context, desired outcome, and even the process to arrive at the outcome. The "issues" surrounding the change that's being encouraged have to be understood and at some level "bought into." There's a kind of cognitive process we go through in evaluating the possible change to be made. I have certainly experienced this.

When I recently called Paul, one of my ministry mentors, to share a frustration about some of our awkward staffing challenges, he said to me, "Ron, congratulations. You are normal. Let me tell you what you may be able to expect for the next six to twelve months as you work through the next growth barrier..." His ability to enter into my dilemma (having been there himself), assuring me it wasn't unusual, and telling me there were certain things that could get worse before they got better was creating a framework for my understanding of the situation. In helping me understand the context, he was shaping for me the first moment of paraklesis, the moment of understanding. Part of his encouragement was helping me come to grips with a contextual understanding of what was going on.

When someone is encouraging us, there's some idea about what they are encouraging us toward. They're pointing us to the "why" and even the "how" of "hanging in there" until we experience the change and growth being sought. The first moment is setting up a frame of reference for us. Framing our understanding of the potential change is what we're calling the moment of understanding.

The Moment of Action

The choice to change and act on our frame of understanding is the moment of action. This is the moment when the encouragement "sinks in" to the point of pushing someone over the edge. Ideally, all paraklesis ends in action, but in practice that isn't the case. When Paul says, "I urge you [paraklesis] to live a life worthy of the calling you have received" (Ephesians 4:1b), the Ephesians may come to understand why that's important and how they're supposed to do so (the moment of understanding). At this time they're faced with the weight of responding to the prompting of God's Spirit to change (the moment of action).

To return to our Hebrews discussion, divine weight coming through paraklesis is what eventually catalyzes change. The Holy Spirit "breathes" on that word of encouragement, comfort, or exhortation, and in so doing provokes and prolongs an incubative process leading to change.

How might this service our leadership definition discussion? Almost every definition of leadership has embedded in it some form of motivation or inspiration. Even the brief and most often quoted definition of "leadership is influence" presumes some sort of motivation is used to influence. I think the function of paraklesis and its coupling with the moments of understanding and action holds promise for us in coming to understand and identify a uniquely Christian definition of leadership.

Three in One

Jesus has given the church a very definite goal and desired outcome. In one passage we see the convergence of all three concepts developed by Firet. Matthew 28:18-20: "Then Jesus came to them and said, 'All authority in heaven and on earth has been given to me. Therefore go and make disciples of all nations, baptizing them in the name of the Father and of the Son and of the Holy Spirit, and teaching them to obey everything I have commanded you. And surely I am with you always, to the very end of the age.' " Jesus, in an act of paraklesis, invites his eleven-man team to go make disciples (a function of kerygma) and to teach them (didache) to obey (an outcome-based indicator that people have reached the moment of understanding, implying change as the measure of success).

Every local church leader, then, is attempting to cast vision for the fulfillment of this Great Commission. While the specific way this mission is fulfilled is unique to each local church, it remains clear that the local church is the primary vortex of power out of which God expects missional accomplishment.[5] If the local church leader is casting vision and helping a congregation listen to Spirit soundings, isn't this a parakletic function? Isn't the local leader attempting to inspire, motivate, encourage, and exhort the local troops to actually act on Jesus' injunctions in the Great Commission? Further, isn't every leader relying on the power of the Holy Spirit to breathe on his or her vision-casting so it's God motivating the local body for the accomplishment of his mission?

I think the answer to all of these is yes, yes, yes! Local leaders paint a picture of God's mission—its scope, magnitude, heart, and rationale (the moment of understanding). Then through encouragement from the intersection of our words and the breath of God's Spirit, they ultimately move to change (the moment of action) and fulfill the Great Commission. Paul's concern was that the Corinthians not simply be moved from great oration or rhetoric (Paul's concern in Corinth in 1 Corinthians 2:4), but from the power of God's Spirit.

Pointing the way toward missional fulfillment is one of the primary functions of the leadership gift; some would say *the* primary role. Furthermore, it appears this vision-casting component doesn't just have a different goal in mind when compared to its marketplace counterpart, but also a different mode of bringing about that goal. Everyone would agree that Jack Welch is a great motivator and in that way similar in mode to how Bill Hybels motivates his team. But it seems the spiritual gift of leadership brings with it the added freight of divine paraklesis, the breath of God on our encouragement and motivation. This isn't simply a little higher octane in the same fuel.

This may begin to get at the core of how Christian leadership is significantly different from marketplace leadership. The goals, of course, are different. But there seems to be more. The mode of the entire vision-casting and motivating process is different, and so is the receiver's experience of that process.

Leadership as Art

Observing a great leader painting the picture of a preferable future, sculpting in detail the clay of tomorrow so we can see it today, is a thing of beauty. Painting that picture, sculpting that clay, sketching those contours is part and parcel of what makes the leader the leader. The leader must first hear from God and then translate what he or she has heard into three-dimensional realities for the followers. In this way the leader is both painter and poet. For what the leader hears and sees must be translated into visual images through his or her words.

One more time we're at the moment of understanding, the leader painting the picture that is the framework where the followers decide if they will act, move, change, and proceed. An artistic rendering of the context is precisely leadership *as* art, and the greatest leaders among us are great artists, poets, sculptors, and painters.

The picture of tomorrow and its specific contours are very person specific, however. In other words, what God does is always mediated through a personality. Some will instantly cry "personality cult" and claim the direction for a church or ministry should be team-designed. I'm afraid American democratic sentiments are entering the fray. Moses got the commission at the burning bush. It wasn't a committee. Joshua said, "This is the direction." It wasn't a team. Paul appointed elders. It wasn't a vote. From first to last, Scripture is clear that direction is mediated through a leader.

Our concern with the personality cult is to curb abuses, and rightly so. But God's solution wasn't to entrust the picture of tomorrow to a team, as if that ensured a better result. God's approach was to entrust the picture of tomorrow to leaders who shared his heart and values. Values motivated vision, mediated through a God chosen personality, is God's approach.[6]

Leadership Beyond Influence

What kind of definition emerges for leadership? Several streams have to be taken into consideration as we think about this from a Christian perspective.

Hopefully this will open up fresh discussion about our leadership conceptions. All constructs are "works in progress." With that in mind, here's a first pass.

By their very nature, definitions are dense and pregnant with meaning. What does this definition say?[7]

> **Leadership is the convergence of picture and paraklesis; releasing God's "what ifs" in the team and church.**

Unpacking the Freight

A couple of factors must coalesce or intersect for there to be any leadership going on. If I have a great picture of tomorrow, I'm merely daydreaming until I encourage some others to jump in and pursue the picture with me. The meeting is between the picture and those so moved by paraklesis. We have already noted that the picture is person specific. It's leader defined. It's personality mediated. A picture of tomorrow mediated through personality instantly brings to the surface the issue of servanthood. This requires the people of God to engage in a number of things they, as individuals, maybe don't want to do. But because it's part of the picture for the whole, it must be done.

The balance between "I will do only that which I am gifted to do" versus "I will do whatever it takes to see God's mission accomplished here in this place" is an interesting tension. Jesus never said you would always do only that which you are gifted to do. Servanthood always wins out. In fact, quite a case could be made that God uses us most in areas in which we are least gifted.[8] Capturing the picture and then painting it with metaphors and images was talked about at length in Chapter 9. Leadership starts with some picture, destination, and preferred state. Without this component, there's nowhere to go and, therefore, no need for a leader.

Converging

The picture must converge with paraklesis. You'll never reach the picture of God's destination without some travelers being motivated toward the goal. Leadership is exactly about travelers with God's destination. We acknowledge that not all who see the picture will be moved by paraklesis to jump in for the ride. The painted picture is only one phase of the paraklesis—the moment of understanding. The follower is given the opportunity to see if he or she wants to make the trip. Those compelled by the picture are moved to change (the moment of action), and we have convergence of picture and paraklesis.

The purpose of paraklesis is first "releasing." Inherent in the idea of "releasing" is something that latently exists already. There's an assumption that God has already planted something deep down inside, waiting for expression. I deeply believe that God really has a destiny for each and every team and church. Of course, we could say God simply wants every church to prevail and fulfill the Great Commission. And while that's true, I think it is far more interesting, colorful, and unique.

When I finally understood the unique future God had for my local church and had some idea how he wanted us to fulfill the Great Commission in this particular setting, life and ministry took on a whole new dimension. For me it was figuring out the creative elements in the picture, understanding and creating a permission-giving environment, building an enviable staff ambiance, and designing a place visitors longed to be in. When the unique features of who we were to become became clear, that's when ministry entered a whole new sphere.

Paraklesis is simply encouragement with divine freight to enlist others into the travel itinerary. The destination is the picture painted, the sculpture shaped, the ambience dreamed of, the new births envisioned. These are exhortational, motivational, inspirational, encouragational (oops! that isn't a real word) attempts to reach God's wildly outrageous possibilities for a team and church. I think this is where we see a big difference between Christian leadership and simply talented leaders in the marketplace.

Great Leadership and Insomnia

When I hear of great leadership getting really artistic in its painting of the picture, I'm moved as the leaders try to get me to buy a ticket for the trip. It has happened to me many times. Sleepless nights due to paraklesis are not bad insomnia. I can lay awake in bed at night contemplating what it's like to be called into something of this scope and magnitude, to spend this kind of creative energy, and to build this kind of team. When things are moving toward "the picture," life doesn't get much better. Do it with family, with friends you love, and in an enviable ethos...wow! I honestly doubt that most General Electric employees ever lay awake in bed at night and have the same thoughts. New initiatives introduced into the marketplace, no matter how compellingly presented, cannot come with the freight of divine paraklesis.

I've opted to articulate leadership in terms of uncovering God's "what ifs." I have in mind here Paul's prayer for the Ephesian church. Ephesians 3:20: "Now to him who is able to do immeasurably more than all we ask or imagine, according to his power that is at work within us."

Paul's prayer for that local church was not for individuals to soar and realize their full potential (as if we have here a precursor to the human potential movement). Paul was challenging a local church to move beyond the confines of its thinking and to get outlandish in its expectation that God could exceed its wildest dreams for the people as a community.

Ultimately, paraklesis helps people come to full life development in Christ. The challenge is for the individual to move beyond self-serving ends in life and instead to place the kingdom of God and the living organism of the church ahead of personal acquisition. Selfless servanthood to see local mission accomplished is the end toward which paraklesis points. In kingdom terms, this is about seeing the local church become a fully leveraged redemption center for God.[9]

My hope in this appendix has been more about opening fresh and creative discussion than actually landing a definitive definition. Further, I hope it's more evident than ever that the kind of leadership definition you adopt will have a rippling effect in the way you do the leadership task and accomplish the leadership goal.

The definition you adopt forms the first strand of your leadership DNA. Everyone has a definition of leadership. It may be conscious or unconscious, thought through or thoughtless, articulate or inarticulate...but everybody has one. Here in this first strand of DNA, you begin to uncover and bring to expression your uniqueness as a leader. From this place your morphic leadership springs and will impact countless lives.

InnerAction

1. What is your current definition of leadership? Is this what the whole team operates with, or are there various definitions floating around?

2. What are the differences in the mind of your team between Christian leadership and marketplace leadership?

3. What implications does a paraklesis-based definition have for you and your context? What skills all of a sudden become important?

4. In your mind, what seems harder to accomplish: painting the picture or exercising the paraklesis muscles of encouragement and motivation? What do you think you can work on? How will you work on it?

5. Craft a leadership definition of your own, or tweak the above.

Endnotes

1. Jacob Firet, *Dynamics in Pastoring* (Grand Rapids, MI: Wm. B. Eerdmans Publishing Company, 1986). While the construct framework is entirely Firet's, I am developing this in an entirely new direction and fleshing out the details in a way he does not. Any criticisms of this construct into the leadership arena will have to fall on me, not Firet. I am sure Firet never had any intention of this being reconfigured under the rubric of Christian leadership.

2. Firet, *Dynamics in Pastoring*, 68.

3. These are all passages in which the paraklesis group of words is used: Matthew 2:18; 5:4; Luke 2:25; 6:24; John 14:16, 26; 15:26; 16:7; Acts 4:36; 9:31; 13:15; 15:31; Romans 12:8; 15:4ff; 1 Corinthians 14:3; 2 Corinthians 1:3ff; 7:4, 7, 13; 8:4, 17; Philippians 2:1; Colossians 2:2; 1 Thessalonians 3:2; 2 Thessalonians 2:16; 1 Timothy 4:13; Philemon 7; Hebrews 6:18; 12:5; 13:22; 1 John 2:1. This list was generated from Bibleworks 5.0 on a parakle* search.

4. Firet, *Dynamics in Pastoring*, 94.

5. Most surely this is the intent of Jesus' statement that he would build his church and the gates of hell would not prevail (Matthew 16:18).

6. We don't have to explore the types of values or principles we would have in mind here. Obviously, as we are talking about Christian leadership, we imply that Christian character and values stand at the foundation of all of this. Much has been written on values-driven and principle-centered leadership from a secular

and Christian perspective. I have, therefore, opted to spend my time on the less familiar and new concepts found in this definition.

7. I prefer this to the "leadership is influence" types of definitions. I like them; I just believe they need refinement. Some may say, "Why not just use the word *encouragement* and skip the Greek word no one understands?" In most contexts I would agree and think that wise. But by keeping the Greek word in this definition in this context, I hope to keep front and center two things otherwise lost in the usage of one English word. One English word hardly does justice to the variegated coloration of *paraklesis*. Comfort is paraklesis helping people toward a goal of wholeness so they can move on in life. Exhortation is no less important, however, and brings with it an entirely different delivery system from comfort or consolation. Motivation brings yet a third category of terms quite core to how we are using *paraklesis* here. So, far from simply flashing a Greek word around to be cute, the dimensionality of the word begs for its survival. A second reason for retaining *paraklesis* has to do with the connection to the noun form in the usage of *Paraclete*. I think lots more work could be done here in helping us understand just what resources are brought to bear by the Holy Spirit in a parakletic encounter. Clearly this is Paul's argument in 2 Corinthians 1:3-4 where part of the goal of paraklesis is taking the divine help received from God and returning it to the community as paraklesis. While this is a "comfort" text, there's no doubt that more reflection on these types of passages could yield helpful insight.

8. Many of those called have excuses as to why they weren't gifted. Moses said he couldn't speak, Jeremiah said he was too young, and the list could go on and on. Paul said clearly the Lord's strength is made perfect in weakness, not giftedness (2 Corinthians 12:9).

9. *Redemption center* is a term Bill Hybels used at the 2001 Leadership Summit. It has never left my heart. I came to realize its presence in my heart weeks later. It was, in fact, an instance of paraklesis in my own life.

Group Publishing, Inc.
Attention: Product Development
P.O. Box 481
Loveland, CO 80539
Fax: (970) 679-4370

Evaluation for
Morph!

Please help Group Publishing, Inc., continue to provide innovative and useful resources for ministry. Please take a moment to fill out this evaluation and mail or fax it to us. Thanks!

● ● ●

1. As a whole, this book has been (circle one)

not very helpful   very helpful

1   2   3   4   5   6   7   8   9   10

2. The best things about this book:

3. Ways this book could be improved:

4. Things I will change because of this book:

5. Other books I'd like to see Group publish in the future:

6. Would you be interested in field-testing future Group products and giving us your feedback? If so, please fill in the information below:

Name_____

Church Name _____

Denomination _____ Church Size _____

Church Address _____

City _____ State_____ ZIP _____

Church Phone _____

E-mail _____